CONFRONTING THE BLUE REVOLUTION

Industrial Aquaculture and Sustainability in the Global South

Like the Green Revolution of the 1960s that resulted in massive increases in agricultural production around the world, the recent "Blue Revolution" has transformed global aquaculture. However, these greater yields – to satisfy the growing demand for seafood by privileged consumers in the developed countries of the North – have come at a high price for the global South: ecological ruin, displacement of rural subsistence farmers, and labour exploitation. The uncomfortable truth is that food security for affluent consumers is built on a foundation of social and ecological devastation in the producing countries.

In *Confronting the Blue Revolution*, Md Saidul Islam uses the shrimp farming industry in Bangladesh and across the global South to demonstrate the social and environmental impact of industrialized aquaculture. Providing a wealth of factual information and fresh insights, the book pushes us to reconsider our attitudes towards consumption patterns in the developed world, neoliberal environmental governance, and the question of sustainability.

MD SAIDUL ISLAM is an assistant professor in the Division of Sociology at Nanyang Technological University, Singapore.

MD SAIDUL ISLAM

Confronting the Blue Revolution

Industrial Aquaculture and Sustainability in the Global South

UNIVERSITY OF TORONTO PRESS
Toronto Buffalo London

ISBN 978-1-4426-4638-4 (cloth)
ISBN 978-1-4426-1440-6 (paper)

Printed on acid-free, 100% post-consumer recycled paper with vegetable-based inks.

Library and Archives Canada Cataloguing in Publication

Islam, Md Saidul, author
Confronting the blue revolution : industrial aquaculture and sustainability in the Global South / Md Saidul Islam.

Includes bibliographical references and index.
ISBN 978-1-4426-4638-4 (bound).   ISBN 978-1-4426-1440-6 (pbk.)

1. Aquaculture – Environmental aspects – Developing countries.
2. Aquaculture – Government policy – Developing countries.   3. Aquaculture – Social aspects – Developing countries.   4. Manpower policy – Developing countries.   5. Globalization – Developing countries.   I. Title.

SH135.S86 2014   338.3'718091724   C2013-906596-2

This book has been published with the help of a grant from the Canadian Federation for the Humanities and Social Sciences, through the Awards to Scholarly Publications Program, using funds provided by the Social Sciences and Humanities Research Council of Canada.

University of Toronto Press acknowledges the financial assistance to its publishing program of the Canada Council for the Arts and the Ontario Arts Council.

University of Toronto Press acknowledges the financial support of the Government of Canada through the Canada Book Fund for its publishing activities.

This book is dedicated to the communities engaged in struggles to sustain their livelihoods, ecosystems, knowledge systems, cultures, and a sense of place in a complex world.

Contents

Tables, Figures, and Boxes

Tables

Figures

Boxes

Acknowledgments

Confronting the Blue Revolution was made possible by research funding from the International Development Research Centre, the Social Science and Humanities Research Council of Canada, and Nanyang Technological University (NTU) in Singapore. I would like to acknowledge my debt to these funding agencies.

I am grateful to Douglas Hildebrand, the Acquisitions Editor of Social Sciences at the University of Toronto Press, for his diligent editorial work, which included providing insightful comments, finding critical and constructive external reviews, and moving the project along in a timely manner; and to freelance copy editor Barry Norris.

Over the past several years, many people and organizations have helped me in various ways to complete this book. First and foremost, I am greatly indebted to Peter Vandergeest, Hira Singh, and Stuart Schoenfeld of York University; the reviewers of the book for their thoughtful comments and suggestions; informants in various sites of my fieldwork; all of my Sociology colleagues at NTU; members of Sustaining Ethical Aquaculture Trade (SEAT), including Dave Little and Francis Murray; and the community of scholars who enriched my thoughts and understanding including Nesar Ahmed, Laurence Busch, Simon Bush, Jennifer Clapp, Jason Clay, Catherine Dolan, Harriet Friedmann, Derek Hall, Maki Hatanaka, Syed Serajul Islam, Stewart Lockie, Philip McMichael, and Laura Raynold, to name a few.

Finally, my family members have been loving and supportive through the long years of this project. I am grateful to my parents, brothers and sisters, and in-laws and their relatives for their assistance, encouragement, and crucial mental support. Last, but not least, I will never forget the understanding and unceasing support of my beloved wife, Salma Sultana, my daughter Ulfat Tahseen, and my son Rawsab Said. They all have endured long periods of separation from me during my fieldwork and write-up phases.

Glossary of Terms and Acronyms

Note: In the literature, spellings of Bengali (or Bengalicized Arabic and Persian) words vary. The entries below are the spellings adopted in this book. Variant spellings, as may appear in quoted passages, are shown in parentheses.

ACC	Aquaculture Certification Council
ADB	Asian Development Bank
AFCD	Agriculture, Fisheries and Conservation Department (Hong Kong)
AFDB	African Development Bank
AIDS	Acquired Immune Deficiency Syndrome
Aman	Seasonal paddies
AquaNIC	Aquaculture Network Information Centre
Aratdar	Commission agent or intermediary who buys and sells products
ASC	Aquaculture Stewardship Council
ATJ	Alter Trade Japan
BAP	Best Aquacultural Practices
Bagda	Saltwater shrimp
Beel	Floodplain
CAAQ	Conseil des appellations agroalimentaires du Québec
CAIA	Canadian Aquaculture Industry Alliance
CARE	Cooperative for Assistance and Relief Everywhere
CBNRM	Community-based natural resource management
COs	Conscientious Objectors
CQL	Carrefour Quality Line
Dadon	Loan extended to shrimp farmers by *faria*

EJF	Environmental Justice Foundation
ERNs	Environmental regulatory networks
ETI	Ethical Trading Initiative
EurepGAP	Euro-Retailer Produce Working Group protocol on Good Agricultural Practices
FAO	Food and Agriculture Organization of the United Nations
Faria	Intermediary who buys and sells products
FIQC	Fish Inspection and Quality Control
FLO	Fairtrade Labelling Organizations
FSC	Forest Stewardship Council
GAA	Global Aquaculture Alliance
GCC	Global commodity chain
GEF	Global Environmental Facility
Ghers	Ponds inside polders used for the cultivation of fish or shrimp
GAP	Good Agricultural Practices
Golda	Freshwater prawns
Haat	Village market
HACCP	Hazard Analysis and Critical Control Points
Huri	Leasing arrangements
IADB	Inter-American Development Bank
IBRD	International Bank for Reconstruction and Development
IDA	International Development Association
IFOAM	International Federation of Organic Agriculture Movements
ILO	International Labour Organization
ISA Net	Industrial Shrimp Action Network
ISEAL	International Social and Environmental Accreditation and Labelling Alliance
ISO	International Standards Organization
Jatra	Stage drama
Khas	Government-owned lands under the supervision and control of the Bangladesh Ministry of Land, typically allocated to the landless for cultivation
Lathi	Bamboo sticks
MAC	Marine Aquarium Council
Mahajon	Great people
Mayender	Bondage or indentured labour
MoE	Ministry of Environment (Bangladesh)
MSC	Marine Stewardship Council

MSCS	Marie Stopes Clinic Society
NACA	Network of Aquaculture Centres in Asia-Pacific
NACs	New Agricultural Countries
NCS	National Conservation Strategy
NCSRA	National Code System for Responsible Aquaculture
NEMAP	National Environmental Management Action Plan
NGO	Non-governmental organization
NSMD	Non-state market-driven
OIE	Office international des épizooties
PAI	Product Authentication International
Polder	Area of low-lying land reclaimed from the sea by construction of a perimeter dike
QAI	Quality Assurance International
Salish	Community hearings
SAPs	Structural Adjustment Programs
SEMP	Sustainable Environment Management Program
ShAD	Shrimp Aquaculture Dialogue
ShAD GSC	ShAD General Steering Committee
SIPPO	Swiss Import Promotion Programme
SPS	Agreement on Application of Sanitary and Phytosanitary Measures
SQF	Safe Quality Food
SSOQ	Shrimp Seal of Quality Organization
Thana	Local police station in Bangladesh
TPCs	Third-party certifiers
TQM	Total Quality Management
UBINIG	*Unnayan Bikalper Nitinirdharoni Gobeshona* (Policy Research for Development Alternatives), a non-governmental organization in Bangladesh
UKAS	United Kingdom Accreditation Service
UNDP	United Nations Development Programme
UNEP	United Nations Environment Programme
UNESCAP	United Nations Economic and Social Commission for Asia and the Pacific
Upazila	Subdistrict (local government)
USAID	US Agency for International Development
WB	World Bank
WWF	World Wildlife Fund

CONFRONTING THE BLUE REVOLUTION

Industrial Aquaculture and Sustainability
in the Global South

1 Introduction: Globalizing Food and Industrial Aquaculture

Only after the last tree has been cut down, Only after the last river has been poisoned, Only after the last fish has been caught, Only then will you find that money cannot be eaten.

– Cree proverb

Subsistence farmers in the global South have caught fish for centuries without causing any significant social or ecological destruction. Over recent decades, however, the massive growth of industrial aquaculture, or aquafarming – hailed as the "Blue Revolution," the water equivalent of the Green Revolution – has integrated the region with the world's food network, transforming the global South's environmental and agrarian landscapes. Although the Blue Revolution initially referred to the management of water resources to steer humanity towards adequate drinking water and crop irrigation security, the term is now used for the exponential growth and productivity of industrial aquaculture – mainly commercial shrimp[1] – in the tropical nations. Mirroring developments in the Green Revolution, the Blue Revolution has seen companies breeding fish to improve traits such as their growth rate, conversion of feed into flesh, resistance to disease, tolerance of cold and poor water, and fertility (*Economist* 2003). Opponents of industrial aquaculture argue that the practice of feeding "fish to fish" – the conversion of small wild fish into fishmeal and fish oil for use in formulated diets for farmed fish – is inefficient and wasteful, and that it can take more than 6 kilograms of wild fish to produce 1 kilogram of farmed fish (Stanford 2002). Critics also express concern about industrial aquaculture's use of chemicals and other substances harmful to human and environmental health, and the risk of sustainability of food production by transforming the food crops of the many into cash crops for the benefit of a few by an industry that directs fish away from human needs towards industrial needs (Mangrove Action Project 2009). The Blue Revolution, therefore, has generated widespread controversy and, inevitably, has produced winners and losers.

Governments in the global South argue that aquaculture is a form of economic development and poverty alleviation, and, as a result, they have encouraged the boom in production of pond-raised fish. Commercial fish farming is now big business: aquaculture production has grown at about 9 per cent per year since 1970, and aquaculture now provides 40 per cent of the world's fish supply for direct human consumption, bringing new challenges to the sustainable use of aquatic resources and environments (World Bank 2012). World aquaculture production attained an all-time high in 2010 of 60 million metric tons (excluding aquatic plants and non-food products), with an estimated total value of US$119 billion (FAO 2012, 24–5). But has this latest technological fix aimed at boosting world food production actually helped to feed the hungry? Consider the cultivated shrimp industry. Shrimp ponds, which now stretch in coastlines from Taiwan to Ecuador, are capital intensive and have led to the destruction of, among other things, thousands of hectares of mangrove forests, the generation of steady flows of polluted wastewater, and the decline of wild shrimp fisheries (Boychuk 1992; EJF 2003a, 2003b).

Over the past thirty years, studies of the global agri-food system have tended to overemphasize the industrialization and standardization of food production and processing, as well as the process of increasing local or regional integration into the global market. Although this focus still dominates the literature, a number of recent studies have shown the dynamics of local or regional changes and the transformations generated by global commodity networks. In this study of the Blue Revolution, I explore not only how food products and processes have been industrialized and standardized on a global scale, but also how the processes of industrialization and standardization have generated significant changes in local settings in terms of environmental politics, employment patterns, gender relations, and agrarian transformations.

Directions in Global Agri-Food Studies

In recent years the global agri-food system has become increasingly complex, multifaceted, and all-encompassing. Scholars, non-governmental organizations (NGOs), and policy makers accordingly are turning their attention towards analysing the trajectories of the development of agri-food and understanding its possible implications. Among the diverse trajectories, one can discern at least three conspicuous yet overlapping themes in the study of the global agri-food system: (1) the evolution and changing contours of regulations governing the system;[2] (2) issues of environmental and social (in)justice, with particular attention to labour and gender patterns;[3] and (3) agrarian transformation.[4] In the midst of both consensus and disagreement in each of these areas, a central question in agri-food dynamics is how these trends influence wider social and rural economic development and change.

Over the past three decades, scholars in the sociology of agriculture and the global agri-food system[5] have studied the global restructuring of agri-food relations, paying particular attention to the predominance of transnational corporations in coordinating global supply chains, the concentration of capital, and the newfound influence of downstream actors such as retailers. More recently, however, scholarly attention has turned towards the emergence of privately regulated supply chains organized more around principles of "quality." As part of a generalized restructuring of the agri-food system based on foods marketed as "fresh," "quality," "organic," and "natural,"[6] heavily audited, privately regulated supply chains have begun to replace or supersede forms of public regulation (see Busch and Bain 2004; Campbell 2005; Friedmann 2005). In this transformation, quality, rather than price or quantity, has become the basis around which production, commodities, and markets are organized. The rise of the "private regulation of the public" (Busch and Bain 2004, 337) following "the rise of consumer sovereignty"[7] has had a significant affect on the global agri-food system. Table 1.1 shows that quality is the most significant factor influencing seafood purchasing decisions, followed by availability.

Against the backdrop of this transformation, multinational firms are now implementing "certification" arrangements under increasing pressure from various actors in their home countries, including environmental and labour activists, multilateral organizations, and regulatory agencies. The certification schemes include "codes of conduct, production guidelines, and monitoring standards that govern and attest not only to the corporations' behaviour but also to that of their suppliers around the world" (Gereffi et al. 2001, 1).[8] Supporters of certification believe that such efforts symbolize a new model for global corporate governance and accountability – no mean feat when national

Table 1.1. Factors Driving Seafood Purchasing Decisions

Factors Important in the Decision to Buy Seafood	"Extremely Important"		
	Chain Restaurant	Retail	Wholesale
	(per cent mentioning factor)		
Quality of fish available	85	88	81
Availability	66	59	69
Customer demand	64	80	77
Whether species is caught in a way that harms marine environment	54	62	49
Whether aquaculture causes harm to marine environment	n.a.	57	62
Whether fish is fresh or previously frozen	54	47	38
Whether species is overfished	50	58	57
Price	49	49	53
Health benefits	45	61	69
Environmental impact associated with catching or producing fish	40	43	40
Whether fish is wild or farmed	19	46	51
Whether fish is certified organic	14	22	17
Whether fish is caught or produced locally	12	19	43

Source: Seafood Choice Alliance (2008, 30).

governments appear unable to constrain powerful multinational corporations.[9] Among the important mechanisms used in such certification schemes are identity preservation, segregation, and traceability[10] systems, allowing for the "field-to-plate" monitoring of supply chains. Prefiguring a new set of conditions for accumulation in the global agrifood system, this movement suggests a bifurcation of supply chains providing "quality" commodities to rich consumers and cheap commodities to poor consumers (Friedmann 2005). The shift to "quality," however, creates new dilemmas for various agricultural sectors and regions as well as for individual producers, as privately regulated supply chains produce different sets of winners and losers (Busch and Bain 2004; Campbell, Lawrence, and Smith 2006; Clapp 1998). For farmers, the exact contract specifications required for participation in quality chains can increase costs, so such chains tend to marginalize smaller, less sophisticated producers (Busch and Bain 2004; Islam 2008a; Vandergeest 2007).

The shift to privately regulated supply chains is driven, in part, by the neoliberal turn in agri-food regulation, with states ceding responsibility for regulation just as corporate actors step in to provide a proliferating array of quality assurance schemes and voluntary standards (Cadman 2011; Campbell, Lawrence, and Smith 2006). European countries have led the way in this transition, largely in response to various food scares such as bovine spongiform encephalopathy ("mad cow disease") and wariness over genetically engineered foods. The United Kingdom's 1990 Food Safety Act, which outsourced government oversight of food safety to retailers, is a symbolic marker of the shift (Campbell, Lawrence, and Smith 2006). Large seafood buyers, such as Walmart, Darden Restaurants, and Lyons Seafood, have already committed to buying only certified seafood (Islam 2010; Walmart 2006). Although consolidation of the regime remains uncertain, as social movements are already regrouping (Friedmann 2005), this remarkable development has given rise to a number of questions. Why are buyers moving towards private regulations and regulators (third-party certifiers)? What is the significance of this trend? What are the implications of this shift for supply chain governance? What role will states and communities play in the wake of private certifiers? Does this new regime marginalize or empower them? Does it offer any "invited spaces" for communities and small players to participate meaningfully? Does it signal a new form of governmentality (see Chapter 2)? The broader sociological effects of this newly emerging global regime of regulation and certification – such as how the state, working conditions in local communities, agrarian relations, and the environment are restructured and reconstituted – need to be explored fully.

The second direction of study, sometimes fused to the first, takes various forms and focuses on environmental effects on communities and ecologies, the displacement of local residents, the exploitation of labour, gender disparity, and so forth. The precarious conditions brought about by the evolution of the global agri-food system have given rise to a number of environmental NGOs and labour and human rights organizations, working on scales ranging from the village to the global. Although considerable diversity and dynamic positions exist among these organizations – some working to oppose current practices and others engaging industry or corporations to push for change from within – most of them claim to address issues of social justice. Consequently, powerful industry players such as large supermarkets have come under pressure to improve the returns to small producers and conditions of employment in the supply chain (Barrientos and Dolan 2006). Local and global environmental and civil rights movements have launched campaigns to address social justice issues by making sure that agri-food products are environmentally friendly and socially responsible as well as meaningful in terms of community participation. These characteristics are sometimes known as "credence," or the non-material aspects of "quality," which consumers cannot detect after purchase in the same way that they can detect freshness and taste (Josling, Roberts, and Orden 2004; Vandergeest 2007). Vandergeest elaborates:

> These credence qualities include the environmental and ethical conditions of production. For example, is the item produced organically? Are beef cattle fed hormones? Do crops include genetically modified varieties? Are coffee producers being paid a fair price? Are tuna caught by methods that minimize dangers to dolphins? Under what conditions were animals raised? Because these qualities are process based and not readily apparent in the physical product that reaches the consumer, consumers can respond only if the product has trustworthy labels. The effect is to make the regulation of food production a way of producing new quality-based values that can be marketed to consumers. (2007, 1154)

From this second focus, several questions arise. How are agri-food corporations and buyers responding to the opportunities and pressures resulting from emerging environmental movements and awareness? How are agri-food corporations changing their business practices to develop new environmentally friendly products, services, and methods of production? Do these environmental movements offer a genuine chance to balance the interests of multinational corporations and the poor, or are they simply examples of corporate whitewash? Can the movements genuinely address the problems facing workers and producers in the global food system? Do they represent a new form of northern protectionism, or can southern initiatives be developed to create a more sustainable agri-food system and ensure social justice? How can the rights and participation of workers, particularly women and small producers, be enhanced, given the power and dominance of large supermarkets in the global food chain? What role can civil society and multistakeholder initiatives play in ensuring social justice for both producers and consumers?

Scholars have also documented that a great deal of agrarian restructuring, along with a new agrarian division of labour, has taken place, with substantial local variation, since the colonial era. The process of local or regional integration into global markets was intensified during the "First Green Revolution" of the 1960s, which was characterized by a technical package of bio-engineered hybrid seeds requiring chemical and mechanical inputs designed to improve agricultural productivity in basic grains such as wheat, maize, and rice (Atkins and Bowler 2001; McMichael 2008). Green Revolution technology gradually extended from basic to luxury, or "high-value," foods. This extension has been called the "Second Green Revolution" (Raynolds et al. 1993; Raynolds 1994a; Sanderson 1986).

A similar shift, the Blue Revolution, has occurred in the global aquaculture sector (see Chapter 3). Its aim has been to increase global aquatic production significantly and to stave off widespread hunger. By 1985, the World Bank, the Asian Development Bank, and a variety of other international aid agencies were pouring over US$200 million a year into aquaculture projects. Mangrove forests in the global South, including in the Philippines, Thailand, Bangladesh, and Ecuador, have been chopped down to make way for shrimp ponds, and carp and tilapia farms have been staked out on the flood plains of the Ganges, Irrawaddy, and Mekong rivers. As a result, the production of pond-raised fish has boomed (Boychuk 1992; Public Citizen 2005). The United Nations Food and Agriculture Organization (FAO 2010) reports that eight of the top ten aquaculture producers are in the global South, with China the top producer, followed by India, Vietnam, Indonesia, Thailand, and Bangladesh (see Figure 1.1). Among aquaculture commodities, shrimp is perhaps the most critical because of its massive social and environmental effects.

Although the Blue Revolution has been geared to quenching the appetite of wealthy consumers in the North, it has come at a price. Many writers have characterized it as a transformation of agrarian landscapes in the South to large farms in a few hands, at the cost of ecological

Figure 1.1. Major Aquaculture Producers in the Global South, 1990–2008

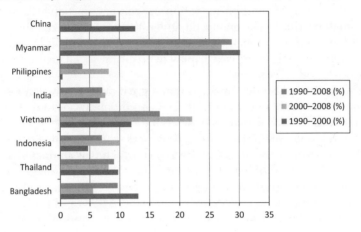

Source: Adapted from FAO (2010, 21).

devastation, the displacement of rural subsistence farmers, rural tension and violence, peasant movements and resistance, exploitative labour relations, and so forth. It has been argued that, in India, for example, every dollar of foreign exchange earned on meat exports destroys US$15 worth of ecological capital stemming from the use of farm animals in sustainable agriculture (McMichael 2008). In Thailand, as Boychuk (1992) reports, the poor living in coastal communities took up arms to prevent corporations from seizing commonly owned mangrove forests for shrimp ponds. In this context, one can pose some striking questions. Does export-oriented high-value aquaculture production mean displacement, violence, and food insecurity? Does it not produce any positive outcomes for local communities? Must food security for affluent consumers in the global North be founded on social and ecological devastation in the global South?

Industrial Aquaculture in the Global Agri-Food System

Industrial aquaculture is a prime candidate for further exploration of these questions for several compelling reasons. First, its products are among the major high-value transnational agri-food commodities (FAO et al. 2006; Vandergeest 2007). Over the past three decades, industrial aquaculture has become a major global industry, regarded as the "pinnacle of the Blue Revolution's achievement" (Public Citizen 2005, 9). Commercial shrimp dominates the industrial aquaculture of the global South, with total annual production worth more than US$14 billion at the farm gate (FAO 2010; Resolve 2012).

Second, the tropical coastal zones of countries such as China, Bangladesh, Thailand, Indonesia, Malaysia, and Vietnam dominate the production and export of commercial shrimp to the United States, Europe, Canada, Japan, and other wealthy areas. For many developing countries, therefore, industrial aquaculture has become a major source of foreign exchange and has integrated often previously marginal coastal communities into high-value commodity networks (Islam 2008a; Roheim 2004; Vandergeest 2007).

Third, industrial aquaculture has been the subject of heated debate and close scrutiny, targeted by environmental groups that claim it has negative environmental and social effects on ocean ecologies and local communities that far outweigh the benefits (Vandergeest, Flaherty, and Miller 1999). One reason shrimp farming has come under close scrutiny on a global scale is that, whereas open (capture) shrimp production is generally seen as self-sustaining, closed (culture) shrimp production requires direct input and human care, involves property rights, and, although renewable, generates a wide range of externalities[11] that make sustainable development a critically important issue (Asaduzzaman and Toufique 1998; Battacharya, Rahman, and Khatan 1999).

Fourth, although coastal zones in tropical regions are important hubs for industrial aquaculture, particularly commercial shrimp, the people living there are mainly poor and heavily dependent on natural resources. Since the early 1990s, numerous researchers and local and international NGOs have voiced serious concerns regarding local-level environmental and social disruptions caused by industrial aquaculture, including displacement, environmental hazards, conflict over access to natural resources, and the violation of human rights.[12] Despite major efforts to resolve these issues, however, the debate surrounding the sustainability of industrial aquaculture remains largely unsettled (Béné 2005), and the industry is still growing quite rapidly (see Figure 1.2). A report by the UK-based Environmental Justice Foundation (EJF), in partnership with the US organization WildAid, suggests that shrimp farming has been accompanied by intimidation, aggression, and threats against those who attempt to oppose its expansion (EJF 2003a, 2003b).

Figure 1.2. World Fish Production, 1950–2010

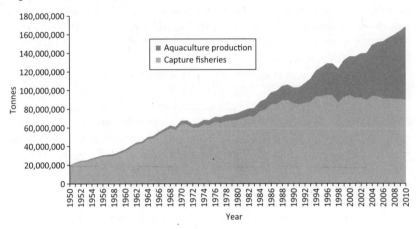

Source: Adapted from FAO (2012).

The Global Aquaculture Alliance,[13] in contrast, claims that the EJF is "strong on attack [but] weak on facts" and that it "ignores industry progress" (AquaNIC 2003). Although recognizing some troubled legacies in the earlier phase of industrial aquaculture, governments in the global South and industry proponents suggest that interventions of various kinds have led to positive outcomes and improved conditions. Why, then, are the claims of environmental NGOs and industry groups so polarized? What are the missing links? Why is the issue of sustainability still unsettled? Exploring shrimp aquaculture is an excellent way to address these critical questions, which are centred around the broader issues of global social justice.

Finally, although shrimp is the most popular seafood in North America (Table 1.2), consumers in North America, Europe, Japan, and other wealthy countries and regions rarely know how it is produced or with what consequences. The EJF (2003a, 12), for instance, quotes a respondent in India as saying, "to those who eat shrimp – and only the rich people from industrialized countries eat shrimp – I say they are eating the blood, sweat, and livelihood of the poor people of the Third World." Although this view might contradict industry players' claim that they have introduced best-management practices and created institutions for certifying producers who follow these practices (Béné

Table 1.2. Seafood Consumption, Top 10 Species, United States, 2009–11

| | 2009 | | 2010 | | 2011 | |
	Species	Pounds per capita	Species	Pounds per capita	Species	Pounds per capita
1	shrimp	4.1	shrimp	4.0	shrimp	4.2
2	canned tuna	2.5	canned tuna	2.7	canned tuna	2.6
3	salmon	2.0	salmon	2.0	salmon	2.0
4	pollock	1.5	tilapia	1.5	pollock	1.3
5	tilapia	1.2	pollock	1.2	tilapia	1.3
6	catfish	0.8	catfish	0.8	pangasius	0.6
7	crab	0.6	crab	0.6	catfish	0.6
8	cod	0.4	cod	0.5	crab	0.5
9	clams	0.4	pangasius	0.4	cod	0.5
10	pangasius	0.4	clams	0.3	clams	0.3
Total, all species		15.0		15.8		15.8

Source: *About Seafood* (2013).

2005; Vandergeest 2007), even industry personnel acknowledge that problems persist (Boyd and Clay 1998).

Central Questions and Themes

Drawing on the foregoing contextualization of the problem, and using the global commodity chain, environmental governance, agrarian transformation, and gender relations as conceptual frameworks (see Chapter 2), I unpack the emergence of the Blue Revolution in the global South, with particular emphasis on shrimp aquaculture; explore the emergence and role of certification in the industrial aquaculture commodity chain; and extend commodity chain analysis to a study of environmental and agrarian transitions, employment, and gender relations in a local supply chain that links large global buyers with farms and farmers in the global South. I also explore how global competitive pressures (certification, in this case) are transmitted through the supply chain, creating new forms of social relations that engender both risks and opportunities.

More specifically, the book has two main objectives. The first is to examine the context of the emergence of transnational environmental regulation and certification in industrial aquaculture. Is this emergence the result of environmental movements, consumer demand, or competition for customers on the basis of quality among supermarkets, restaurants, and retailers, or of something else altogether? Who or what is setting environmental standards: locals,[14] consumers, environmental groups, supermarkets? What is the role of certification vis-à-vis other actors, especially supermarkets, in governing industrial aquaculture? What are the long-term sociological implications of the emergence of third-party certification agencies for different stakeholders, including rural communities in the global South?

The second objective is to examine the intersections among changes in livelihood, the environment, and conflict, as sites of industrial aquaculture in the global South become integrated into the global agri-food commodity chain. How does industrial aquaculture enter into and change agrarian relations, particularly with respect to land ownership, land tenure, the organization of labour, and access to other resources needed for shrimp farming? What do people in farming sites identify as the major effects, both positive and negative, of aquaculture farming? What, if anything, is being done in aquaculture farming areas to control or manage these effects? For example, do villagers take direct action? Do they appeal to the government, and if so, in what form? Do they work with NGOs? Who are the main actors – villagers, men, women, specific classes, local governments, specific government ministries, NGOs? What, if any, is the local effect of regulation through the commodity chain (including food safety, the environment, and labour relations)? Is there an intersection between what public and private quality and other commodity-chain-based regulations seek to change and what are identified as priorities at the local level?

To address these crucial questions comprehensively, the analysis integrates a number of relevant disciplinary lenses, including insights from social movements, international relations, organization and rural sociology, economics, and geography. For the same reason, I also explore, among other issues, international rules-making development, global economic dynamics, domestic policy-making issues, and firm-level sustainability initiatives. This broad agenda makes a sustained contribution to understanding of the emergence of a "twin-driven commodity chain" in global governance (see Chapter 2). Known generally as environmental and social certification programs, which recognize and reward individual firms operating according to pre-established rules, the twin-driven commodity chain is important because its growth in the global aquaculture sector – shrimp, in particular – has led stakeholders to promote the model to address a range of other key global policy problems, including fisheries depletion, mining destruction, environmental and social deterioration associated with global coffee production, the effect of tourism in ecologically sensitive areas, and sweatshop labour practices. All of these international development issues are strongly tied to social and environmental justice.

Methodology

I explore the complex intersection and negotiation between global and local forces and processes surrounding industrial aquaculture that define the central dynamics of environmental politics, agrarian restructuring, and gender relations in the global South through a robust analysis of secondary sources found in various social science disciplines and a content analysis of "grey" literature (see Cadman 2011, 21) generated by NGOs and other non-refereed sources. This analysis has been substantiated by a primary study conducted in various sites in the global South, including Bangladesh, China, Indonesia, Malaysia, and Mexico, as well as in the global North. The primary research uses a variety of techniques, such as ethnography, qualitative interviews, and focus group discussions with various stakeholders in the Blue Revolution in both the global South – notably, through ethnographic field visits to Bangladesh in 2005–06 and subsequent follow-up visits between 2007 and 2011 – and the global North (specifically in Canada, Singapore, the United Kingdom, and the United States).

Although a clear definition of ethnography is elusive, Hammersley and Atkinson (2003, 1) suggest that it entails participating, for an extended period of time, in the research environment, "collecting any data available to throw light on the issues that are the focus of the research." Ethnographic techniques offer flexibility and the ability to engage with theoretical assumptions while embarking on the practical process of data collection. For Herbert (2000), ethnography is singularly capable of exploring the complexities of meanings, place, and process. As for commercial shrimp, both domestic and international forces intersect, configuring the parameters of change. My ethnographic research, therefore, was conducted at both the local level (at sites of production) and the global level (at sites of consumption). During my visits to Bangladesh in 2005–06, for example, along with direct and sometimes participant observation, I conducted informal interviews – largely in the mode of purposive conversation – with a diverse range of people, including more than a thousand shrimp and prawn farmers in the greater Khulna, Bagherhat, and Satkhira regions, where more than 80 per cent of the nation's shrimp farming takes place. Indeed, I continued to talk with local people until I reached a stage of data saturation, where no new or additional information was being generated. For a final consistency check, I then conducted focus group discussions with various representative groups, such as fry catchers, fry traders, hatchery owners, shrimp and prawn farmers, traders and middlemen, NGOs, workers (both male and female) in shrimp and prawn ponds and processing factories, *upazila* (subdistrict) fisheries officers, and informed villagers. Field visits to China, Indonesia, and Malaysia were relatively short, but they nonetheless provided in-depth insights into local dynamics and the trajectories of the Blue Revolution.

At the global level, I draw on data collected from Web sites maintained by research organizations, industry organizations, certification institutions, NGOs, the FAO, and governments to map out transnational commodity networks, with specific attention to the Blue Revolution and how certification regimes are initiated in key consumption sites. I obtained a deeper understanding of these data through interviews with key actors representing the aquaculture industry, retailers, wholesalers, restaurant chains, environmental groups, government regulators, academics, development organizations, and research institutions in Canada, the Unites States, and the United Kingdom. As key points of access, I participated in various world forums, conferences, and meetings, such as those of the World Aquaculture Society (Veracruz, Mexico, 26–29 September 2009); the Shrimp Aquaculture Dialogue (organized by the World Wildlife Fund and the Indonesian Ministry of Marine Affairs and Fisheries, Jakarta, 9–10 March 2010);[15] the Asian Food Security Workshop (organized by the International Development Research Centre and Nanyang Technological University, Singapore, 3–4 June 2010); the Rural Sociological Society (Atlanta, 12–15 August 2010); and the Asian Fisheries Forum (Shanghai, 21–25 April 2011). I also talked to representatives of a variety of global actors, such as the World Bank Group; the Global Aquaculture Alliance in the United Kingdom; the Environmental Law Institute, the Food and Drug Administration, and the Ocean Conservancy in the United States; Oxfam Novib in the Netherlands; GlobalG.A.P. in Germany; the Asian Institute of Technology in Thailand; the Network of Aquaculture Centres in Asia-Pacific; the World Wildlife Fund; and a number of investors, traders, consumers, and researchers from Asia, Europe, and North America. Taken as a whole, these data sources provided a robust and in-depth understanding of complex issues and questions regarding the Blue Revolution and the global agri-food system driven largely by neoliberal restructuring and its implications for the global South.

Outline of the Book

In Chapter 2, I take up four conceptual threads to provide an analytical framework for a comprehensive understanding of the Blue Revolution: global commodity chains, environmental governance, agrarian transformation, and gender relations. I define the global commodity chain approach broadly; I then show how it has been used, with substantial variation, by scholars of the global agri-food system, and examine the extent of its usefulness for the current study. Taking important insights from scholars of the agri-food system and environmental governance, as well as ongoing debates over supply chain governance, I use environmental governance to describe the ways the actors in a commodity chain organize to employ power to manage natural resources and the environmental and social effects of their use. The term includes the activities not only of governments, but also those of other actors, including businesses, NGOs, and networks or communities of affected and concerned people, each with competing claims to authority over particular issues. The concept of agrarian transformation builds on two divergent yet complementary research traditions: agrarian political economy, and industrial restructuring and regulation. The chapter thus also examines how the rapid process of transformation in the globalization of the agri-food system has affected and redefined work and gender relations in a variety of ways.

Combining the four conceptual tools, I argue that the complex nature of most agri-food commodity chains goes beyond Gary Gereffi's traditional buyer- and producer-driven dichotomy, the non-state, market-driven system, and private regulation of the public. Upon identifying two divergent streams of the literature on governance, I call for an integrated analysis of the agri-food system that incorporates both institutional developments and various discursive shifts and constructions as part not only of "good governance," as propounded by the mainstream development literature, but also of an environmental governance that potentially marginalizes and displaces certain actors. I also call for a more appropriate global-commodity-chain model for the agri-food system, one that identifies different sources, forms, and levels of control across commodities. As the environment is a compelling issue in the global agri-food system, particular attention must be paid to environmental governance within the chain, as it has an influence on the chain's structure. Examination of the social relations of production in the commodity chain, with particular attention to environmental governance, should divulge who owns and controls what, why, and to what effect. A key contribution is the development of a new model, the aforementioned twin-driven commodity chain, moving beyond Gereffi's "buyer-driven" versus "producer-driven" dichotomy.

In Chapter 3, I examine how neoliberalism has driven and accelerated the Blue Revolution in the global South to quench the appetite of wealthy consumers in the global North. Although the key aim of the Blue Revolution, as presented and heralded, has been to feed the hungry in the global South, I show how it has been largely a part of the structural adjustment programs introduced by neoliberal global managers to promote – largely through World Bank loans – the opening of national resource pools for transnational corporations in the interest of rapid national revenue generation to facilitate debt repayment. I then examine in particular how debt crises and consequent structural adjustment policies have made national governments more likely to respond like private landowners to opportunities for quick profit and less likely to prioritize long-term sustainable development goals.

Chapter 4 examines the environmental and social effects of the Blue Revolution that various NGOs and human and labour rights movements consider to be serious, with particular emphasis on commercial shrimp farming. I identify three phases of the Blue Revolution in the global South – namely, an era of resistance and violence, an era of depoliticization and negotiation, and, finally, an era of a strong ambivalence – and describe the environmental and social effects of industrial aquaculture at each stage. I also examine different politics and discourses over industrial aquaculture by linking it to the global arena.

In Chapter 5, I examine regulatory regimes of industrial aquaculture in the global South. I first adumbrate the emergence of the "hazards analysis and critical control point" regime and its effects on the aquaculture sector, and then examine the emergence of third-party certifiers.

I outline the campaigns for privatizing environmental governance, shifts in these campaigns, and the involvement of local and global environmental and regulatory NGOs. I then examine likely trends in, and the social implications of, industrial aquaculture in the wake of private certification.

Chapter 6 investigates changes in agrarian structure brought about by farmers switching from rice cultivation to fish and shrimp production. I examine the local supply chain, the ownership of land and tenancy agreements, the organization of labour, sources and management of rural tensions, and, finally, patterns of culture and consumption generated by the new production regime. The effect of these changes – their significance, their effect on the rural community, and their implications for rural development – is an important part of this chapter.

In Chapter 7, I explore how the twofold pressures transmitted from lead firms and environmental groups – particularly through certification in this case – via global commodity chains and other local influences create new forms of employment in the aquaculture sector that engender both risks and opportunities for workers. In response to the high degree of female participation in the sector – quite new in the global South – I highlight gender issues in the production and processing segments of the chain, especially the working conditions of women in shrimp-processing factories.

Finally, in Chapter 8, I draw together the common and differing insights from earlier chapters and discuss the complex implications of the Blue Revolution. I offer some concluding remarks about the key questions raised in the book and about the research problem in general, and I discuss the implications for theory, policy, and practice.

Industrial aquaculture – the pinnacle of the Blue Revolution's achievement – is a critical part of the global agri-food system, and a prime candidate for further exploration of the changing contours of regulations governing the agri-food system, social justice, and changes in the environmental and agrarian landscapes of the global South. The proliferation of different certification schemes is a recent phenomenon in the globalization of the agri-food system and hence a new area of academic inquiry. Most agri-food industries, including industrial aquaculture, are now adopting the certification system to survive in the competitive global market, as "quality" becomes a major concern for both consumers and environmental groups. More research thus is needed as to why and how different regulatory regimes have emerged, and what are the broader sociological implications of this new phenomenon. Through my use of the relatively new global-commodity-chain model to delineate changes in environmental politics, agrarian relations, and gender and employment patterns, I hope to make a sustained contribution to the existing literature and to the broader debate surrounding the global agri-food system.

2 The Analytical Framework

Globalization of the agri-food system can be understood as "agriculture's continued incorporation into the general dynamics of capitalist accumulation," to quote Le Heron (1993, 17). Expanding on this view, and drawing on other writers (including Atkins and Bowler 2001; Bonnano et al. 1994; Clapp and Fuchs 2009; Goodman and Watts 1997b; and McMichael 1994), this trend has seen the fragmentation of agri-food production processes and the integration of producing countries into global commodity networks, the increasingly liberal international trading of food and agricultural products, dominance of that trade by corporately restructured agri-food capital (that is, food processing and retailing), the emergence of a new international division of agri-food labour, and the partial displacement of national institutions by such international bodies as the World Trade Organization in the regulation of trade relations for agri-food products.

Over the past few decades, the global agri-food system has undergone various transformations. The approaches sociologists and other scholars have adopted to investigate this evolution include those of the French regulation school (Aglietta 1979; Boyer 1990; Buttel 2001); Fordist and post-Fordist regime theory (Busch and Bain 2004); the theory of food regimes (Friedmann 1982, 2000, 2005; Friedmann and McMichael 1989; Le Heron 1993; McMichael 1992, 1994, 1999; Robinson 1997); post-Foucaultian developmental governmentality (Watts 2003); and global commodity chain (GCC) analysis, although, in most cases, scholars have incorporated more than one approach at a time. In this chapter, I first provide a conceptual review of the widely used GCC approach. In adopting this model to identify problems in the study of agri-food dynamics, I suggest a somewhat revised GCC approach.

I then delineate the important conceptual debates surrounding the chain of governance. The term "environmental governance" has been used to capture the power and actor dynamics at work in governing the contemporary agri-food system. To define agrarian transformation, I then draw on two competing, yet complementary, traditions: political economy and industrial restructuring and regulation. The final conceptual thread I examine in this chapter is gender relations in the context of the globalization of export-oriented industries, including agri-food. The combination of these four conceptual threads provides a solid analytical framework in which to examine environmental politics, agrarian change, and gender patterns brought about by the emergence of the Blue Revolution in the global South.

The Global Agri-Food Commodity Chain

The GCC model, which "draws on the simple idea that the design, production, and marketing of products involve a chain of activities divided between different enterprises" (Dolan and Humphrey 2000, 148–9), is one of the most widely used approaches in sociology to study inter-firm relations in the global agri-food system. There are several reasons for its popularity among scholars. First, as Collins (2005, 4) notes, the GCC is "well-suited to capturing the complex transactions of an era of globalization and corporate domination of agriculture." Second, the method makes sense at a time when diversified farming is giving way to the specialty production of particular crops or animals (Friedland 1984). Third, it provides a way to encompass the array of actors and institutions involved in what Friedmann (1993) calls "private global regulation" in a context in which the relevance of national accounts data to understanding trade and policy is declining (Collins 2005).

Within the GCC framework, however, is a plethora of overlapping names and concepts, such as global value chains, the value system, production networks, value networks, commodity system analysis, and so forth, as various authors have developed the concept in different ways (Islam 2008a, 2008b). In the well-known framework developed by Michael Porter (1990, 40–4), for instance, "the value system" is a set of interlinked "complete" firms that comprise the network of business functions. Porter asserts that "[c]ompetitive advantage is increasingly a function of how well a company can manage this entire system. Linkages not only connect activities inside a company but also create interdependencies between a firm and its suppliers and channels" (43–4).

Analysts such as Gereffi and Korzeniewicz (1994) and Dolan (2004) believe that the GCC approach originated with the work of Hopkins and Wallerstein, who define a GCC as "a network of labor and production processes whose end result is a finished commodity" (1986, 159). Ruigrok and van Tulder (1995) use "industrial complex" to discuss the restructuring strategies leading global firms have adopted in organizing suppliers, workers, and dealers and maintaining relations with governments and financiers. Similarly, Wilkinson (1995, 1), using the concept of the "productive system" to analyse the knitwear industry, notes that "[i]t is possible to describe as a 'productive system' the combination of design, product development, marketing, production, and retailing by which products progress from their conception to the final consumer. In the markets for knitwear, different types of 'productive systems' coexist and compete." Among agri-food scholars, Friedland (1984) was perhaps the first to adopt this approach, which he called "commodity systems analysis." The concept of a chain of inter-firm linkages is the key to the analyses of all these authors, who have applied it to particular circumstances, concentrating on specific linkages and their characteristics. Accordingly, their different perspectives and priorities have generated different but overlapping approaches.

The GCC analysis that facilitated mapping of the world division of labour (Hopkins and Wallerstein 1986) was further elaborated upon by Gereffi and Korzeniewicz (1994) in the sixteenth Political Economy of the World System conference proceedings (see McMichael 1995). Gereffi and Korzeniewicz, whose model offers a more direct empirical line of inquiry, explore how the production, distribution, and consumption of products are globally interconnected along commodity or value chains. According to the authors (1994, 2), "[a] GCC consists of sets of inter-organizational networks clustered around one commodity or product, linking households, enterprises, and states to one another within the world-economy. These networks are situationally specific, socially constructed, and locally integrated, underscoring the social embeddedness of economic organization."

Although Gereffi and his colleagues took as their starting point the work of Hopkins and Wallerstein (1986), their concept of the GCC contains four new elements that are particularly useful for analysis of the global agri-food system. First, they emphasize the fact that these chains frequently involve the cross-border coordination of the activities of independent firms. Second, they emphasize the issue of governance, drawing attention to the fact that large retail and brand-name companies create inter-firm networks characterized by a high degree of coordination. Third, they highlight the increasingly important role played by international buyers, retailers, and brand-name companies in the trade of labour-intensive manufactured products such as garments (see also Gereffi 1994). Last, in recognition of these elements, Gereffi (1994, 1999) himself postulates two types of commodity chains: buyer driven and producer driven.

The GCC model, therefore, has become a useful analytical tool in identifying the central role that global buyers such as Walmart, Nike, Gap, Darden Restaurants, and Lyons Seafood play in organizing activities within commodity chains (see Dolan 2004; Islam 2008a). Gereffi (1994, 1999), for example, emphasizes the importance of what he calls "buyer-driven commodity chains," observing that, in some industries, large retailers, marketers, and brand-name companies play a pivotal role in establishing and driving geographically dispersed production and distribution systems without necessarily owning any themselves. The UK-Africa horticulture value chain, for example, exhibits several characteristics of a buyer-driven commodity chain, in which powerful lead farms[1] (supermarkets) govern supply networks that cross several African countries, defining not only what is to be produced, but also how and under what conditions it is to be produced (Dolan 2004; Dolan and Humphrey 2000). According to Dolan (2004, 100), "[t]hese supermarkets increasingly determine the production imperatives of horticultural farms upstream in the chain and, indirectly, the employment strategies they adopt." In Raynolds's (2004) analysis, the Gereffi GCC framework is used to examine the interlinking of products and services in a sequence of value-added activities, the organizational and spatial configuration of enterprises forming production and marketing networks, and the governance structure determining resource allocation along the commodity chain.

GCC analysis is similar to supply-chain analysis in that "both focus on the institutional arrangements that link producers, marketers, distributors, and consumers" (Gammage et al. 2006, 2). More precisely, supply-chain analysis focuses on "the way goods move from producers to consumers; the exchange of payment, credit, and capital among actors; price signals, pricing behavior, and value added; the dissemination of technology; and the flow of information across the chain" (2). GCC analysis augments this approach by identifying and exploring the spaces in which returns are generated. It also recognizes that "different configurations of actors may influence capabilities, relative bargaining power, and subsequently affect outcomes along the value chain" (2). Overall, the GCC approach defines product chains in terms of actors and their objectives, the structure of the respective markets, the strategies or instruments that actors use to influence that structure, and, finally, the product itself, as different product chains might have different characteristics.

The GCC model[2] has thus become an important framework for analysing economic development and the evolution and complexity of export-oriented industries in the context of globalization, thereby proving fruitful for delineating the power relations or governance within chains and their prospects for broad-based growth (Dolan and Humphrey 2000). The framework also provides, to quote Collins (2005, 7), "an alternative to the totalizing frameworks of development theory" such as determinism, economism, and Western bias. The point of departure for GCC analysis is the fact that some firms directly or indirectly influence the organization of global production, logistics, and marketing systems. Through the governance structures they create, the decisions that these firms make have important consequences for the access of developing country farms to international markets and their range of activities (Gereffi 1999). The governance structures also generate changes in local landscapes (Dolan and Humphrey 2000).

Whereas, in his earlier writings, Gereffi (1994, 1999) distinguished between two basic types of governance in commodity chains (buyer driven and producer driven), recent studies have extended this model beyond this dichotomy to, for example, the "international trader-driven" chain (Gibbon 2003). Gereffi et al. (2001, 4), for example, identify some features of governance in the global value chain that is now appearing. First, coordination within value chains can take various forms. In addition to coordination through arm's-length market relations,[3] there are three forms of governance in value chains: inter-firm networks, quasi-hierarchical relationships between powerful lead firms and independent but subordinate firms in the chain, and vertical integration within enterprises. Where powerful lead firms do exist, their power stems from two factors: their market power (measured in part by concentration or market share) and their positioning in chain segments in which they can create and/or appropriate high returns. Second, governance structures, as opposed to arm's-length market relationships, arise primarily in response to two distinct needs for coordination: the greater involvement that companies have in specifying the products their suppliers must make, the likelier they are to develop a governance structure to coordinate supplier activities; and the greater their exposure to the risks resulting from suppliers' failures, the likelier they are to intervene directly to coordinate and monitor the supply chain. Third, governance involves the ability of one firm in the chain to influence or determine the activities of another firm in the chain. This influence can extend to defining the products to be produced by suppliers (in extreme cases, even those of suppliers' suppliers) and specifying the processes and standards to be used. The power to exert such influence is exercised through lead firms' control over the key resources needed in the chain, decisions about entry to and exit from the chain, and the monitoring of suppliers. It might also involve the provision of technical support to suppliers to enable them to achieve the required performance. Chains differ significantly with respect to how strongly governance is exercised, how much governance is concentrated in the hands of a single firm, and how many lead firms exercise governance over chain members.

A number of significant questions about governance in the global value chain have been raised (see, for example, Gereffi et al. 2001), but have yet to be addressed. For example, what role do government agencies and other external forms of regulation (such as environmental certification) play in determining both product and process parameters? To what extent is there a trade-off between coordination and control within the chain and the use of external agencies to certify and regulate firms? Taking governance as a core element of GCC analysis, such economists as Humphrey and Schmitz (2001) and Sturgeon (2001) have further expanded Gereffi's model. Humphrey and Schmitz (2001, 21–2), for instance, clarify why chain governance is needed in export-oriented industries in the age of globalization. At any point in the chain, they explain, the production process (in its broadest sense, including quality, logistics, and design) is defined by a set of parameters, and the five key parameters that determine what is to be done are: (a) what is to be produced (production definition); (b) how it is to be produced (definition of production processes, including the kinds of technology to be used, quality systems, and labour and environmental standards); (c) when it is to be produced (for example, production and supply deadlines); (d) how much is to be produced; and (e) what the price will be.[4] Underlying these variables is the question of chain governance. In addition to all of these parameters and risks, Humphrey and Schmitz (2001) further identify the factors that necessitate chain governance, such as market access, the acquisition of production capabilities, the distribution of gains, leverage points for policy initiatives, the funnelling of technical assistance, the sale of technology, and so forth (see also Islam 2008a).

Gereffi and his colleagues used the GCC model primarily in analysing export-oriented manufacturing industries (see, for example, Dicken 1998; Gereffi and Korzeniewicz 1994; Henderson and Dicken 2002). The basic GCC framework has also been used and elaborated upon, with substantial variation, by many agri-food scholars,[5] who suggest that powerful buyers increasingly govern and drive production definition, specification, production processes, and enterprise participation in the international supply chain. Some analysts, however, have linked their discussion of GCCs to the complementary use of earlier traditions of producer-consumer networks, such as commodity systems (sometimes termed "production chains," "food chains," or "filières") (Bowler 1992; Friedland 1984) and food networks (Arce and Marsden 1993). The theoretical underpinnings of these approaches can be traced back further to the actor-network theory, which itself was introduced into the literature (in English) on the sociology of science and technology by such analysts as Callon (1986), Latour (1986), and Law (1986). The GCC approach has thus become what Collins (2005, 15) has described as "a richly promiscuous approach" that has helped to "concretize and situate a broad range of theoretical perspectives."[6]

Although scholars' extension of Gereffi's producer- and buyer-driven analogy to the agri-food sector seems quite insightful, one can discern some critical scrutiny of and challenges to what Raynolds (2004, 727) calls "a simple dichotomous characterization of producer- versus buyer-driven chains." First, the nature of globalization's effect on the agri-food system differs from that of other export-oriented manufacturing industries. Goodman and Watts (1997a), for example, show that, due to their inherent characteristics and dynamics, most agri-food industries do not display the vertically integrated transnational production that Gereffi (1999) found in the apparel industry. In the agri-food commodity chain, the nature of lead firms varies significantly (Raynolds 2004). Among buyer-driven agri-food commodity chains, some are driven by large supermarket retailers, whereas others are dominated by processors, international traders, or global branders (Dolan and Humphrey 2000; Gibbon 2001a, 2001b; Ponte 2002a, 2002b). Some chains are also influenced by environmental and labour rights movements (Islam 2008a; Vandergeest 2007). Second, although buyers in the current global agri-food system are increasingly opting for linkages to fewer but larger producers to ensure traceability and a timely supply, and are therefore tightening chain governance (Busch and Bain 2004), the characterization of an agri-food system simply as "buyer driven" obscures the potential influence of other actors in the chain. Third, referring to Fold (2002), Ponte (2002a), and Talbot (2002), Raynolds (2004, 727) observes that agri-food commodity chains are often characterized by "important internal variations, with different types of enterprises dominating different segments or different regional strands." Fourth, in the traditional GCC model, economic actors are given primacy, and political conditions are treated as contextual (Gereffi 1999; Sturgeon 2001). In agri-food networks, however, economic, social, and political forces are central to chain governance (Dolan and Humphrey 2000; Islam 2008a; Ponte, 2002a, 2002b; Raynolds 2004).

Although economic actors are important, agri-food chains sometimes contain non-human actants, such as viruses, bacteria (Vandergeest 2007),[7] and other elements of nature. According to Fine (1994), for instance, agri-food chains should include nature to permit a more complex understanding of the ways in which biology and the organic "temper," to use his language, the political economy of the food system. In this sense, Goodman and Watts (1997a, 19) suggest that "the question of risk, perishability, seasonability, sustainability, and non-identity of production and labor time ... are necessary to grasp the commodity-specific dynamics of production systems ... but should be linked with food consumption as integral elements of global food networks." Finally, the analysis of Humphrey and Schmitz (2001) is helpful in delineating how environmental groups and recently emerged third-party certifiers play roles in defining and enforcing the production and process parameters of the global agri-food system. One can argue that many agents traditionally presented as "external to the chain" are no longer "external" but now constitute an indispensable and intrinsic part of the commodity chain.

These critical accounts of traditional GCC analysis ardently call for more appropriate analysis of the agri-food system, one that identifies different sources, forms, and levels of control across the commodity. This is all the more critical given that the dynamics and characteristics of the agri-food chain differ from those in export-oriented manufacturing industries and that agri-food commodity areas are strongly influenced by consumer and environmental groups and deeply embedded in non-market norms, such as the need to expand the commodity chain to ensure socially and environmentally friendly food (Busch and Bain 2004; Raynolds 2004; Vandergeest 2007). Accordingly, Raynolds (2004,

728) suggests that "governance [be] understood not as a pre-existing structural feature of commodity chains, but as the relations through which key actors create, maintain, and potentially transform network activities."

Agri-food scholars have also used the GCC approach, albeit in different ways, primarily to explore production-consumption networks,[8] which traditionally has tended to favour analyses of buyers and to some extent suppliers (Dolan 2004). Recent studies, however, have extended GCC analysis to explore local labour relations (see, for example, Dolan 2004; Islam 2008b) and gender issues (Barrientos, Dolan, and Tallontire 2003; Gammage et al. 2006; Islam 2009). As governance is a key factor in GCC analysis, a conceptual synthesis of a broader dynamics of GCCs and environmental governance offers a better understanding of the global agri-food system.

Environmental Governance

Governance: Good and Bad

The notion of governance, which has long featured in both political and academic discourse, is not only one of the most pervasive features of human society, but also one of the vaguest terms in the social sciences. In the development literature, for example, "governance" has been used both as a viable route to positive social change and a critique of development. One can therefore discern at least two broad trajectories of the development literature dealing with governance: the mainstream and the critical. The concept of "good governance" has recently gained widespread use in the mainstream development literature, promoted largely by what McMichael (2008) calls "global managers,"[9] to distinguish the concept from the critical literature on development and "governance" and from "bad governance."

In the mainstream development literature, definitions of governance vary widely among development actors. The Institute on Governance,[10] for example, defines it as "the process whereby societies or organizations make important decisions, determine whom they involve and how they render account" (Plumptre, n.d.). The World Bank first picked up the issue of governance in the late 1980s when it started to advocate civil service reforms, although the term did not come into Bank parlance until 1989 (Wood 2005). The Bank defines governance as "the manner in which power is exercised in the management of a country's economic and social resources for development" (quoted in Santiso 2002, 2). Many elements of and principles underlying the concept of good government have become an integral part of the meaning of "governance." The World Bank (2007b, 1) further defines governance as "the traditions and institutions by which authority in a country is exercised for the common good. This includes (i) the process by which those in authority are selected, monitored and replaced, (ii) the capacity of the government to effectively manage its resources and implement sound policies, and (iii) the respect of citizens and the state for the institutions that govern economic and social interactions among them."

The World Bank's focus on governance reflects the worldwide thrust towards political and economic liberalization. Such an approach highlights issues of greater state responsiveness and accountability, as well as the effect of these factors on political stability and economic development. In *From Crisis to Sustainable Growth*, the World Bank (1989) expresses the notion of "better governance" as "political renewal" achieved through curbing corruption at the highest and lowest levels by strengthening accountability, encouraging public debate, and nurturing a free press. To the Bank, better governance also means fostering grassroots and non-governmental organizations (NGOs) such as farmers' associations, cooperatives, and women's groups.

The United Nations Economic and Social Commission for Asia and the Pacific (UNESCAP 2007, 1) similarly defines governance as "the process of decision-making and the process by which decisions are implemented (or not implemented)." For UNESCAP, there are different layers and characteristics of governance, and the concept can be used in several contexts, including corporate governance, international governance, national governance, and local governance. UNESCAP identifies eight major characteristics of good governance: it should be participatory, consensus oriented, accountable, transparent, responsive, effective and efficient, equitable and inclusive, and follow the rule of law. Similar to the World Bank's definition, UNESCAP's view of good governance specifies that "corruption is minimized, the views of minorities are taken into account and that the voices of the most vulnerable in society are heard in decision-making. It is also responsive to the present and future needs of society" (2007, 1).

Despite the emphasis placed on governance by the World Bank and the United Nations, many scholars and practitioners working in international development and/or with donor agencies have concentrated almost exclusively on the issue of "political legitimacy" – the dependent variable produced by effective governance. For them, aside from being an instrument of public affairs management or a gauge of political development, governance has become a useful mechanism for enhancing the legitimacy of the public realm. One model of local governance that scholars and practitioners have devised is "community-based natural resource management" (CBNRM). The stated aims of CBNRM, an approach not without criticism, are to (a) promote democracy and participation among local people, including women, who have historically been excluded; (b) create mechanisms for their empowerment; (c) claim natural resources that are extracted mainly by the state elite; (d) reorganize local communities into legal entities and frameworks for the management of resources; (e) create networks from the local to the international level; and (f) render development projects more fruitful by ensuring the participation of local people, thereby also making them more meaningful and accepted (Brosius, Tsing, and Zerner 1998; Li 2000, 2002; Lynch and Talbot 1995). Serving as a bridge between the state, communities, and development agencies, CBNRM offers a comprehensive view of self-governance. Li (2002, 281) elaborates upon the approach:

> A core concern of CBNRM has been to strengthen the capacity of the communities to protect their natural resource base from the more destructive and rapacious activities of ruling regimes, among others. The model envisages a shift in power from states to communities, conceived as separate entities. Instead, as I have argued, states and communities are mutually constitutive. CBNRM offers the state system an opportunity to rearrange the ways in which the rule is accomplished, while also offering the communities an opportunity to realign their position within (but not outside) that system.

In the critical development and governance literature, a key mode of governance is "discursive categorization." Scholars have shown how, for example, capitalist development – by making discursive categories – historically became a governing tool by which the dominating groups exercised control over the dominated. Prominent scholars adopting the poststructuralist and postmodern perspectives explain how capitalist governance and power have been maintained and extended through the discursive creation and re-creation of different domains of thought in the development discourse to justify certain actions and interventions. Escobar (1995), for example, delineates how poverty was "discovered" and "problematized," how the "Third World" was constructed in the discourse of development, and how two-thirds of the world's population was governed under a regime of control by discursive practices: "The poor increasingly appeared as a social problem requiring new ways of intervention in society" (22), and "the treatment of poverty allowed society to conquer new domains" (23). The management of poverty, then, called for intervention and scientific categorization in education, health, hygiene, morality, and employment, and the instilling of good habits regarding association, savings, child rearing, and so on. The result was a panoply of interventions accounted for by the domain of knowledge and intervention. Not only poverty, but also health, education, hygiene, employment, and the poor quality of life in towns and cities were constructed and categorized as social problems, requiring extensive knowledge about the population in question and appropriate modes of social planning (Escobar 1992). According to Escobar (1995, 23), the "most significant aspect of this phenomenon was the setting into place of apparatuses of knowledge and power that took upon themselves to optimize life by producing it under modern, 'scientific' conditions." By constructing the discourse of sustainable development, and problematizing "global survival," capitalism conquered nature, thereby legitimating its exploitation (see also Brosius 1999; McMichael 2008).

By uncovering these discursive constructions, scholars have shown how categorization becomes an objectifying tool of governance. Such categorization operates by creating an apparent, but always hidden, power relation: prioritizing certain actors while stigmatizing others. The Third World is constructed by distancing it from the "civilized" and developed West, as a result of which the power relation between the agency doing the constructing and the subjects so constructed becomes that of "father-child" or "doctor-patient" (Escobar 1995, 159), and thus governance is maintained in an objectifying and normalizing manner.

Categorization is a dominant mode of governance not only in the broad discourse of development and North-South relations, but also in development projects. It empowers certain actors, spaces, and species, and disempowers others. As Vandergeest (2003a, 47) states, "[a]ll development projects involve reorganizing the meaning and control of space" and have "the potential of causing displacement," not only for human beings but also for other species. Scott (1998, 13) writes: "Plants that are valued become 'crops,' and the species that compete with them are stigmatized as 'pests.' Thus, trees that are valued become 'timber,' while species that compete with them become 'trash trees' or 'underbrush.' The same logic applies to fauna. Highly valued animals become 'game' or 'livestock,' while those animals that compete with or prey upon them become 'predators' or 'varmints'."

With such powerful vocabularies and discursive practices, development projects create categories, make different spaces, and disempower those that appear inimical to or compete with them. Thus, through the processes of "reorganizing nature" (Scott 1998), "racializing space" (Vandergeest 2003b), "producing and reproducing differences" (Soja and Hooper 1993), and "labeling identities" (Islam 2013) – by both empowering and disempowering – governance in development projects works through discursive categorization. An apparent implication of this type of governance is that it "privilege[s] certain actors and marginalize[s] others" (Brosius 1999, 38). As Doty (1996, 3) puts it in the case of North-South relations, "one entity has been able to construct 'realities' that were taken seriously and acted upon and the other entity has been denied equal degrees or kinds of agency." The central character of capitalist governance is not merely an economic one; rather, it is a whole package of power, production, governance, and social relations (Islam 2005, 2007).

Another critical stream of the governance literature in the environmental realm centres around Foucault's notion of *gouvernementalité*, a neologism he first presented and explored at the end of the 1970s (see Foucault 1979, 1984, 1991). The term implies the establishment of complex social techniques and institutions to intensify and expand mechanisms of control and power over the population in the name of what has become known as "reasons of state." Governmentality, for Foucault, refers to a "conduct of conduct" (2000, 211), a more or less calculated and rational set of ways of shaping conduct and securing rules through a multiplicity of authorities and agencies inside and outside the state and at a variety of special levels – or what he calls, albeit negatively, the "art of government" (1979, 5).

In a similar vein, Goldman turns our attention to the World Bank's attempt to "enlist scores of social actors and institutions to help generate a new development regime that is coherently *green* and *neoliberal*" (2004, 167; italics in original) in order to transform modern states such as Laos into what he calls "environmental states." The social actors and institutions he refers to include ministries of the environment, natural resources, and finance and some of the Bank's best-funded international environmental organizations, such as the International Union for Conservation of Nature and the World Wildlife Fund. Contrary to what ecological modernization theorists suggest – that is, that states are unified rational actors that eventually graduate into eco-rational modernity[11] – Goldman argues that emerging "environmental states" are "marked by new global forms of legality and eco-rationality that have *fragmented, stratified,* and unevenly *transnationalized* Southern states, state actors, and state power" (2004, 167; italics in original). Drawing on a Foucauldian understanding of power, he calls this new form of green governance "eco-governmentality," which is having an impact on "the production of, first, national and global truth regimes on nature; second, rights of regimes to more effectively control (and increase the market value of) environments, natural resources, and resource-dependent populations; and third, new state authorities within national boundaries and in the world system" (167). Taking Laos as an example, Goldman argues that "much of a borrowing country – its nature, populations, governance, and knowledge – has the potential of becoming reconstituted as subjects of new forms of government according to new cultural logics of eco-rationality, enabling new and old frontiers of World Bank-fostered capital accumulation" (171–2).

One of the fundamental ways of extending the realm of governmentality is "institutionalization," which, for Foucault (1979), is the process of centralizing power around the government (the army, the educational system, government ministries, the justice system, and the like), and thereafter intensifying the effects of power at various levels: that of the entire population, the economy, and the individual. The process also requires new forms of (scientific) knowledge, which eventually create "institutionalized subjectivity." To understand this concept, one must look not at the elements themselves, but at the system of relations established among them. As Escobar (1995, 40–1) explains, "[i]t is a system that allows the systematic creation of objects, concepts, and strategies ... the system of relations establishes a discursive practice that sets the rules of the game: who can speak, from what point of view, with what authority, and according to what criteria of expertise. It sets the rules that must be followed for this or that problem, theory, or object to emerge and be named, analyzed, and eventually transformed into a policy plan."

In highlighting the indicators of the scale of contemporary environmental institutionalization, Brosius (1999, 38) turns our attention to "the accelerating pace of professionalization," particularly "the remarkable growth of the field of environmental management and ... the proliferation of environmental studies programs at universities." With respect to the latter, Brosius argues that such proliferation represents efforts to train a transnational cadre of planners to design and execute various forms of environmental intervention. This process of environmental institutionalization can be viewed as a positive development, particularly in terms of raising environmental concerns to a level of legitimacy they previously lacked. Some concerns, however, remain, as Brosius explains:

> There are reasons to be concerned about this process of institutionalization. Such institutions, whatever they may do, inscribe and naturalize certain discourses. While they create certain possibilities of ameliorating environmental degradation, they simultaneously preclude others. They privilege certain actors and marginalize others. Apparently designed to advance an environmental agenda, such institutions in fact often obstruct meaningful change through endless negotiation, legalistic invasion, compromise among "stakeholders," and the creation of unwieldy projects aimed at top-down environmental management. More importantly, however, they insinuate and naturalize a discourse that excludes moral or political imperatives in favor of indifferent bureaucratic and/or technoscientific forms of institutionally created and validated intervention. (1999, 39)

These two broad trajectories of the governance literature – the mainstream and the critical – call for agri-food research to incorporate an examination of institutional developments and various discursive shifts and constructions, not only as part of the "good governance" propounded by the mainstream development literature, but also as part of an environmental governmentality that has the potential to marginalize or displace certain actors. Such an examination, in fact, offers a number of important insights into how a regime of environmental governmentality is established and amplified to the possible marginalization of other forms of engagement, such as NGOs and community-led institutions, in the politics of nature and the environment.

Privatizing Environmental Governance in Global Commodity Chains

Governance is at the analytical core of GCC analysis, and is conventionally understood as the "non-market coordination of economic activity" (Gereffi et al. 2001, 4). More precisely, governance refers to "the inter-firm relationships and institutional mechanisms through which [the] non-market coordination of activities in the chain is achieved" (Humphrey and Schmitz 2001, 22). Although many export-oriented industries previously exhibited this kind of chain governance, more recently they have become less vertically integrated and more network oriented (Gereffi, Humphrey, and Sturgeon 2005). In addition to this shift in governance, the past few decades have also witnessed the proliferation of crucial environmental and ecological attributes and regulations governing the global agri-food system (Goodman and Watts 1997b; Henson and Reardon 2005; Vandergeest, Flaherty, and Miller 1999). Hence, the environment has become an indispensable ingredient of, and an overarching framework for, governance. As noted at the beginning of this chapter, one can call this "environmental governance."

The agri-food system increasingly is governed by an array of complex interrelated public and private standards that Caswell, Bredahl, and Hooker (1998, 548) call "quality metasystems." Since the late 1980s, a number of such metasystems and metastandards have emerged in widely varying areas: product quality (ISO 9000 and QS 9000 standards), environmental management systems (ISO 14000 standards), worker empowerment and quality (total quality management), customer feedback (efficient consumer response), supply-chain management, inventory control (just in time), and, more narrowly, food safety (hazard analysis and critical control points, and statistical process control).[12] These systems – mostly dominated by environmental, social, and safety concerns, which can also be viewed as "codes of conduct" – increasingly govern the way in which the entire supply chain operates, from primary production through retail distribution. At the same time, the evolution of such systems has stimulated and been facilitated by the development of a multitiered system of conformity assessment based around certification and accreditation (Henson and Reardon 2005; NRC 1995).

Scholars and practitioners of environmental regulation have discerned different forms of environmental governance, but they are all more or less embedded in three broad pillars: environmental, economic, and social. Cashore (2002) and Cashore, Auld, and Newsom (2003), for instance, use the term "non-state market-driven" (NSMD) governance to characterize the turning of some states to market-based incentives and the abandoning of their traditional key roles for the sake of "collective interests." Prominent examples include the Forestry Stewardship Council, the Marine Stewardship Council, and ISO 14000 certification (Cadman 2011; Clapp 1998; Taylor 2005; Vandergeest 2007). Although these institutions focus primarily on environmental qualities, other certification regimes – such as Fair Trade (Raynolds 2002), the new Ecotourism Council, and organic food certification (Hamilton 2004; Vandergeest 2007) – pay less attention to environmental impacts but claim "sustainability" as one of their goals. This broader trend in the environmental movement has shaped the global agri-food system significantly. Cashore and his colleagues use the term in the context of sustainable forestry certification, but it is also highly relevant to the global agri-food system, as both are moving towards private forms of environmental regulation. Although the NSMD model has attempted to challenge existing state-centred authority in the wake of private regulatory regimes, evidence shows that the roles and authority of states in the new regimes have not been totally ceded, but rather have taken different forms (Cadman 2011; Islam 2008a; Vandergeest 2007).

In the context of agri-food studies, the emergence of private regulations and regulatory agencies has transformed governance. Traditionally, government agencies were responsible for monitoring safety standards and other food quality attributes. Recently, however, the emergence of certification has precipitated a shift in responsibility for this task to third-party certifiers.[13] This transformation, which Busch and Bain (2004, 337) call the "private regulation of the public," has shaped the global agri-food system significantly as new regulatory practices are being extended across national borders – from consumption sites in the North to production sites in Asia, Africa, and Latin America (Vandergeest 2007).

Contesting the ideas of "the private regulation of the public" and NSMD governance in relation to the environmental dimensions of new commodity-based forms of regulation, Vandergeest (2007) turns our attention towards new environmental regulatory networks (ERNs), arguing that they allow us to get around the framing of regulatory practices as either state or market driven, permitting us instead to think through the way in which regulatory regimes can mobilize a dispersed network of actors in the regulatory process. The ERN concept was devised in response to the clear-cut demarcation of regulation as privatized, market-driven, or non-state driven, a demarcation that Vandergeest (2007, 1154) finds "difficult to sustain." The actors in these networks typically do not eliminate state involvement in shaping regulatory regimes; rather, they relocate specific state institutions as actors in a network of regulatory actors, although still acting within the broader dynamics that characterize state-based institutions and the regulatory network. In comparison to other models, Vandergeest fairly claims that his model – being accommodative rather than exclusionary – is "a more open and accurate way of understanding certification," one that includes "different state institutions, environmental groups, the World Bank and other multilateral and bilateral development agencies, UN organizations, trade agreements, consumers, retailer organizations, farmers, policy and research centers ... and non-human actants such as viruses [and] bacteria" (1154). Vandergeest also shows us that the human and non-human actors in the network are driven by multiple factors and motives, such as "reducing harmful environmental impacts, promoting economic growth, harmonizing certification standards for the purpose of facilitating trade, ensuring safe food, protecting domestic industries, and creating new food qualities that can be marketed to consumers" (1154). His model therefore goes beyond the simple characterizations of NSMD (Cashore 2002; Cashore, Auld, and Newsom 2003), buyer driven (Gereffi 1994), demand driven (Reardon and Berdegué 2002), and "the private regulation of the public" (Busch and Bain 2004, 337).

Vandergeest's (2007) position is reinforced and supported by a broad array of the agri-food literature.[14] In organic coffee certification, for example, Mutersbaugh (2002) finds that the active involvement of producer organizations and village and regional leaders, along with "a new producer logic" (market-price interdependence), plays a significant role in governing the coffee chain. Similarly, in their discussion of the coffee chain, Muradian and Pelupessy (2005, 2031) report that "the relationship between the degree of coordination and power asymmetry is not straightforward," but, rather, takes diverse forms such as "market transactions" (typical arm's-length transactions with no or a low degree of coordination), "weak coordination" (complex but not very specific information exchange; low monitoring costs for buyers; low cost of switching to other commercial partners), "strong coordination" (considerable, complex, and specific information exchange; high monitoring and switching costs), and "vertical integration" (complex and very specific information that is secret most of the time; standards, processes, and logistics that are controlled through ownership).

In his analysis of the fish commodity chain, Wilkinson (2006, 139–40) argues that "long-established food chains, where multiple actors, both public and private, have cumulatively defined and redefined policies and strategies through complex procedures of conflict and compromise, may often assume a more systemic dynamic that is less amenable than sectors such as fresh fruit and vegetables to clear governance, whether by supply or demand." In their study of the implementation of private standards, Hatanaka, Bain, and Busch (2006) find a multiplicity of actors whom they classify into four stakeholder types: retailers, NGOs and activists, suppliers, and third-party certifiers. A more nuanced approach to governance can be found in Raynolds's examination of commodity networks, in which she refers to "the complex web of material and nonmaterial relationships connecting the social, political and economic actors enmeshed in the life of a commodity." She suggests that "agri-food network analysis can refine its political edge by increasing its attention to governance – the analytical core of commodity chain analysis – where governance is understood not as a preexisting structural feature of commodity chains, but as the relations through which key actors create, maintain, and potentially transform network activities" (2004, 728).

Taking important insights from such authors as Hatanaka, Bain, and Busch (2006), Ponte (2002b), Raynolds (2004), Vandergeest (2007), and Wilkinson (2006), as well as from the ongoing debates surrounding chain governance discussed thus far, "environmental governance" can be understood as the way in which the actors or actants in the commodity chain organize and use power to manage natural resources, and the environmental and social impacts of its use. The term encompasses the activities not only of governments, but also those of other actors, including business, NGOs, and the networks or communities of individuals affected and concerned, each with competing claims to authority over particular issues. Although not entirely situated in the agri-food arena, Lemos and Agrawal's (2006) hybrid model of environmental governance across state-market-community divisions (co-management, public-private partnerships, and social-private partnerships) is also useful for agri-food research. Governance thus involves many social structures and processes that influence how decisions are made, rules are enforced, conflicts are resolved, and projects are funded, monitored, and evaluated. The interplay between actors and institutions can be complex, especially when several scales are involved – as is typical in decision making concerning commodity chains. This environmental governance framework allows us to understand why and how private regulation or certification emerges and is implemented; to explore the various ways in which agri-food production is regulated and driven by various human and non-human agents or actants and local ecologies; to look into the current practice of certification and its future impact on the global agri-food system; to examine environmental and agrarian changes; and to study gender and employment relations.

Agrarian Transformation

Agrarian transformation in this book builds on two divergent yet complementary research traditions: agrarian political economy, and industrial restructuring and regulation. Agrarian political economy can be traced to the writings of Marx, Lenin, Kautsky, and Chayanov that deal with the nature of the production process and peasant culture, the contours of rural transition, and the character of rural class politics (Newby 1987).[15] Many scholars of political economy use the term "commoditization" to denote the process of agrarian transformation from a subsistence (non-market) economy to market-based production. During this process, according to Atkins and Bowler (2001, 56), "as farm business and farm households are drawn into a dependency on non-farm goods and inputs purchased in the market, they are compelled to produce agricultural commodities with an exchange value in order to obtain a cash income." Smaller and economically unsuccessful farm businesses usually become marginalized through competition in commodity markets, whereas the owners of more successful and larger businesses are able to purchase the land of small farmers, thereby further enlarging the size of their own farms. Consequently, theorists posit, a polarizing trajectory in farm-size structure emerges in which fewer but larger farms dominate, with medium-sized farms the least able to resist the economic pressure towards marginalization (Atkins and Bowler 2001; Bowler 1992). Medium- and small-scale subsistence farmers gradually become wage labourers in the new economy of commodity production. To quote Marx (1999, 146), the emergence of wage labour is nothing but "the historical process of divorcing the producer from the means of production."

For classical Marxists, the process of capitalist accumulation unleashed by the logic of commoditization generates a polarized agrarian class structure: a capitalist land-owning class (the bourgeoisie), which occupies or owns large-scale, wage-labour farms, and a proletariat comprising the marginalized and ultimately landless peasant class that supplies the wage-labour for capitalists' farms (Atkins and Bowler 2001). Some researchers, such as Friedmann (1986) and Small (2007) have contested this notion of an agrarian class dichotomy, however, based on the existence of medium- and small-sized family farms that rely exclusively on family labour and experience no pressure to enlarge their businesses beyond demographic and cultural factors. Marsden and Symes (1984) argue that many large-scale, capital-intensive farm businesses can be owned and operated almost exclusively by multigenerational family labour, and therefore do not produce what neo-Marxists call the "proletarianization of farm labour" (see, for example, Araghi 1995; Davis 2006; Harvey 2003; Walker 2006). Other writers, such as Moran, Blunden, and Greenwood (1993), emphasize the importance of farmer cooperatives in the defence of small- and medium-sized farms. Although these scholars contest the inevitability of the agrarian class dichotomy posited by the neo-Marxists, they cannot ignore the increasing power of capital and the concomitant increasing vulnerability of family farms. As Marsden et al. (1986, 512) write, "[t]he legal ownership of farm business and land remains [with the farm family] whilst they become increasingly separated from effective control, as management depends on external technical and economic factors governed by monopoly industrial and finance capitals." What becomes increasingly apparent, as Atkins and Bowler (2001, 59) point out, is that "non-farm capital extracts surplus value from the farm sector indirectly, for instance through interest paid on farm finance (e.g., mortgages and credit facilities) and obtaining raw materials for food processing by production contracts with individual farms rather than through the open market."

A more recent approach to agrarian change is based on industrial restructuring and regulation. Focusing largely on the United States and Europe, this approach investigates how, at the national level, particular social and institutional ensembles temporarily might uphold particular regimes of accumulation and how, at the farm level, common technical and economic organizational changes are institutionalized (Raynolds 1997). This approach, drawn largely from the French regulation school (Buttel 2001), argues that capitalism develops through a series of distinct phases, each phase comprising a "regime of accumulation" and its associated "mode of social and political regulation" (see Aglietta 1979; Boyer 1990). A regime of accumulation, as defined by Busch and Bain (2004, 322), is "a stable and reproducible relationship between production and consumption." A mode of regulation, they explain, comprises "the state and private institutional forms, social practices, habits, and norms that regulate relationships and individual behaviors to ensure economic stability" (323). From the regulationist perspective, the Fordist regime was dominant throughout the post–Second World War period, during which economic accumulation was based on "the mass production and mass consumption of uniform, standardized, manu-factured goods supported by Keynesian state policies and institutions" (323). The post-Fordist regime of "flexible accumulation," which was founded on "the fragmentation of the market, since workplace and la-bor flexibility are required to produce customized, non-standardized goods and services" (323), was born out of the economic crisis of the 1970s and was accompanied by the demise of Keynesianism and the welfare state. Under Fordism, price and quantity were the primary cri-teria for characterizing production. Today, in contrast, the economic focus has turned to quality (see also Hatanaka, Bain, and Busch 2005).

Despite its major research contributions – such as highlighting the importance of the state in the regulation of economic activities, recog-nizing temporal and spatial regularities, and identifying the shifting competitive conditions of firm organization – the industrial restructur-ing and regulation approach generally suffers from a US and Eurocen-tric bias that, as Raynolds says (1997, 120), "glosses over real-world inequalities and variations, [and] when exaggerated, [the above] strengths become this literature's central weaknesses."

Until the relatively recent emergence of the industrial restructuring and regulation tradition, research on the multifaceted and dynamic na-ture of agrarian transformation was dominated by the agrarian political economy perspective. Although the former has provided a divergent body of literature on this transformation, the two perspectives share considerable common ground (Goodman and Redclift 1982; Jessop 1990; Raynolds 1997). Despite their different substantive focuses, the two approaches are, at heart, "theoretically and methodologically com-patible," provided they "eschew overly essentialist and deterministic models of development and pursue a dialectical analysis of the complex social forces and institutions shaping concrete economic processes and the multiple, recursive, trajectories of change" (Raynolds 1997, 120). A theoretical synthesis of the two approaches provides what Raynolds calls "a promising starting point for analyzing current restructuring dy-namics" (121). Such a synthesis helps us to examine the striking unity and diversity of the ongoing transformation in the global South, as it allows sensitivity to both sectoral differences and commonalities.

Gender Relations

Over the past three decades, research on the globalization of agri-food production[16] and other export-oriented industries[17] has revealed the rapid transformation that has opened up opportunities for women to enter new areas of paid employment, earn an income, gain independence, and participate more actively in social life. This transformation, however, has also created new challenges for women. Much of this employment is informal in nature, with poor working conditions and a lack of labour rights, and must be carried out in addition to household and family responsibilities.

From the contemporary literature on gender and work[18] in the context of the globalization of the agri-food system, one can discern at least three paradoxical patterns: *feminization alongside masculinity*, characterized by an increasingly large female workforce in processing factories, which remain dominated by men; *flexibility and informality with rigidity*, in which an increasingly precarious and vulnerable workforce, being casual, temporary, and part time, finds itself in an inflexible and formal workplace with various codes of conduct; and *human mobility*, with movement from rural to urban areas and from one form of subsistence to another. Wage labour, notes McMichael (1996, 40), "is undergoing a profound transformation, signalled by the increasingly unstable terms on which people are hired across the world, and the growing range of forms of labor in industry and agriculture – from stable cores of wage work through contract- and piece work to new forms of indentured, slave, and child labor – incorporated into global commodity chains under the restructuring of the global economy."

The enthusiastic neoliberal ideological patina that has been laid over the myriad technological innovations and organizational adjustments that have taken place has served to obscure what is a hard reality for increasing numbers of workers around the world: good jobs are getting harder to find – *and to keep* – while bad jobs are in plentiful supply, but working conditions seem to be getting worse. Countless low-wage labourers in the global South who produce primarily for the consumption of wealthy buyers in the global North encounter this bitter reality almost every day (Islam 2008b). Labour in the global South is always gendered, and its endless supply depends on complex patriarchal and subcontracting hierarchies. For corporations, subcontracting is a way of reducing labour costs and controlling labour power while evading responsibility for exploitation (Ong 1997; Ortiz and Aparicio 2007). The agri-food and other export-oriented industries prefer young, unmarried, and relatively uneducated women. Employers argue, as McMichael (2008, 92) writes, that "women are suited to the jobs because of their dexterity and patience, the qualities assumed of female employees are required as much by the construction of jobs as by patriarchal and repressive cultural practices produced within the factories, sweatshops, and homework units." Job construction also depends on changing conditions, as Raynolds (2001) shows in his research on plantations in the Dominican Republic. In times of economic downturn, displaced men in turn displace women via the use of local patronage networks, with work "regendered" to reward masculine competition. Mass layoffs of female workers lead to what Barrientos, Dolan, and Tallontire (2004, 5) call the "de-feminization of industry."

"Gender" is understood here as created through both practical activities and a culture of "representation" expressed in, for example, gendered labour relations. Acker (2006, 5–6) reminds us that "gender is best understood as pervasive patterns of difference, in advantage and disadvantage, work and reward, emotion and sexuality, image and identity, between male and female, created through practical activities and representations that justify these patterns that result in the social categories of women and men. Gender may include more than these two social categories. Gender is a basic principle of social organization, almost always involving unequal economic and social power in which men dominate. Gender is socially constructed and diverse, and varies historically and cross-culturally." This conceptualization helps us examine the trajectories of gender and employment relations in the sites of the Blue Revolution.

Conclusion

The global-commodity-chain approach was popularized by Gereffi and colleagues and applied initially to the study of export-oriented manufacturing industries such as apparel, shoes, and automobiles. Agri-food scholars subsequently adopted Gereffi's "buyer-driven" model, albeit in different ways, but recent changes to the global agri-food system suggest that we need to go beyond Gereffi's simple dichotomous model of governance. Although there is no clear consensus in the agri-food literature on how and to what extent the GCC concept can be used in the study of the global agri-food system, partly because of the dynamics inherent in the system – a move towards networks and the environment is becoming increasingly prominent.

In agri-food studies, the GCC approach has been used mainly to explore production-consumption networks and traditionally has favoured analyses of buyers, and only secondarily suppliers. Recent studies, however, have extended GCC analysis to explore local labour relations and gender issues, elucidating not only how food products and processes have been industrialized and standardized on a global scale, but also how the processes of industrialization and standardization has generated significant changes in local settings. What is apparent is that, although governance is the analytical core of the GCC model, the broader dynamics of governance are often more suitable. Distinguishing between the two major streams of the governance literature – the mainstream and the critical – can be useful in this regard. In this chapter, I have suggested the efficacy of integrated analysis of the agri-food system, incorporating both institutional developments and various discursive shifts and constructions as part not only of "good governance," as propounded by the mainstream development literature, but also of an environmental governmentality that potentially marginalizes or displaces certain actors. Because governance is a key factor in GCC analysis, and environmental regulations increasingly constitute a crucial issue, a conceptual synthesis of the broader dynamics of GCCs and environmental governance offers us a better understanding of the Blue Revolution and its effect on the global South.

Applying the GCC approach to industrial aquaculture – for example, the shrimp commodity chain that links the global South to Japan, the European Union, and the United States – might demonstrate, in part, several characteristics of a buyer-driven commodity chain. However, contrary to Gereffi's (1994, 1999) view on the sole governing role of powerful lead firms (supermarkets), a network of diverse local and international environmental groups and labour rights movements also defines – and intends to define – not only what kind of shrimp is produced, but also how and under what conditions it is produced. In this way, the shrimp commodity chain exhibits not a unilinear buyer-driven commodity chain, but a twin-driven commodity chain in which lead firms govern the supply network while environmental and non-profit groups and recently emerged third-party certifiers lay out and govern the regulatory aspects of shrimp aquaculture, sometimes working in an overlapping manner. Figure 2.1 illustrates what a twin-driven commodity chain might look like.

This chapter's brief conceptual background on the process of agrarian transformation in the global South – which has moved from subsistence shrimp and fish capture to farmed aquaculture, thereby linking itself to the global capitalist club – gives rise to a number of questions. Who are shrimp farmers today – locals or outsiders? Have small farmers

Figure 2.1. A Twin-Driven Commodity Chain

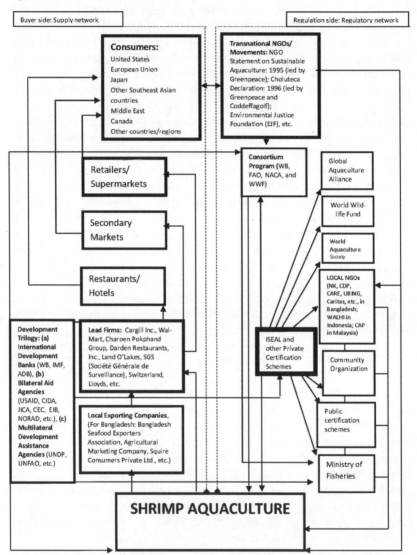

Source: Islam (2008a, 218); reprinted with permission from Elsevier.

been marginalized by the emergence of large-scale farms? Is a polarizing trajectory evident in shrimp aquaculture between large-scale farms in a few hands and the marginalization of small-scale farms? How is labour organized, and to what extent has wage labour emerged? Does social structure exhibit the agrarian class dichotomy propounded by classical Marxists? Does non-farm capital extract surplus value directly or indirectly from the production regime? I explore these questions in Chapter 6.

Similarly, the discussion on gender and employment also raises questions. What kind of development is realized through the manipulation of gender inequality? To what extent can certification agencies that have incorporated social principles address labour and gender issues? Do working conditions in industrial aquaculture in the global South follow the patterns outlined above, and if so, why and how? What are the sociological implications of work and gender issues in global agri-food studies? I address these crucial questions in Chapter 7.

3 Neoliberalism and the Emergence of the Blue Revolution in the Global South

Green Revolution technologies deepened the integration of local or regional agriculture into global markets. In the 1960s these technologies were gradually extended from staples – basic grains such as wheat, maize, and rice – to luxury high-value foods such as animal protein products and fruits and vegetables, a process dubbed the Second Green Revolution (McMichael 2008). A decade later, echoing the Green Revolution (Khor 1994), aquaculture underwent a similar shift in the form of the neoliberalism-driven, so-called Blue Revolution. In particular, shrimp farms – which rely on intensive, monocultural stocking, mechanized water exchange, antibiotics, and processed feeds – were set up by many commercial companies in the coastal areas of tropical nations as part of national government policies in this period, often with technical or financial aid from international agencies. Shrimp, including large tiger prawns, are exported primarily to the rich countries of the global North, where they fetch a high price and have become a fashionable and expensive cuisine item and a major source of export earnings for a number of countries in the global South (Hall 2004). Many are now members of a club known as the New Agricultural Countries (NACs). As alluded earlier, for centuries, subsistence farmers caught shrimp and other aquatic food products without causing any significant social or ecological disturbance. Now, however, these countries' convergence with the world's food network through the Blue Revolution has transformed their environmental and agrarian landscapes, generating widespread controversy and, inevitably, producing winners and losers.

As with the Green Revolution, whose problems are becoming increasingly apparent, the Blue Revolution has been plagued by a wide range of negative environmental and social effects. The emergence of the Blue Revolution, in fact, is largely due to the neoliberal global governance project to open up the natural resource pool of the global South to satisfy the appetites of wealthy consumers in the global North. Although tropical countries of the global South have embraced the Blue Revolution, overconsumption in the North is profoundly connected to ecological and social changes taking place in the South. In this chapter, I present some examples, including a detailed case study of Bangladesh.

From the Green to the Blue Revolution

The Green Revolution was facilitated by a package of plant-breeding agricultural technologies that increased the production of corn, wheat, and beans by 300 per cent from 1943 to 1963. Developed by the Rockefeller Foundation in Mexico, in conjunction with the Ford Foundation in the Philippines, Nigeria, and Colombia, and promoted heavily by the US land grant university system and large, capitalized farmers, the Green Revolution was the primary means by which the US chemical agriculture model was introduced to the global South. The revolution was accelerated and legitimized on the basis of several factors: the conversion of wartime nitrogen production and nerve gases to inorganic fertilizers and insecticides, which created political pressure to expand chemical agriculture; the spectre of population growth, which led to technological solutions focusing on national output; and the inability of native varieties of seeds, although not inherently low yielding, to absorb high doses of chemicals, thus requiring the use of high-yielding varieties of hybrid seeds that need fungicides, pesticides, and herbicides (Gupta 1998; McMichael 2008).

Green Revolution advocacy symbolized the idealized prescriptions of what McMichael (2008) terms the post–Second World War era's "development project," with its focus on output despite the known ecological and social consequences. These consequences include the displacement of millions of rural Americans with the expansion of corporate farming, the growth in the number of urban slum dwellers in the global South (who now constitute up to 50 per cent of its population), and the displacement of agri-ecological methods of crop rotation, thereby compromising soil fertility and preventing natural regeneration and renewal. The long-term social and ecological effects of the Green Revolution have been blamed for as many as 100,000 farmer suicides in India between 1993 and 2003 (Newman 2006). The Green Revolution has also generated "development subjectivity," whereby farmers have begun to devalue traditional farming. The anti-rural biases of the development project have also seen the development policies of governments in the global South systematically privilege urban interests and discriminate against peasant cultures, resulting in growing rural poverty, the marginalization of rural populations, and increasing land reform movements (London 1997; McMichael and Kim 1994; Rich 1994).

In Latin America, the 1961 US Alliance for Progress program coordinated nationally planned agrarian reforms to undercut insurgencies, stabilize rural populations, and promote the US family farm model of smallholder owner-occupancy. These land reforms exempted commercialized farmland and focused on what was left: frontier lands. Resettlement schemes on frontier lands privileged males, excluded women, relocated rural poverty, and destroyed tropical forests (Deere and Leon 2001). In Brazil, for example, roughly 28 million small farmers were displaced between 1960 and 1980 by their government's sponsorship of industrial farming, which aimed to enhance foreign-exchange earnings from agricultural exports, notably soy products. These displaced farmers spilled into the Amazon region, burning the forest to clear new and often infertile land (McMichael 2008; Rich 1994).

In the 1960s, in an effort to alleviate poverty, the World Bank devised a credit program for smallholders, although half of eighty-two agricultural projects initiated between 1975 and 1982 were unsuccessful in achieving this goal. Instead, their outcomes included the allocation of credit funds to more powerful rural operators, the displacement of hundreds of millions of peasants, and the incorporation of surviving peasant smallholders, via credit, into commercial cropping at the expense of basic food farming (Rich 1994). The long-term assault on peasant agriculture has continued through colonialism, food dumping, and institutional support for commercial and export agriculture, resulting in the creation of a "planet of slums" – the migration of displaced peasants to overcrowded urban centres. Thus, a key lesson of the Green Revolution is that neither the resettlement of peasants nor their integration into the money economy is a sustainable substitute for supporting agri-ecological methods.

The Blue Revolution that began in the 1970s has followed a similar trajectory, but has generated even more debate, controversy, and resistance (see Box 3.1). There is no doubting the Blue Revolution's huge increase in output. In 1990, for example, Asia produced 556,500 metric tons, of cultured shrimp, or 80 per cent of world output, from approximately 820,000 hectares of coastal area (Khor 1994). Before 1939, Japan produced about 76,000 metric tons of shrimp a year, but by 1987, production had increased to 1.1 million metric tons. Along their coastline, the Japanese farm salmon, prawns, flounder, yellowtail, red sea bream, and other species with a high market value (Boychuk 1992). The UN Food and Agriculture Organization reports (FAO 2010) that, in 2008, nearly 3.4 million metric tons of commercial cultured shrimp were produced worldwide, with an annual growth rate of more than 7 per cent in the 2000s. Table 3.1 shows the aquaculture and commercial catches of different species.

Table 3.1. World Aquaculture and Commercial Catches of Fish, Crustaceans, and Molluscs, by Species, 2010

Species	Aquaculture	Catch	Total
		(metric tons)	
Herring, sardines, anchovies	–	17,096,817	17,096,817
Carp, barbels, cyprinids	24,237,303	1,371,685	25,608,988
Cod, hake, haddock	22,558	7,426,888	7,449,446
Tuna, bonito, billfish	9,412	6,620,373	6,629,785
Salmon, trout, smelt	2,411,136	979,590	3,390,726
Tilapia	3,497,391	801,542	4,298,933
Flatfish	146,330	955,350	1,101,680
Sharks, rays, chimaeras	–	738,924	738,924
Shad	–	644,388	644,388
River eels	271,536	8,440	279,976
Sturgeon, paddlefish	40,273	547	40,820
Other fish	8,538,357	38,674,468	47,212,825
Shrimp	3,787,706	3,129,250	6,916,956
Crab	254,395	1,470,447	1,724,842
Lobster	1,611	279,685	281,296
Krill	–	215,175	215,175
Other crustaceans	1,681,482	1,008,122	2,689,604
Clams, cockles, arkshells	4,885,179	669,169	5,554,348
Oysters	4,488,544	103,985	4,592,529
Squid, cuttlefish, octopus	10	3,652,632	4,375,448
Mussels	1,812,371	88,943	1,901,314
Scallops	1,727,105	840,876	2,567,981
Abalone, winkles, conches	383,811	142,157	525,968
Other molluscs	861,825	1,139,566	2,001,391
Sea urchins, other echinoderms	137,160	101,207	238,367
Miscellaneous	677,104	443,600	1,120,704
Total	59,872,600	88,603,826	148,476,426

Note: Data for marine mammals and aquatic plants are excluded.

Source: United States (2011, 47).

Aquaculture farms, which require mainly brackish water, consist of huge tanks or ponds constructed on land near the sea. Sea and ground water is pumped into the tanks, and pesticides and chemicals are also added. The polluted waste water from the ponds is then released into the sea and onto neighbouring lands. In constructing the ponds and pumping stations, land, forests, and mangroves in the coastal areas are bulldozed and excavated, resulting in massive forest losses (EJF 2003b). The salt water in the ponds seeps into the groundwater, the increased salinity of which damages both the drinking water supply and surrounding agricultural land. The waste water from the ponds also pollutes the sea and marine environment, reducing and poisoning fish life (Khor 1994). According to the Environmental Justice Foundation, "[d]estruction of wetlands, including mangrove forests, together with shrimp fry collection to stock ponds, have been linked to declines in capture fisheries. Shrimp farms have also blocked traditional users' access to coastal and estuarine resources, leaving rural communities increasingly marginalized in degraded environments. Loss of mangroves has also increased risks to coastal communities from tidal waves and cyclones. Given the large range of such hidden costs generated by shrimp farming, there are serious concerns over the sustainability of this industry" (EJF 2003b, 2).

The initial phase of the Blue Revolution forced farmers from their lands to make way for aquaculture through either the invasion of gangs controlled by shrimp farm owners or the acquisition of their land at low prices by the state or entrepreneurs. Furthermore, the flow of salt water from aquaculture ponds into the surrounding fields damaged many farms, subsequently reducing their output. Fishing communities were also badly hit, as the ponds blocked their access to the sea and displaced villagers from areas in which they previously had landed, parked their boats, and spread their nets. Their catch was also depleted by pollution from the ponds and by the aquaculture farms' capture of shrimp fry for their hatcheries (Khor 1994).

Box 3.1: The Blue Revolution

From salmon cages anchored in icy Norwegian fjords to prawn ponds carved out of Thailand's mangrove forests, fish farming is big business. The question is: has this new techno-fix to boost world food production helped to feed the hungry? ... In Ecuador, shrimp-pond investors include Coca-Cola and General Foods. In Thailand, the poor living in coastal communities have taken up arms to prevent corporations from seizing commonly owned mangrove forests for shrimp ponds. Nonetheless, the industry continues to expand. In ... El Salvador ... the government is offering foreign aquaculture investors a 10-year tax holiday and unrestricted repatriation of profits [and] a local [non-governmental organization] is offering to finance up to 80 per cent of the capital costs and 60 per cent of the operating costs for aquaculture projects.

"People have been killed defending their land along the coast," says Ian Filewod of the Canadian Council for International Co-operation. The owners of the ponds tend to be businesspeople and urban investors. And the shrimp produced don't grace the dinner dishes of the hungry poor. The compelling attraction of intensive commercial aquaculture is that it generates export revenue that can be used to pay foreign debt. In addition, it's relatively efficient: beef cattle require seven pounds of grain to produce a pound of meat. Catfish require only 1.7 pounds of grain to produce a pound of fish ...

Critics believe ... the increase in the commercial fish harvest will come at the expense of both wild fish stocks and the environment. Fisheries expert Brian Davy of the International Development Research Centre says major disease and pollution problems are already emerging in Japan. Fish waste and uneaten fish food have accumulated on the sea bottom. In some places the sludge below cage sites is more than 30 centimetres thick. The waste stifles the growth of aquatic organisms and causes water quality to deteriorate. Intensive coastal fish farming has also been linked to "red tides" – an explosive growth of toxic algae that can kill fish and fatally poison people who eat contaminated seafood ...

In the 1980s, along Canada's Pacific coast, ITT and other corporations invested heavily in salmon farming. There are now 125 salmon operations along what is known as the Sunshine Coast. Ten Dawe of the Ocean Resources Conservation Alliance says the farms have been a disaster ... [T]he salmon pens have triggered red-tide outbreaks and polluted the foreshore with waste and the biocides, antibiotics, and other medicines used to treat the fish ... In addition ... the pens frequently break, and the farm-bred salmon then make their way into rivers where they force out wild salmon – a kind of genetic pollution ... Genetically homogenizing the salmon makes the fish much more vulnerable to environmental change ... [F]armed salmon are also responsible for infecting wild salmon with a variety of diseases, including sea lice, which deform the fish, and bacterial kidney disease ... [I]f salmon are to be farmed they should be raised in tanks on land, and all of the effluent should be treated ...

Gary Spiller, a fisheries consultant[,] ... says disease is common where fish farms are not closely regulated. In 1987 Taiwan became the largest prawn producer in the world. A year later disease struck, and production dropped by 70 per cent. The industry never recovered ... The Philippine prawn industry is currently suffering from disease problems, and experts predict prawn farms in Thailand will be hit next. The Brundtland Commission, which endorsed the promise of aquaculture, noted that the major constraint to expansion of the industry is science: "Because marine biologists have not been able to get some commercial species to reproduce in captivity, fish farmers are still largely dependent on the gathering of eggs or the capture of fingerlings." Fisheries scientists across the globe are now working to overcome that technical barrier to expansion of the industry. Their efforts are characterized by industry supporters as a race against hunger: if natural stocks of fish are not enough to meet demand, then fish farmers will come to the rescue. That line of reasoning troubles many. Philippine prawn farms are not producing food for the hungry, nor are they providing employment for hundreds of jobless sugar workers ...

[I]n Java ... as prawn and fish farming expanded so did the landholdings of the wealthy. The losers were villagers who, for generations, had been cultivating fish in small ponds for local consumption. The environmental problems posed by attempts to assume nature's responsibility for managing fish stocks are even more troubling. Ray Hilborn, a biologist at the University of Washington, says there is a danger that science will provide a smokescreen for environmental degradation ... Money that should be spent on habitat protection or restoration is instead being spent on restocking[,] ... [an] approach [that] both encourages careless exploitation and reduces species diversity ... The Blue Revolution's promise of precious protein to feed the world's hungry appears now to be hollow rhetoric. And its enduring legacy may be the gradual but calamitous decline of wild fish stocks.

Source: Boychuk (1992); reprinted with permission.

Neoliberalism and the Blue Revolution

The Blue Revolution was a product of the neoliberal globalization project, initiated largely by those who saw it as a way for the poorer countries of the global South to service their debts, although the much heralded – and seemingly laudable – stated aim of the Revolution was to stave off widespread hunger. By 1985 the World Bank, the Asian Development Bank (ADB), and a variety of other international aid agencies were pumping millions of dollars a year into aquaculture projects in countries such as China, Vietnam, the Philippines, Thailand, Bangladesh, and Ecuador. The Sundarbans, the world's largest mangrove forest, spread across Bangladesh and India, was chopped down to create shrimp ponds (Boychuk 1992; Public Citizen 2005), and the flood plains of the Ganges, Irrawaddy, and Mekong rivers were transformed into homes for less environmentally destructive species such as carp and tilapia. Although there were some positive economic returns, the common outcomes of such commercial farming were population displacement through land grabbing, loss of access to natural resources, and a massive degree of social disparity and tension.

Loans for aquaculture development and direct aid for aquaculture expansion came from three main external sources that Public Citizen (2005, 2) has termed "the development trilogy": international development banks, bilateral aid agencies, and multilateral development assistance agencies. The World Bank Group – particularly the International Bank for Reconstruction and Development (IBRD) – played a central role, along with various regional development banks such as the ADB, the Inter-American Development Bank (IADB), and the African Development Bank (AFDB) (see Table 3.2).

Portraying and heralding the Blue Revolution as a means to feed the hungry in the global South largely served as an ideological guise to occlude structural adjustment programs (SAPs) introduced by neoliberal global managers. SAPs promote the opening of national resource pools for transnational corporations in the interest of rapid national revenue generation to facilitate debt repayment. Debt crises and consequent SAPs therefore have made national governments more likely to respond like private landowners to opportunities for quick profit and less likely to prioritize long-term sustainable development goals. Under SAPs, "policies that had limited trade were replaced with new policies that encouraged exports," and "the changes created an environment in which private investments in shrimp culture, shrimp processing, and shrimp exports flourished" (Roheim 2004, 277). Following crucial World Bank loans and subsequent policy changes – Bangladesh, for instance, received World Bank loans totalling US$1.76 billion over the 1979–96 period (Battacharya, Rahman, and Khatan 1999) – countries in the South became an important part of the global agri-food system, inspiring many rice farmers to adopt low-salinity culture systems that

Table 3.2. Shrimp Aquaculture Funding Sources, 1974–96

Year	Donor	Recipient	Loan Amount (US$)
1974	Asian Development Bank (ADB)	Vietnam	6,000,000
1976	World Bank Group (WBG)	Bangladesh	20,000
1976	WBG	Philippines	12,000,000
1977	WBG	Mexico	500,000
1977	Inter-American Development Bank (IADB)	Colombia	800,000
1977	Asian Development Bank (ADB)	Bangladesh	18,000,000
1978	ADB	Thailand	14,000,000
1978	ADB	Myanmar	24,880,000
1979	WBG/International Finance Cooperation (IFC)	Costa Rica	2,100,000
1980	IADB	Peru	8,200,000
1981	WBG	Bangladesh	300,000
1982	WBG	Mexico	200,000
1982	ADB	Indonesia	23,000,000
1983	IADB	Panama	13,200,000
1984	ADB	Philippines	21,840,000
1985	WBG	Philippines	4,800,000
1985	IADB	Mexico	4,500,000
1986	WBC/United Nations Development Programme (UNDP)	Bangladesh	25,285,000
1987	WBG	Indonesia	24,500,000
1987	ADB	Thailand	11,100,000
1988	ADB	Bangladesh	36,074,000
1988	WBG	China	36,200,000
1988	WBG	China	67,900,000
1988	WBG	Belize	600,000
1990	WBG	Bangladesh	35,800,000
1990	WBG	China	9,300,000
1990	World Bank Group	China	39,800,000
1990	ADB	Indonesia	12,000,000
1991	African Development Bank (AFDB)	Guinea	28,000,000
1991	European Investment Bank (EIB)	Madagascar	6,500,000
1992	WBG	Indonesia	106,100,000
1992	WBG	India	85,000,000
1992	WBG	China	121,000,000
1993	UK Commonwealth Development Cooperation (CDC)	Nicaragua	1,000,000
1994	WBG	India	90,000,000

Table 3.2. *(Continued)*

Year	Donor	Recipient	Loan Amount (US$)
1995	AFDB	Madagascar	6,000,000
1995	WBG	Mexico	100,000,000
1996	EIB	Madagascar	300,000
1996	WBG	China	70,000,000
1996	WBG	Indonesia	150,000,000
Total			1,272,299,000

Source: Public Citizen (2005, 24).

rely upon sea water or on salt farm effluent that is trucked inland and mixed with fresh water. As farmers continued to convert paddy fields to shrimp ponds, the amount of land under shrimp production skyrocketed, creating profound changes to the environmental and agrarian terrains of the global South (Islam 2009; Vandergeest, Flaherty, and Miller 1999). Aquaculture now means billions of dollars worth of global business for the transnational giants. Critics of the Blue Revolution argue, however, that the goal of feeding the hungry in the global South has largely failed (Deb 1998). Instead, neoliberal global managers have proved themselves to be even hungrier to feed their own appetite for accumulation and governance.

Against this backdrop, a key impetus of the Blue Revolution was to find an alternative means of feeding the growing appetite of wealthy consumers worldwide. Between 1950 and 2007, the total landed catch from open- and inland-sea fishing almost quintupled, from around 20 million to about 95 million metric tons. Greater demand from rising world incomes and a larger supply caught by larger and more efficient fishing vessels, mediated by global supermarkets and restaurant chains, were the prime contributors to the surge in fish catches and consumption. Large and misguided subsidies to fishing fleets, reflecting the political power of geographically concentrated fishing communities and industries, also contributed to the surge (Sachs 2007). The protein loss and devastating consequences for ocean ecosystems due to the exhaustion of many marine species through commercial fishing led global managers to initiate pond-based aquaculture in the global South (see Table 3.3).

Table 3.3. World Aquaculture and Commercial Catches of Fish, Crustaceans, and Molluscs, by Country, 2010

Country	Aquaculture	Catch	Total
		(metric tons)	
China	36,734,215	15,418,967	52,153,182
India	4,648,851	4,694,968	9,343,819
Indonesia	2,304,828	5,380,266	7,685,094
Vietnam	2,671,800	2,420,800	5,092,600
United States	495,499	4,369,540	4,865,039
Japan	718,284	4,044,185	4,762,469
Peru	89,021	4,261,091	4,350,112
Russia	120,384	4,069,624	4,190,008
Burma	850,697	3,063,210	3,913,907
Norway	1,008,010	2,675,292	3,683,302
Chile	701,062	2,679,736	3,380,798
Philippines	744,695	2,611,720	3,356,415
Thailand	1,286,122	1,827,199	3,113,321
Bangladesh	1,308,515	1,726,586	3,035,101
South Korea	475,561	1,732,928	2,208,489
Malaysia	373,151	1,433,427	1,806,578
Mexico	126,240	1,523,889	1,650,129
Egypt	919,585	385,209	1,304,794
Brazil	479,399	785,369	1,264,768
Spain	252,351	968,662	1,221,013
All others	3,564,330	22,531,158	26,095,488
Total	59,872,600	88,603,826	148,476,426

Note: For the United States, the weight of clams, oysters, scallops, and other molluscs includes the shell weight, which is not included in the US landings shown elsewhere. Excluded are data for marine mammals and aquatic plants.
Source: United States (2011, 48).

As a result, aquaculture yields in the global South increased from around 2 million metric tons in 1950 to almost 50 million metric tons in 2007. Thus, even though the global fish catch peaked in the late 1980s, aquaculture has enabled human consumption of fish to continue to rise. China now accounts for around two-thirds of total aquaculture production worldwide by weight and roughly half by market value (Sachs 2007), and Glitnir Bank's 2007 China Seafood Industry Report (Glitnir 2007) confirms that China is the world's leader in both the output (some 35 per cent of total global production) and consumption of seafood. In 2007, China's annual per capita seafood consumption was 26 kilograms, and this is expected to increase by 40 per cent over the next decade to 36 kilograms. China is also by far the largest exporter of seafood, outstripping its closest competitor, India, more than fourfold. The Glitnir Bank report further highlights shrimp as an increasingly important species, noting that, in 2006, shrimp production in China rose by 14.7 per cent. Given the ease of raising shrimp and the ability to fetch a relatively quick profit thanks to the industry's cost-effective production system, Glitnir Bank predicts that shrimp might soon join tilapia and other farmed species in importance to China's aquaculture industry, although ABN Newswire (2007) reports that "the growth and success of Chinese seafood production in 2007 has been overshadowed by a series of import bans from trading partners relating to antibiotic contamination, carcinogens, and in earlier years traces of chloramphenicol. In response to sharp criticism from abroad, the Chinese government has implemented a series of measures to address product quality control and monitoring, including over 700 national standards, almost 2,000 industrial standards and 1,780 quality inspection agencies at [the] provincial, municipality and county level."

Divergent Views of the Blue Revolution

As we have seen, shrimp is a major high-value transnational commodity, generating revenues worth more than US$10 billion per year (Roheim 2004, 227), or more than one-sixth of all aquaculture trade (Béné 2005, 585). Accordingly, shrimp aquaculture is considered a great development opportunity in a large number of developing countries in the global South, and has become a basis for rural development and foreign-exchange earnings. Its troubling social and environmental legacies mean, however, that the industry has been the subject of heated debate and scrutiny by environmental groups.

Since the early 1990s, numerous researchers and local and non-governmental organizations (NGOs)[1] have voiced serious concerns about the negative environmental and social effects of commercial shrimp farming in many producing countries, including salt intrusion in paddy farms, the destruction of mangrove forests and other species, the displacement of local residents, and rural conflict. Despite major efforts to resolve these issues, however, the debate about the sustainability of shrimp culture remains unsettled (see, for example, Béné 2005; Roheim 2004; USAID Bangladesh 2006; Vandergeest, Flaherty, and Miller 1999), and NGOs remain actively involved in the sector. A joint report by the UN Economic and Social Commission for Asia and the Pacific (UNESCAP) and the Asian Development Bank (ADB) estimates

that more than 60 per cent of Asia's mangroves have already been converted to aquaculture farms, primarily for the production of shrimp
(UNESCAP and ADB 2000), even though such forests are not ideal locations for this activity.

Bangladesh, one of the world's major shrimp-producing countries, is
a prime candidate for the investigation of the effects of the Blue Revolution (see Figure 3.1).[2] Battacharya, Rahman, and Khatan (1999, 19) note
that these effects are "well articulated, if not always well evidenced."
Most research has found the expansion of shrimp culture in Bangladesh
to be unregulated, uncontrolled, and uncoordinated – Deb (1998, 63),
in fact, calls it a "fake blue revolution." The general outcomes of this
unregulated expansion include overfishing (as the industry is dependent on primarily wild sources of fry); the loss of shellfish and fin fish
(due to the catching of wild tiger shrimp fry); the destruction of fragile
mangrove ecosystems (which provide numerous benefits to society, the

Figure 3.1. Areas of Coastal Bangladesh Suitable for Prawn and Shrimp
Farming

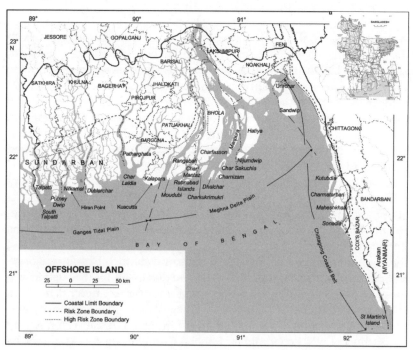

ecology, and other species); and increased soil acidity and salt incursion, with flow-on effects on other coastal agricultural activities, including paddy farming. In addition, intensive shrimp farming requires large amounts of fresh water (approximately 25–30 million litres to raise one metric ton of shrimp), and shrimp pond effluent (ammonia, nitrate, phosphate, and bacteria) makes a significant contribution to both inorganic and organic coastal pollution.

Studies carried out in the mid-1990s also indicate that shrimp farming in Bangladesh has led to changes in land-use patterns, which have affected traditional agricultural activities and practices (Nijera Kori 1996). Aggravating the situation is that the major beneficiaries of shrimp farming are non-local entrepreneurs[3] with no long-term stake in the development of the local community. As a result, sharecroppers whose livelihood traditionally depended on the leasing or renting of cultivable land have been deprived of access to their major productive resource and thus have become unemployed. Furthermore, traditional economic activities such as cattle grazing, poultry keeping, household vegetation, and social forestry are no longer possible in many areas that have been under shrimp cultivation for relatively long periods. These negative effects have not gone unchallenged, and have often led to violent confrontations between shrimp cultivators and local people, with local administrations, the police, and other law enforcement agencies siding with the shrimp cultivators (Islam 2009; Manju 1996; Nijera Kori 1996; Tutu 2004). In response, NGOs such as Nijera Kori (1996) have called for a complete ban on shrimp cultivation in Bangladesh or, at the very least, the imposition of restrictions on cultivation in areas where there is clear proof of overwhelming negative effects.

In contrast, documents prepared by the Bangladesh government, shrimp entrepreneurs, and shrimp farm owners usually focus on the industry's potential role in the economy, pointing out its mounting significance as the country's second-largest non-traditional export-earning activity, after the garment sector (see Bangladesh 1983, 1992, 1996, 1998, 1999, 2001, 2002, 2004a, 2004b, 2005). According to these documents, the benefits of increased foreign-exchange earnings, rising employment, and income generation far outweigh any short-, medium-, or long-term negative effects of shrimp aquaculture. They further assert that the underlying benefits are not confined to the entrepreneurs involved, but that there is a substantial multiplier effect accruing to the whole of the local community.

The Bangladesh government's favourable disposition towards shrimp cultivation played a critical role in stimulating entrepreneurial activity in the industry through favourable land-acquisition arrangements, the leasing of *khas* (government-owned) land to shrimp farmers, and the provision of fiscal and financial incentives for the production and processing of shrimp. When the negative implications of the industry gradually began to emerge and the debate on ecological and environmental concerns grew more heated, the government took a number of initiatives to contain the situation, including enacting laws governing the leasing of land, designing guidelines for the setting up of shrimp farms, requiring the consent of local farmers before the farms could be set up, and establishing shrimp culture steering bodies at the national, regional, and local (*thana*) levels (Aftabuzzaman 1996). Such initiatives have been criticized, however, on the grounds of their inadequacy, weak enforcement, and lack of sensitivity to environmental concerns (see Habib 1998; Islam 2009; Manju 1996; Nijera Kori 1996).

A review of the literature surrounding the social and environmental effects of the Blue Revolution in Bangladesh reveals at least three major perspectives. First, there is the pessimist view, which accentuates the environmentally unsustainable character of shrimp culture in the coastal-ecological conditions of Bangladesh. This view maintains that the negative externalities are systemic, endemic, and irreversible, and hence there is a need to impose an outright ban on shrimp cultivation. The optimist view, in contrast, highlights the potential benefits of the industry, such as increased income, employment, and the capacity to earn foreign exchange, and maintains that these benefits far outweigh the costs associated with the industry's possible negative effects. Finally, the reformist view, although not disputing the negative environmental effects, stresses that these could be addressed satisfactorily through an effective set of policies and instruments.

The question that then arises is how to address the problems associated with aquaculture in an effective manner. Taking the reformist view, a number of studies illustrate different micro aspects of shrimp aquaculture by linking it to the broader debate on the environment, sustainability, and global trade. One thread of research analyses rural women's participation in Bangladesh's shrimp industry and their possible empowerment through the extent to which they have extricated themselves from discrimination and exploitation. Such research also analyses the possible conflict between employment conditions and local norms and value systems, and finds that a range of factors influences the pattern and extent of women's employment in the country. Although women increasingly participate in the shrimp industry, relative to their male counterparts they are marginalized and confined to less important nodes of the local supply chain.[4]

Another thread of research investigates the changes in the agrarian structure brought about by the development of export-oriented freshwa-ter prawn and brackish-water shrimp cultivation in Bangladesh. Ito (2002, 2004), for example, finds that prawn farming in this particular context has spread among agricultural producers so rapidly within the decade that many of the agrarian institutions have been carried over from, or have adapted to, the new production regime. Thus, the institutions gov-erning the landholdings and contractual labour arrangements involved in prawn farming have many things in common with those involved in rice production. She finds that landholders have generally benefited from the new prawn economy, but expresses doubts about whether the posi-tion of landless men and women from poor households has improved on a sustainable basis. The employment gain of local male workers is under threat from cheaper migrants, whereas new jobs for women from poor households are highly intensive, potentially hazardous, and poorly paid.

An Overview of the Bangladesh Shrimp Sector

Production, Export, and Employment

As a result of the Blue Revolution, shrimp export and cultivation in Ban-gladesh have undergone rapid expansion over the past two decades (see Deb 1998). Between 1980 and 1995, the area under shrimp cultivation in-creased from 20,000 to 140,000 hectares (Metcalfe 2003, 433). The Depart-ment of Fisheries estimates that, in 2003, approximately 203,071 hectares of coastal shrimp farms were producing an average of 75,167 metric tons of shrimp annually, an average of 370 kilogram per hectare per year (Gammage et al. 2006). Shrimp cultivation is concentrated in the coastal areas of the Khulna (80 per cent of the total, particularly in the districts of Khulna, Satkhira, and Bagerhat) and Chittagong (the remaining 20 per cent) (Alam et al. 2005, 48). Table 3.4 provides some details about the prawn and shrimp industry as it stood in fiscal year 2008/09, and Table 3.5 illustrates the expansion of the industry from 1986 to 2007.

The exponential growth in the production and export of shrimp re-sulted from a combination of factors, including increased demand from abroad and a large supply of low-wage local labourers. The demand for shrimp products stemmed primarily from the United States, Japan, the Middle East, and Europe – indeed, the European Union remains

Table 3.4. Prawn and Shrimp Farming, Bangladesh, fiscal year 2008/09

Item	Prawn	Shrimp	Total
Number of species	24	36	60
Main aquaculture species	M. rosenbergii	P. monodon	–
Total farming area* (hectares)	50,000	167,877	217,877
Average farm size (hectares)	0.2–05	2–4.5	–
Number of farmers	120,000	200,000	320,000
Production (kilograms/ hectare/year)	350–600	300–550	
Total production (metric tons/year)	*	*	145,585
Export volume (metric tons/year)	23,377	26,991	50,368
Export value (US$ millions/year)	174	230	404

* Statistics often do not distinguish between prawn and shrimp, and thus information has been obtained from personal communications with the relevant authorities from the Department of Fisheries.

Source: Adapted from Bangladesh (2010).

the largest importer of Bangladeshi shrimp today (Islam 2008a; Khatun 2004; Pokrant and Reeves 2003). As the country's second-largest industry after the garment industry, shrimp brings in foreign-exchange earnings of about US$400 million from the approximately 50,000 metric tons that are exported to the world annually (Bangladesh 2010). Experts estimate that the proper use of shrimp fry and other measures could raise this amount to 300,000 metric tons (Islam 2008a). Several years ago, the Bangladesh government set itself the ambitious target of raising export earnings from shrimp to about US$1.5 billion by 2010 (*IntelAsia* 2005), but the various challenges that confront the industry have prevented it from meeting that target (Islam 2010). In addition to earning foreign exchange, the shrimp sector employs more than 600,000 people, who support approximately 3.5 million dependents (USAID Bangladesh 2006).

The Introduction of Private Regulation

In response to global competitive pressure from buyers, consumers, and environmental groups for quality shrimp in the shrimp commodity

Table 3.5. Prawn and Shrimp Production, Bangladesh, 1986–2007

Year	Khulna Division			Chittagong Division			Total		
	Area	Prawn	Shrimp	Area	Shrimp	Prawn	Area	Shrimp	Prawn
	(ha)	(metric tons)		(ha)	(metric tons)		(ha)	(metric tons)	
1986	62,120	4,432	12,016	24,775	2,597	846	87,300	14,658	5,293
1987	62,120	5,977	11,361	24,755	3,354	1,279	87,300	14,773	7,277
1988	68,363	6,064	13,793	24,755	4,244	1,250	94,010	17,889	7,359
1989	79,728	6,938	15,049	27,453	2,983	1,905	108,280	18,235	8,937
1990	79,728	6,905	15,193	27,453	3,226	1,882	108,280	18,624	8,881
1991	79,728	7,286	15,951	27,453	3,323	1,558	108,280	19,489	8,942
1992	79,728	8,210	16,685	27,453	3,425	1,492	108,280	20,335	9,812
1993	79,728	8,571	19,198	27,453	4,073	1,558	108,280	23,530	10,243
1994	79,728	–	–	27,453	–	–	108,280	–	–
1995	104,625	11,619	26,750	29,792	6,651	1,485	137,996	34,030	13,301
1996	104,625	18,200	35,830	29,792	9,734	3,634	137,996	46,233	22,125
1997	104,625	22,084	40,443	29,792	11,127	4,354	137,996	52,272	26,748
1998	104,625	–	–	29,792	–	–	137,996	–	–
1999	107,962	–	–	29,792	–	–	141,353	–	–
2000	107,962	–	–	29,792	–	–	141,353	–	–
2001	107,962	–	–	29,792	–	–	141,353	–	–
2002	107,962	25,327	50,864	29,792	13,993	6,296	141,353	65,579	32,026
2003	107,962	27,052	51,289	29,792	14,586	6,542	141,353	66,703	34,101
2004	163,849	29,811	59,616	29,792	13,322	8,319	203,071	75,167	39,494
2005	171,505	27,946	65,559	34,704	14,648	8,611	217,877	82,661	38,049

(Continued)

Table 3.5. (Continued)

Year	Khulna Division			Chittagong Division			Total		
	Area	Prawn	Shrimp	Area	Shrimp	Prawn	Area	Shrimp	Prawn
	(ha)	(metric tons)		(ha)	(metric tons)		(ha)	(metric tons)	
2006	171,505	31,152	67,487	34,704	15,126	9,598	217,877	85,510	42,419
2007	171,505	31,307	68,222	34,704	15,695	9,362	217,877	86,840	42,320
				Increase in Area, 1986–2007(%)					
	276.09	706.39	567.76	140.08	604.35	1,106.62	249.57	592.44	799.55
				Productivity, 1986(kg/ha)					
		71.35	193.43		104.82	34.15		167.90	60.63
				Productivity, 2007(kg/ha)					
		182.54	397.78		452.25	269.77		398.57	194.24

Source: Rahman, Barmon, and Ahmed (2010, 667–8).

chain, the leading shrimp-processing plants in Bangladesh have shifted continuously towards new regulations and the rearrangement of local institutions, with significant implications for the local landscape. In 1997, for example, EU buyers imposed a ban on shrimp exports from Bangladesh because of what they called "sub-standard products." At the same time, other large buyers in the United States and Japan pressured Bangladeshi producers, via the commodity chain, to use the Hazard Analysis Critical Control Point (HACCP) system (see Chapter 5) to maintain shrimp freshness and quality (Islam 2008a; Pokrant and Reeves 2003), at which point the EU ban was lifted.

Despite the quality upgrade obtained through the use of the HACCP system, Bangladeshi producers continued to receive at least 10 per cent less for their shrimp in international markets due to the relatively poor quality of their product compared with that from other suppliers (Islam 2010). To address this continuing problem of quality, and in line with US and EU food safety standards, in 2002 USAID Bangladesh established the Shrimp Seal of Quality (SSOQ), a private, independent, non-profit organization that, until recently, oversaw compliance of shrimp production with international codes of conduct in the areas of food safety and hygiene, human rights, fair labour practices, and sound environmental management. The organization also monitored production standards and promoted finished products in international markets, and provided training, technical support, laboratory analysis, and market research and development services (Gammage et al. 2006; SSOQ 2002). The SSOQ began certifying shrimp processors and hatcheries in February 2005 with the aim of fetching premium prices in the international frozen food market (*Independent*, 18 February 2005).

Shrimp exported from Bangladesh is inspected in Singapore by Switzerland's Société Générale de Surveillance and UK-based Lloyds to ascertain whether it meets importer standards before it is sent on to buyers. Inspections are also carried out in Bangladesh by appointed quality inspectors for processors and exporters, buyer-designated quality assurers, and EU-delegated government bodies (Gammage et al. 2006).

The Shrimp Commodity Chain

Shrimp aquaculture in Bangladesh lies at the extraction, production, and processing end of an extended global commodity chain that is dominated by restaurants, supermarkets, seafood companies, and buying agencies located in Europe, North America, and Japan. The chain is also influenced by environmental groups working at scales ranging from the local to the global. Although vertical integration in the sector has increased since the mid-1990s, it remains limited. Processors in the country – the main interface between domestic shrimp suppliers and external markets – generally have been reluctant to incorporate shrimp cultivation into their operations. Instead, they prefer to leave what they consider to be the environmentally, politically, ecologically, and economically risky business to the country's tens of thousands of shrimp farmers and to purchase shrimp directly from them or through advanced payment arrangements (*dadon*) with the help of company agents, independent suppliers, shrimp depot owners or parties, and commission agents (*arotdars*). Shrimp farmers, in turn, obtain shrimp fry and other inputs from wild fry collectors, hatcheries, feed mills, and feed supply traders. Figure 3.2, adapted from Khatun (2004) and the author's ethnography, provides a brief illustration of the cultured shrimp production supply chain in Bangladesh.

Compared with brackish-water shrimp farming (*bagda*), freshwater prawn farming (*golda*) has attracted relatively little attention, most likely because the former tends to involve large amounts of capital and to arouse the concern of environmentalists and social activists. Many of the producers of freshwater prawn, in contrast, are small farmers who switched from rice farming to prawn farming en masse in the 1990s; many recently have begun to practise rice-*cum*-shrimp cultivation. Indeed, the local economy boomed until, in more recent years, ecological and managerial problems began to threaten the sustainability of farming activities. Furthermore, the introduction of global standards of food safety and sanitation is changing the structure of the local supply chain. The combined effect of these changes has been to increase the marginalization of small-scale shrimp farmers, as I discuss in later chapters.

Conclusion

The coming of the Blue Revolution was the result of complex dynamics driven largely by the neoliberal global governance agenda. "Feeding the hungry" in the coastal communities of the global South served as a legitimizing tool and ideological guise for the managers of this agenda to expedite capitalist accumulation even from the distant terrains of tropical nations. The Revolution has integrated many countries of the global South into the global agri-food commodity chain, thereby creating both complex intersections and tensions. It has also been an indispensable ingredient in global managers' structural adjustment programs, which advocate short-term profit to service debt, rather than long-term social and environmental sustainability. As a result, the

Figure 3.2. The Supply Chain of Cultured Shrimp, Bangladesh

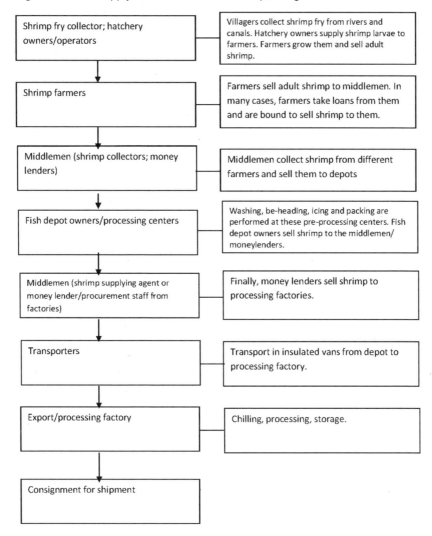

troubling social and environmental effects of the Blue Revolution now loom large in the coastal countries of the global South.

From the exponential rise of shrimp aquaculture, in particular, in the global South, one can glean several significant implications. First, although the negative environmental and social legacies of shrimp aquaculture are well documented and have generated a variety of environmental and social justice movements (discussed in Chapter 4), conflicting views of the effects of the industry leave a question mark hanging over its sustainability.

Second, private certification schemes have been launched as a viable means of mitigating tensions and addressing the troubling social and environmental problems associated with the shrimp industry, although no comprehensive study of the effects and sociological implications of these private schemes is currently available. In Chapter 5, I delineate the trend towards privatizing environmental governance in the form of certification regimes to highlight further the intensity of neoliberal governance.

Third, although some researchers have offered important insights into the issue of gender in the shrimp sector in Bangladesh and elsewhere, further exploration is of crucial necessity to determine the effects of global competitive pressure in the shrimp commodity chain, particularly on employment patterns. Why are men and women working in particular areas and not others? Are there any "invited spaces" available, or can they be made available for equal participation? Do the new productive activities of women enhance their social status and family decision-making power or have any effect on gender relations? To what extent are labourers, both male and female, aware of their rights and of emerging regulations? I address these questions in Chapter 7.

Finally, most research on the Blue Revolution has taken a country-focused approach, and fails to provide a link to the broader debate about the effect of the global commodity chain on politics at the local level. In this age of neoliberal globalization, global market pressures are critical in restructuring agrarian institutions in the shrimp and other supply chains. In the case of shrimp farming, access to financial capital on the part of small farmers has been reduced and ownership patterns of shrimp farms have changed (see Chapter 6). Busch and Bain (2004, 340) rightly argue that "a focus on nation-state regulation is no longer adequate in light of the growing influence of the private sector and new forms of private institutions in shaping the global agrifood system."

4 The Blue Revolution and Environmental Dilemmas: Resistance and Response

What environmental and social damage has aquaculture – particularly commercial shrimp farming – caused, and what kinds of resistance has it provoked? How have governments, international buyers, and donor agencies responded to environmental movements aimed at resisting shrimp aquaculture? Is sustainable aquaculture possible? What are the current priorities at the local and international levels with regard to the troubled environmental legacy of shrimp farming? In this chapter, I discuss the environmental dilemma and politics surrounding the Blue Revolution across the global South, and then present a case study of Bangladesh.

Contesting the Blue Revolution

Since the early 1990s researchers and local and international non-governmental organizations (NGOs) have voiced serious concerns about the social, economic, and environmental consequences of the aggressive deployment of the Blue Revolution in the global South.[1] They argue that industrial shrimp farming has caused social dislocation, ecological damage, and environmental destruction to an arguably worse extent than many earlier Green Revolution technologies. Some of the most serious environmental problems they identify include the destruction of coastal wetlands, water pollution, the disruption of hydrological systems, the introduction of exotic species, and the depletion and salinization of aquifers. Critics also claim that local people regard one of the most serious problems to be the loss of communal resources – including mangrove areas, estuaries, and fishing grounds – on which they depend for subsistence and commercial economic activities. Commercial shrimp farming, in particular, has displaced local communities, exacerbated conflicts, provoked violence involving property and tenant rights, decreased the quality and quantity of drinking water, increased local food insecurity, and threatened human health. The World Wildlife Fund (WWF) (1997, 201), for example, claims that

> in many locations commercial shrimp farming has devastated fragile coastal ecosystems, causing mangrove destruction, coastal erosion, pollution of surface and ground-waters including salinisation of vital coastal freshwater aquifers, and in some cases introduced exotic species. The few cost-benefit analyses performed to date have indicated that the cost of natural resource depletion and environmental damage far outweighs the direct economic returns from the industry ... Shrimp aquaculture, as currently practiced in many areas, provides a striking example of unsustainable use of natural resources for export markets. As well as seriously damaging the environment, it also undermines food security at the local level and reduces prospects for future development and poverty alleviation. The industry has triggered serious social conflicts in some locations by marginalizing village communities and the poor. In many cases, while a few individuals benefit from this industry, many more see their livelihoods and local environment damaged and destroyed.

In 2003 a report compiled by the Environmental Justice Foundation (EJF 2003b, 7) revealed some striking patterns in the global South.

- In Thailand, where an estimated 65,000 hectares of mangroves have been converted to shrimp ponds since the mid-1980s, it is estimated that, for every kilogram of shrimp produced, 434 grams of fisheries are lost due to habitat conversion alone.
- In Malaysia, within two to three years of large-scale mangrove clearance in Kuala Muda, fishers reported their income dropped to one-sixth its prior level.
- In Sri Lanka, lagoon fishers' average catches declined by 62.5 per cent since the advent of shrimp farming.
- In Ecuador, decreased catches of shrimp larvae have been associated with the conversion of mangroves to shrimp ponds.
- In India, a year after shrimp farms began operating in Ramachandrapuram, fishers reported that catches had declined to one-tenth their previous size.

- In Bangladesh, fishers in Chokoria reported an 80 per cent decline in catches since the destruction of mangroves and the creation of dikes for shrimp farming.
- In Burma, the country's mangrove area decreased by 271,000 hectares between 1983 and 1997, leading to a decline in coastal fisheries production of 190,000 metric tons annually.
- In the Philippines, shrimp farming has been linked to declining stocks and to fish deaths and deformities due to the use of chemical inputs.
- In Mexico, mangrove declines of 200 hectares per year from 1980 to 1990 in Campeche State caused fisheries losses of US$140,000 annually.

Such reports of environmental and social setbacks have escalated the conflict between proponents and opponents of industrial shrimp farming. Moreover, conflict has gradually transcended local and national arenas and given rise to the formation of environmental and peasant-based NGOs opposed to shrimp farming, while industry groups have sought to counter the claims and campaigns of the resistance coalition. In May 1995, for example, Greenpeace and twenty-four other NGOs, some representing people living in the communities directly affected by the shrimp farming boom, submitted an unprecedented "NGO Statement on Unsustainable Aquaculture" to the Commission on Sustainable Development meeting at the United Nations in New York. The group urged their governments to move quickly to ensure the compatibility of aquaculture development with the social, cultural, and economic interests of coastal communities and that future development would be sustainable, socially equitable, and ecologically sound (Hagler 1997).

At an NGO Forum on Shrimp Aquaculture held in Choluteca, Honduras, in October 1996, organized by Greenpeace and CODDEFFAGOLF, a Honduran grassroots group, twenty-one NGOs from Latin America, India, the United States, and Sweden adopted the "Choluteca Declaration," reaffirming the demands contained in the 1995 "NGO Statement on Unsustainable Aquaculture." The signers of the Choluteca Declaration insisted that governments apply a precautionary approach to aquaculture development, one that includes integrated strategies for development planning in coastal areas, the use of environmental and social impact assessments prior to aquaculture development, and ongoing monitoring of the environmental and social effects of such operations. They also sought assurances from their governments that coastal fishing and farming communities would not be adversely affected by aquaculture development or operations, including assurances that mangrove forests, wetlands, and other ecologically sensitive coastal areas would be protected, that abandoned or degraded aquaculture sites would be ecologically rehabilitated, and that the companies concerned or the industry as a whole would be held responsible for bearing the cost of such rehabilitation (Greenpeace 1998; Hagler 1997).

Hagler (1997) – who is also a campaigner with Greenpeace International – reports that the NGOs demanded that governments enforce prohibitions against or restrictions on the wholesale conversion of agricultural or cultivable land to aquaculture use, the use of toxic and bio-accumulative compounds in aquaculture operations, the pollution of surrounding areas, the development and use of genetically modified organisms in aquaculture, and the use of exotic and alien species. They also called on governments to prohibit aquaculture practices that cause the salinization or depletion of fresh water and to ban the use of fish feed in aquaculture that could be used to feed people. In addition, the NGOs sought to ensure that ‘the collection of wild larvae to stock shrimp ponds did not adversely affect species biodiversity in the areas in which collection took place. Another key demand was that multilateral development banks, bilateral aid agencies, the UN Food and Agriculture Organization (FAO), and other relevant national and international development assistance organizations cease funding or otherwise promoting any aquaculture development that was inconsistent with the aforementioned criteria.

In October 1997 representatives of major environmental and community organizations from fourteen nations met at the NGO Planning Forum on Shrimp Aquaculture in Santa Barbara, California. At the forum, there was overwhelming support for the formation of a global group to address what was described as the "disturbing" environmental and social legacy of commercial shrimp farming. Accordingly, on World Food Day, 16 October,[2] the Industrial Shrimp Action Network (ISA Net) was formed, consisting of a long list of organizations from both producing and consuming countries (Ramsar 1997): Alter Trade (Japan); CODDEFFAGOLF (Honduras); the Consumers Association of Penang (Malaysia); the Environmental Defense Fund (United States); the Forest Peoples Programme (United Kingdom); Fundación Cimas del Ecuador; Greenpeace Guatemala; Greenpeace International; KONPHALINDO (Indonesia); the Mangrove Action Project (United States); the Natural Resources Defense Council (United States); Organizaciones de

Comunidades Negras de Colombia; PREPARE (India); the Sea Turtle Restoration Project (United States); the Sierra Club of Canada; the WWF; WWF Hong Kong; and the Yadfon Association (Thailand). Leading grassroots groups in the producing countries were also involved in the network – for example, joining Yadfon and the Consumers Association of Penang were Nijera Kori from Bangladesh and WALHI from Indonesia – as were private foundations such as the MacArthur Foundation and the Rockefeller Brothers Fund.

The goals of the new global group were, first, to recognize, support, and empower communities threatened by shrimp farming to enable them to control the use and management of coastal resources to meet their food, livelihood, cultural, and other basic needs; second, to educate consumers about the social, economic, and environmental costs of shrimp production to enable them to make informed decisions about purchasing and eating shrimp; third, to resist destructive industrial shrimp production practices and policies and to encourage the adoption of ecologically responsible and socially equitable alternatives by industry, local communities, national governments, and international institutions; and fourth, to identify and encourage better coastal resource management and to support the restoration of ecosystems degraded by industrial shrimp farming (Ramsar 1997).

ISA Net's growing strength and accomplishments, in turn, elicited an organized response from the shrimp industry (producers, processors, importers, and input suppliers), as well as from government and academic supporters (Stonich 2002). Industry proponents subsequently formed the Global Aquaculture Alliance (GAA) to promote aquaculture and to act as the industry's public relations arm. One of the key supporters of aquaculture over the years has been the World Bank. As Public Citizen (2005, 10) reports, the Bank made loans to China amounting to US$600 million in 1986, US$670 million in 1988, US$430 million in 1989, and US$210 million in 1990. Brazil received US$683 million for aquaculture in 1987, and India US$85 million in 1992. In 1991 the World Bank Group provided a total of US$1.78 billion, and in 1992 a further US$1.68 billion for all types of aquaculture worldwide. In October 1996 Bangladesh received a US$22 million package from the World Bank to promote its shrimp sector. Goldman (2004, 171–2) articulates this substantial monetary support as the "new cultural logics of eco-rationality, enabling new and old frontiers of World Bank-fostered capital accumulation."

Faced with NGO critiques of its role in the shrimp farming explosion, however, the World Bank finally joined the FAO, the Network of

Aquaculture Centres in Asia-Pacific (NACA),[3] and the WWF to form the Consortium Program on Shrimp Farming and the Environment. With a meagre fund of US$600,000, the consortium conducted a series of case studies to analyse and discuss "objectively" controversial issues surrounding the sustainability of shrimp farming, to identify better management strategies, and to develop preliminary guidance for the World Bank and other multilateral and bilateral agencies, among other objectives (Public Citizen 2005, 17). Although the consortium's final report acknowledged "much controversy in recent years about the sustainability of shrimp farming," it omitted the roles of both the World Bank and the FAO, claiming that "the driving forces behind the rapid expansion of shrimp aquaculture include potentially high profitability, buoyant demand for high-quality seafood, increasing demand for farmed shrimp due to limitations and fluctuations in supply from capture fisheries, and its capacity to generate foreign exchange and employment in poor coastal areas" (Consortium Program 2002, 1).[4] The World Bank concluded, moreover, that "there are many positive developments with regard to the social impact of shrimp farming aquaculture throughout the world ... [and] several examples of efforts being made to develop solutions that are economically remunerative, environmentally sound and socially beneficial" (World Bank et al. 2002, 47).

In contrast, the Environmental Justice Foundation (EJF 2003a; 2003b, 15–17) has highlighted the intimidation, aggression, and threats against those who oppose the expansion of shrimp farming, claiming that people have been killed in shrimp-industry-related violence in almost every producing country.

THE PHILIPPINES

In the Philippines, Eliodoro de la Rosa, a forty-three-year-old fisher and leader of a fishers' group, campaigned about the dangers of shrimp pond expansion for the productivity of Manila Bay, and stressed the need to protest the acts of pond owners. He was murdered on 22 January 1990.

THAILAND

In Thailand, shrimp farmers are reported as boasting that the amount needed to silence a protesting rice farmer is equivalent to sales of only 20 kilograms of shrimp. Employees of shrimp farms on the country's Phuket Island are said to have intimidated villagers protesting the impact of shrimp aquaculture on their livelihoods. For example, Sirirpot

Chichang, who campaigned against illegal shrimp farms, was crippled when thugs associated with the shrimp farms ran his car off the road. On 30 January 2001, Jurin Ratchapol, fifty-one, a leading activist against shrimp farm development, was shot dead while collecting nuts near his village, Paklok. He had previously received death threats from workers at the Watchara shrimp farm. Subsequently, nineteen illegal shrimp farms were discovered in the mangroves around Paklok, despite a ban on shrimp farming in protected forest areas. Phuket's governor, Pongpayom Wasaphuti, commented: "No one follows this law." Later that year a Watchara worker was charged with murder, and Somsak Wongsawanont, Watchara's owner and a known associate of the police and the judiciary, was charged with conspiracy to murder. Four months before Ratchapol's death, Queen Sirikit had personally presented him with an award in recognition of his campaigning efforts. It is questionable whether arrests would have followed so quickly had the victim not had this high-profile encounter.

GUATEMALA

In May 2001, police in Champerico shot dead Maytin Castellanos, a fourteen-year-old participant in fishers' protests against the shrimp farming firm Camarones del Sur S.A. (Camarsa) and its subsidiary Pesca S.A., which they claimed had deforested mangroves, constructed a fence that blocked access to the coast, and polluted waters. The following month, Camarsa security guards killed another young protestor, Fernando Chiyoc Albizures, and injured eight more. Company staff were arrested and jailed for a few days before being released without charge, and Camarsa eventually removed the fence and pledged to replant the mangrove forests.

HONDURAS

In Honduras, shrimp farms have blocked local people's access to the Gulf of Fonseca, resulting in numerous protests. Community activists have been shot at, and Goldman Prize–winning anti-shrimp campaigner Jorge Varela has had his life threatened on several occasions. Associates of shrimp producers have been linked to the deaths of fishers, twelve of whom were violently murdered with guns or machetes. Local environmental activists have protested each killing to the relevant authorities, but a culture of impunity persists, and the killers have not been brought to justice.

BRAZIL

In Brazil, João Dantas Brito, an environmental investigator from the Brazilian Institute of Natural Resources and Environment, was shot in the head and back in December 2001. His death has been linked to his denunciation of illegal shrimp farms in the state of Rio Grande do Norte. In April 2002 two men alleged to be connected to the shrimp industry murdered Sebastian Marques de Souza, a fifty-two-year-old father of four who led community opposition to the expanding shrimp aquaculture industry in Piaui state, where shrimp farmers were buying, or appropriating, lands within or surrounding mangrove forest zones to build shrimp ponds.

INDONESIA

In Indonesia, the army has been accused of hunting down, beating, and torturing small-scale shrimp farmers who had protested about their rights on the Wachyuni Mandira farm in Sumatra. Some farmers reportedly were trapped on a farm for three weeks with their food supply cut off by farm officials. In March 2000, during protests about working conditions at a shrimp farm operated by PT Dipasena Citra Darmaja (in Lampung Province), violence broke out, and one farmer and two policemen were killed.

Continuing Controversy

Environmental NGOs opposed to commercial shrimp farming claim that its touted benefits do not outweigh the risks and costs to local people and environments. Employment opportunities do not compensate for declines in access to communal resources and for other social and cultural costs, and the environmental and human costs are not balanced by improvements in local lives, livelihoods, and cultures (see, for example, EJF 2003b; Stonich 2002). Industry proponents, such as the GAA, have responded by saying that the NGOs' "shrimp farming reports [are] strong on attack; [but] weak on facts." The GAA also claims that it is "feeding the world through responsible aquaculture,"[5] whereas the "EJF ignores industry progress" (AquaNIC 2003).

What is clear is that, despite numerous efforts, the issue of the sustainability of shrimp culture remains largely unsettled (Béné 2005). Two conspicuous positions – sometimes identified as "political ecology" (Skladany and Harris 1995; Stonich and Bailey 2000) and "better management practices" (Hempel and Winther 2002; World Bank et al.

Table 4.1. Political Ecology versus Better Management Practices in Commercial Shrimp Farming

Questions or Topics	Political Ecology	Better Management Practices
The issue:	Social disruption and environmental degradation	Farm sustainability and environmental degradation
Focus on:	The causes of the problem (question raising)	The solution of the problem (problem solving)
The conclusion:	The cause is political, but the solution is vague	The solution is technical; political and social issues are never raised
Systems to promote:	Extensive, mixed systems	Intensive, closed systems
Who should be supported?	Poor, small-scale farmers	Large-scale entrepreneurs
Who should be blamed for the environmental impact?	Large-scale entrepreneurs	Poor, small-scale farmers
Who should be blamed for the mess?	Local politicians and international donor agencies	Anyone opposed to the development of the shrimp industry, NGOs

Source: Béné (2005, 592).

2002) – seem to have common goals for improving the sustainability of commercial shrimp farming; they differ substantially, however, on the "what" and the "how." Table 4.1 summarizes the differences between the two approaches, as described by Béné (2005).

Environmental Change in Bangladesh

Although not all scholarly, activist, and institutional approaches fit into Béné's two divergent streams, the environmental changes that have taken place against the backdrop of these debates are quite significant. To take Bangladesh as an example, since the inception of commercial shrimp farming in the 1960s, three stages can be discerned: an era of resistance and violence; an era of depoliticization and negotiation; and an era of normalization.

An Era of Resistance and Violence

Although the demarcation might seem arbitrary, from the 1960s until the end of the 1990s shrimp aquaculture in Bangladesh experienced an era of resistance on the part of villagers, landholders, and NGOs. Lured by the enormous potential profits, and at the expense of local people, shrimp producers, who came primarily from outside the shrimp farming zones, expropriated land and forcibly converted it into shrimp ponds. According to respondents to my survey of the situation (Islam 2009, 2010), shrimp farming during that tumultuous era was sustained through a complex system of political patronage, corrupt officials, local politicians, and a handful of drug dealers; there were even instances of shrimp producers evicting small and marginal rice farmers with the help of hired musclemen.

Then new and largely unregulated, aquaculture in Bangladesh created many social and environmental problems, including overfishing (as the industry is dependent primarily on wild sources of fry); the loss of shellfish and fin fish (due to the catching of wild tiger shrimp fry and the dumping of other species on riverbanks); the destruction of fragile mangrove ecosystems that provided many benefits to society (as mangrove forests were converted to large shrimp ponds); and increased soil acidity and salt incursion with flow-on effects on other coastal agricultural activities, including paddy farming. In addition, because intensive shrimp farming also requires large amounts of freshwater and results in large amounts of shrimp pond effluent (ammonia, nitrate, phosphate, bacteria), it contributes significantly to both inorganic and organic coastal pollution.

Shrimp cultivation also had socioeconomic effects, including the displacement of local residents and the erosion of coastal people's traditional resource-use rights.[6] Hagler (1997, 2) reports that "shrimp farming in Bangladesh's Satkhira region displaced 40 per cent of the area's 300,000 inhabitants into the country's overcrowded cities." Although this figure might be an exaggeration, there is no doubt that there were many displacements. During my field visit in 2006, an NGO worker in Satkhira, pointing to the panoramic view of shrimp ponds, remarked that "there were nice greenery, flora and fauna in these areas before; today the only things we can see are shrimp ponds." A perusal of newspaper reports during this era shows that investors were quick to cash in on the lucrative shrimp business; a relatively small number of investors, however, received the lion's share of benefits, while a large proportion of the rural population, particularly the rural poor, was disenfranchised, marginalized, and left with severely damaged environments.

Duplisea (1998) writes that, in Bangladesh, armed guards were stationed at ponds to protect them from local people and that more than one hundred people were killed resisting shrimp farming. There were also instances of bombings, kidnappings, rape, and assault. Although some respondents in the Satkhira and Bagherhat districts expressed doubts about the number of people killed, they admitted that, at the initial stage of commercial shrimp farming, there were pockets of violent expansion and resistance from local people (Islam 2009). Many respondents expressed the belief that unplanned and unregulated pond construction is the cause of the floods that visit their areas almost every year. During the rainy season, water cannot move due to the hundreds of shrimp ponds. Further, mud brought by floods covers the rivers, thereby affecting river navigation. Although there have always been cyclones, tidal surges usually were stopped by the forest; with the advent of shrimp farming and the destruction of much forest land, however, villagers believe cyclones have become worse (see also, EJF 2003b; Hagler 1997). Climate change is thought to be responsible for most environmental changes in Bangladesh, but aquaculture practices have exacerbated the situation.

All of these problems generated resistance from villagers, rice farmers, and NGOs, ranging from street protests to violent confrontations between the shrimp cultivators – mostly outside entrepreneurs – and local people. These confrontations resulted in adverse law-and-order situations, violence, serious human rights violations, and even deaths (Manju 1996; Nijera Kori 1996; Tutu 2004). In almost all cases, the local administration, the police, and other law enforcement agencies sided with shrimp cultivators rather than with the locals who had been evicted and made landless. In an interview with me, the secretary of the Bangladesh Manabadhikar Bastabayan Sangstha (Bangladesh Human Rights Association) in Satkhira said that the initial stage of commercial shrimp farming "brought disaster to the landless farmers who used to lease ... and cultivate lands. Most of them failed to become shrimp farmers as it was a rich people's business. They became just wage labour in the shrimp ponds."

In response, NGOs such as Nijera Kori and Unnayan Bikalper Nitinirdharoni Gobeshona (UBINIG, Policy Research for Development Alternatives) started working to raise awareness of the negative consequences of the shrimp industry (Pokrant and Reeves 2003). Another NGO, Coastal Development Partnership, began operating with a variety of environmental and social protection agendas. Fieldwork in Bangladesh discovered many local narratives concerning peasant resistance to the environmental damage, land expropriation, displacement, and natural resource exploitation generated by commercial shrimp farming.

THE MOVEMENT AGAINST KHORA ABUBAKAR

According to respondents in Satkhira, shrimp farming there was begun in 1974 by entrepreneurs from outside the region. At that time, the shrimp were exported to India and then, after processing, on to other countries. When Bangladesh began exporting shrimp directly to wealthy countries in the global North in 1985, these outside entrepreneurs became more aggressive in converting *khas* (government-owned) land into shrimp ponds. The government began issuing licences to a few powerful entrepreneurs, and if an entrepreneur managed to lease 80 per cent of a plot, he was entitled to the remaining 20 per cent regardless of objections from the landholders. Land was often occupied by force, often with the help of hired musclemen, and rapes and killings were also reported. There were numerous cases in which the shrimp lords forcibly converted small farmers' land into large shrimp ponds without paying the landholders, rendering many landless.

One such entrepreneur, who made fifty to sixty small farmers landless, was Khora Abubakar. In response, the landless farmers mobilized and, with the help of local sympathizers, launched a vibrant resistance movement against him and land expropriation in general, engaging in street protests and complaining to the local civil authorities. Khora Abubakar hired musclemen to crush the movement, which had the unintended effect of garnering the movement wider public attention and greater acceptance by local people, and spreading the effect of the resistance movement beyond the village arena, with the farmers eventually joined by journalists and NGOs such as Bangladesh Manabadhikar Bastabayan Sangstha. After four long years, the landless farmers got back their land.

THE KHUKSHIR BEEL MOVEMENT

In the greater Khulna region in Keshabpur, Jessore, the livelihoods of hundreds of poor inhabitants were dependent on Khukshir Beel, a low-lying government-owned lake, for fishing. In addition, water from the lake was the main source of irrigation for many farmers. In July 1988 a powerful individual named Majid Golder forcibly occupied the lake

and converted it into a large shrimp farm. Following a resistance movement organized by local people, the farm ultimately was shut down,
but many were injured in the confrontation.

THE DEBHATA-KALIGANJ MOVEMENT

In the Debhata and Kaliganj areas of Satkhira district, landless farmers launched their resistance movement with a street procession. On
27 July 1998, a police force accompanied by the hired thugs of influential shrimp lords opened fire on protestors. Jaheda – a landless house-
wife and mother of five – was killed and hundreds more were injured.
This tragic incident added fuel to the farmers' movement. The landless
farmers, along with the other local people, renamed their village, previously called Baburabad, Jaheda Nagar (the village of Jaheda) to keep
the memory of the deceased alive.

THE DUHURIR BEEL MOVEMENT

Taking advantage of the landowners' absence, a shrimp lord named
Atiar Khan occupied a large part of a lake called Dubrir Beel in the
greater Khulna region and converted it into shrimp ponds, resulting
in the waterlogging of upstream areas. When local people protested,
Khan threatened them with his hired musclemen. Three people, including a school teacher, were killed and many others were injured. The
incident later resulted in a number of court cases.

THE POLDER 22 MOVEMENT

In the Khulna region, a group of people affected by floods, the confisca-
tion of natural resources, and increased salinity launched a campaign
of resistance with the help of the NGO Nijera Kori against commercial
shrimp farming in Polder Number 22, a large shrimp *gher* (pond). In
November 1990, in the midst of the campaign, a woman was killed and
around fifty others were injured. The Polder 22 Movement received
nationwide attention, and became a powerful example and source of
inspiration to anti-shrimp campaigners such as Nijera Kori, UBINIG,
and Coastal Development Partnership.

The Era of Depoliticization and Negotiation

Resistance to shrimp farming during the initial period transcended local
boundaries, with NGOs from both shrimp-producing and -consuming
countries launching a campaign to change farming practices and even

to halt shrimp farming completely (Princen 1994). In so doing, environmental activists succeeded in drawing international attention to the damage caused by the shrimp industry and to the issue of food safety. The Bangladeshi authorities, in turn, responded by introducing a series of environmental programs, as well as inspection and quality-control institutions, to demonstrate their adherence to the principle of "environmentally sound shrimp aquaculture." In addition, in response to buyer and consumer demand for quality shrimp, the leading processing plants began to apply stricter regulations (Pokrant and Reeves 2003). Following a 1997 export ban by the European Union, for example, Bangladesh started implementing the Hazard Analysis Critical Control Point (HACCP) manual in its shrimp aquaculture, in the process restructuring its institutional settings and launching a massive pro-shrimp campaign.

In response to unrest and violence in rural areas, and to counter the campaigns of international and local environmental NGOs, international development agencies and the Bangladeshi government promoted several institutions aimed at ensuring environmentally friendly shrimp aquaculture. The World Bank announced approval of a US$28 million-equivalent credit by the International Development Association (IDA), the Bank's concessionary lending affiliate,[7] and a US$5 million Global Environmental Facility (GEF)[8] grant for the Bangladesh Fourth Fisheries Project. Project task leader Benson Ateng, a senior economist in the Bank's South Asia Rural Development Unit, said that "[t]he objective of the project is to support environmentally-friendly and sustainable fish and shrimp production for domestic consumption and exports and to help fight poverty in Bangladesh by improving the livelihoods of people who depend on fishing ... The project will also provide about 440,000 additional jobs in the fishing industry, especially for the poor and women." Ateng went on to say that, "[w]hile the contribution of the sector to national food supply and [gross domestic product] needs to be optimized in order to support economic growth and employment, it is essential to ensure that fisheries are managed effectively and the aquatic environment is protected at the same time" (World Bank 1999, 1).

In announcing its support for the project, the World Bank exhibited not only a strong tone of depoliticization and negotiation, but also, to quote Goldman (2004, 169), "the more obvious exercises of World Bank power as it seeks to 'green' or ecologically neoliberalize its borrowing country clients, including its efforts to restructure the state itself and related non-state local institutions." The basic objectives of the project, according to the 20 January 1999 news release that accompanied the announcement, were as follows. First, problems facing open water inland fisheries were to be addressed through different management measures with the direct involvement of beneficiaries and NGOs in the design, site selection, management, and monitoring of these interventions. The stocking of fingerlings of indigenous species in the floodplains was one such measure. To increase productivity and biodiversity, the project also was intended to help reopen important canals and tributaries by which river fish breed and graze that were blocked due to siltation. Up to ten pilot habitat restoration sub-projects were to be implemented by communities and NGOs, allowing for more effective fish migration. The project also included passes to allow fish to get through flood control, drainage, and irrigation projects that blocked their migration routes.

Second, the project sought to address some of the environmental and social problems facing the rapidly growing shrimp farming subsector – for example, with respect to water quality, disease, mangrove deforestation, and the degradation of agricultural land. In particular, the practice of alternating shrimp culture and rice farming has often been upset by more intensive use of land areas for shrimp. Potentially destructive methods of shrimp fry collection also have significant environmental implications.

Third, to ensure that these issues were addressed in the improvement of four existing polders and the development of one new polder for shrimp farming, the project was to undertake a full-feasibility study covering the engineering, aquaculture, socio-economic, and community organizational aspects, incorporate the results of consultations with local communities, examine the environmental and economic feasibility of proposed interventions, and determine what was needed to ensure that smallholder shrimp farmers also would benefit from them.

Fourth, the project was to encourage adoption of alternative shrimp fry harvesting systems to reduce wastage and inadvertent effects on non-target species, of particular benefit to the poor and women who harvest shrimp fry.

Fifth, the project was to support freshwater aquaculture extension and training to increase fish supplies from aquaculture through intensified yields and increased areas under production, strengthen extension links by which newly researched technologies reach farmers, and improve the management of fisheries at the district level through greater cooperation between the Department of Fisheries and the private sector.

Finally, the project was to strengthen the basis for aquatic resources policy development, since the Department of Fisheries had a strong focus on the biology and ecology of commercially and artisanally exploited species, but lacked a knowledge base and the technical capacity required to transform itself into an integrated manager of aquatic ecosystems as a whole. The project was to provide the department with the basic tools to make this transformation by strengthening research and monitoring capacity and supporting training and other institutional strengthening activities.

Although such initiatives had some positive effects in terms of boosting local people's awareness of environmental issues, they also facilitated the birth of what Goldman (2004, 166–7) calls "environmental states" that "tell an important political story about new efforts to classify, colonize and transnationalize territory." They contributed not only to depoliticizing the vibrant environmental politics surrounding shrimp aquaculture that environmental NGOs and other social justice groups had initiated, but also to installing a regime of control and governance through a new body of knowledge. These initiatives entail how politics of resistance are normalized through an anti-politics of development (Ferguson 1990). In addition, they had a strong tendency, as Brosius (1999, 36) puts it, to "insinuate and naturalize a discourse that excludes moral or political imperatives in favor of indifferent bureaucratic and techno-scientific forms of institutionally created and validated intervention."

With a view to displacing politics from the shrimp industry debate in Bangladesh, officials vociferously reiterated that the government was committed to ensuring an environmentally sound shrimp culture. Their statements were published in a number of pro-government national dailies, and several government-funded environmental magazines, such as the *Bangladesh Environmental News Letter* and the *Agribusiness Bulletin*, were established. In this period, a variety of government ministries, bodies, and agencies actively worked together to introduce what the government called the "better management of shrimp aquaculture."

The government also introduced a number of programs in the environmental realm. For example, one initiative taken by the Ministry of Environment (MoE) to address environmental degradation was the Sustainable Environment Management Program (SEMP). The MoE also prepared a National Environment Management Action Plan (NEMAP), which was praised by global institutions, including the United Nations Development Programme (Jilani 1999). The SEMP consisted of five major institutional components: Policy and Institution, Participatory Ecosystem Management, Community Based Environmental Sanitation, Awareness and Advocacy, and Training and Education. The SEMP was formulated within the framework of sustainable human development, with the aim of offering a special role to the poor, particularly poor women, as environmental managers. The ultimate objective was to help these groups to build their capacity for decision making and for conserving the environment at the grassroots level (Jilani 1999; Karim 2000).

In addition to the MoE's NEMAP, a National Conservation Strategy (NCS) was also proposed by multilateral banks and bilateral aid agencies. The NCS covered a wide range of areas, including agriculture; conservation of genetic resources; cultural heritage; energy and minerals; environmental education and awareness; environmental pollution; fisheries; forestry and forest conservation; health and sanitation; human settlement and urban development; industry; international dimensions; land management; livestock; natural hazards; population; rural development and NGO activities; transportation; water resources and flood control; and wildlife management and protected areas. Its overall aim was to provide a guide for development practitioners on the means to preserve or improve the environment while pursuing the goal of sustainable development. The two main objectives of the NCS were to collect and analyse data on the key socio-economic indicators of relevance in influencing the environment and development; and to formulate policy and guidelines and prepare documentation on the proper and sustainable use of natural resources (Bennett et al. 1995). Although the Bangladesh government has yet to adopt this strategy formally, the proposed policy played a vital role in depoliticizing the environmental campaign initiated by NGOs.

Through this long series of actions, institutional restructuring, and the provision of monetary and technical help to new entrepreneurs and farmers, the government and its funding agencies succeeded in depoliticizing much of the resistance movement in the second stage of commercial shrimp farming in Bangladesh. In part because of this depoliticization, many Bangladeshis began to see shrimp aquaculture in a positive way. As most of the research funded by the government and donor agencies was based on cost-benefit analyses and focused more on economic returns than on environmental and social costs, and as foreign cash began to flow to the local economy, many rice farmers began to switch to shrimp aquaculture on a trial-and-error basis. Many local

NGOs, such as the Cooperative for Assistance and Relief Everywhere, Proshika, Caritas, the Bangladesh Rural Advancement Committee, and the Grameen Bank, started working with international donor agencies and the Bangladesh government to promote the "better" environmental, social, and economic management of shrimp farms. Only a few NGOs, such as Nijera Kori, remained opposed to any shrimp culture at all (Pokrant and Reeves 2003).

Working through, among other things, institutional reshaping, knowledge production, and the production of what Agrawal (2003) terms the "environmental subjectivities" surrounding shrimp farming, this period of depoliticization and negotiation persisted in Bangladesh until 2003. The worst human and environmental abuses gradually declined, and certain environmental practices began to normalize, as echoed in the testimony of a respondent to me in 2006:

> During the 1980s shrimp industry was at its peak in Bangladesh. Lured by enormous profit, many big shrimp lords in coastal areas occupied the lands of many small farmers to expand their farms. This resulted in – apart from environmental disasters – violence, fighting and even killing. At that time several NGOs resisted the shrimp industry by highlighting the issues surrounding social and environmental damages. Later on, *the resistance was no longer strong. It was as if most people had accepted the industry. The government, with donors' help, not only managed to normalize the issue, but also constantly said that extensive development of the shrimp industry is greatly needed in order to boost the national economy.* (emphasis added)

The Era of Normalization

As NGOs began to shift their activities from resistance to cooperation, and as many local farmers changed their form of subsistence farming from rice to shrimp, local people also began to cope with the resulting new social structure, labour arrangements, and consumption patterns. A number of NGOs left environmental politics in this era. Shrimp aquaculture became more widely accepted by the local population overall, due, among many other factors, to the invigoration of the local economy through the influx of foreign cash. Since 2003, the main issue of concern for shrimp producers has not been opposition to shrimp farming and reversion to rice farming, but ensuring quality and traceability, as buyers demanded. As Busch and Bain (2004) note, in the current global agri-food system, private food safety and quality standards, branding, traceability, contracts, certification, and agreements are the axes around which food retailers organize competition based on quality.

In an interview conducted by the author, one villager said, "[w]ith a very few exceptions, cases of looting, occupation of *ghers* [ponds], local muscle-men, violence, rape – all these are a thing of the past … People are, in general, living peacefully" (see Islam 2009). Although problems remain, many people in the shrimp-farming regions of Bangladesh not only have a positive attitude towards such farming, but also a strong desire to become involved in it. A local farmer said: "Previously a powerful few got licences from the government to cultivate shrimp, and there were numerous examples of expropriation and violence. The government later on banned the licensing system and made the culture open to all. Outsiders used to cultivate [shrimp] before; now locals are involved in shrimp culture. There are still outsiders but they have to work in collaboration with the local people." A village teacher observed that "shrimp is now more community oriented than being the business of a powerful few, although small farmers are more likely to lose out." Indeed, local farmers currently are the main actors in shrimp farming.

Among the rural population, concerns remain about environmental change, and many are nostalgic for the previous environmental state. As one villager complained, "[d]airy milk is no longer available here, as all grazing lands for cows have been converted to shrimp ponds." Another lamented that "[u]nplanned ponds and canals create waterlogging that eventually generates floods in our vicinity." Almost all shrimp farmers – many of them once paddy farmers – believe that shrimp is more financially profitable for and beneficial to the local community than rice (Islam 2009).

Although some environmental NGOs still have concerns about commercial shrimp farming, and although a strong sense of ambivalence persists, many contentious issues have gradually become exposed to the docile supporters of the Blue Revolution as myths or relics of the past (Islam 2012). Three such myths, in particular, merit examination.

Myth 1: *Shrimp farming has created less employment than paddy farming* (Manju 1996; Nijera Kori 1996; Shiva 1995). In fact, because of what Ferguson (1990) calls the "anti-politics machine," most locals currently believe that shrimp farming has created more employment opportunities than paddy farming. Based entirely on some sort of economic logic, they argue that most of the land currently used for shrimp was previously uncultivated or constituted paddy fields with only seasonal paddies (*aman*), thus representing less production and fewer economic and social returns. *Golda* (freshwater prawns) and rice are cultivated in turns in freshwater areas. Locals argue that a huge array of shrimp-related jobs has emerged that rice paddies were unable to generate, including employment in fry collection, fry trading, shrimp hatcheries, fry nursing homes, shrimp pond creation and repair, ice factories, shrimp trading, shrimp feed mills, regulation and quality control bodies, transportation, shrimp-processing factories, and shrimp export.

Myth 2: *Shrimp farming has created greater salinity than did paddy farming.* Water in the southern coastal regions of Bangladesh is brackish – an admixture of saline water from the sea and fresh water from rivers originating in the Himalayas. Due to the Farakka Barrage[9] and other barriers to the flow of fresh water from the Himalayas, the formation of brackish water in fact has been greatly hindered in a way that has had a tremendous impact on the ecosystem of coastal areas, including the Sundarbans. "Shrimp may contribute to salinity, but it is not the main reason, as depicted by many," according to Aftafuzzaman, the president of the Bangladesh Shrimp Farmers Association.

Myth 3: *Shrimp farming is disastrous for women* (EJF 2003b; Shiva 1995; Tutu 2004). In fact, shrimp has created more opportunities for women than they had before. Although women remain marginalized relative to men, shrimp farming has elevated their status and subverted the traditional rigid gender division of labour. As a chemistry professor at Shyam Nagar Mohsin College claimed during my interview with him, "[f]or [shrimp] business and cultivation, people have to move freely day and night. [This is] not feasible for ... women, [as] they are not habituated to do so, nor does the society allow them to do so. Nevertheless, this pattern is changing. Previously we did not see any females in cultivation and business, [and] now we see some."

Thus, with this apparent normalization of resistance, the approach of better management practices seems to have won out. Long-term ecological and social damage has been tolerated and downplayed for short-term economic gain, and priorities at the local level have shifted from resistance to cooperation. Yet, as we shall see in Chapter 6, where I focus on the agrarian transformation, and in Chapter 7, where I examine gender and employment in shrimp aquaculture, the arguments of political ecology remain largely intact in the landscape of the Blue Revolution.

Priorities at the Local Level

Since the early 1990s, research on commercial shrimp farming in Bangladesh[10] has focused – apart from the various gains – on a range of environmental and social concerns. Table 4.2 summarizes the major environmental concerns stemming from certain shrimp farming practices in Bangladesh and the interventions researchers have recommended. Studies have found that, although there have been some positive developments, and although the government, with support from donor agencies and pressure from buyers, has implemented a number of recommendations, contentious issues have not disappeared. Moreover, as environmental movements transcend local boundaries and today's consumers are more aware of product "quality,"[11] the shrimp industry faces a variety of novel problems, such as traceability and labour rights, in addition to that of environmental sustainability. As a result, the government and other stakeholders have taken action to render shrimp farming more responsible, to distribute its benefits more equitably, and to end the worst of the human rights abuses associated with it. Campaigns have continued at the international level, and buyers have begun to commit to buying shrimp that is traceable and about which something is known about the social and environmental consequences of its production. What has thus emerged is the need not only to undertake better practices, but also to document these practices for an international audience. This shift in the global agri-food system has been a major part of the shift in priorities seen at the local level.

Table 4.2. Environmental and Social Effects of Shrimp Farming in Bangladesh and Recommended Solutions

Practices and Actions	Consequences for Development	Environmental and Social Effects	Recommended Solutions
Land leased by outside entrepreneurs	Use of land only to maximize short-term profit without concern for long-term sustainability	• Deforestation • Destruction of mangrove ecosystems (biodiversity) • Destruction of alternative sources of livelihood	• Ensure participation of stakeholders in the management of shrimp farming and stricter implementation of existing laws • Introduce zoning and declare certain parts of the country to be shrimp-free areas

(Continued)

Table 4.2. *(Continued)*

Practices and Actions	Consequences for Development	Environmental and Social Effects	Recommended Solutions
Lease of government *(khas)* land for shrimp culture Salt water penetration of embankments for substantial periods	Traditional rice culture replaced by shrimp culture Increased salinity in the area	• Disentitlement of the landless • Intensification of poverty • Prevalence of environmentally unfriendly practices • Gradual degradation in the quality of land and soil nutrients resulting from accumulation of salt	• Enact laws ensuring participation of landless people in any use of *khas* land • Develop land use policy and environmental guidelines for shrimp culture • Develop optimal practices for rice-shrimp mixed culture
Use of extensive methods of shrimp cultivation causing inundation of large tracts of land	Large areas remaining under water for substantial period of time	• Destruction of homestead cultivation, fruit orchards • Rupture of the subsistence cycle	• Encourage semi-intensive methods of cultivation • Undertake zoning and area mapping
Indiscriminate shrimp fry collection	Destruction of fish biodiversity and increased exploitation of preferred species	• Overfishing	• Develop shrimp hatcheries

Source: Author's Investigation.

Currently, there are no visible resistance movements against commercial shrimp farming in Bangladesh, although some individuals, including some NGO activists, remain highly ambivalent about the industry, as issues of sustainability remain unsettled. Although the production of rice – the local food staple – was already in decline when shrimp aquaculture was introduced and its has largely been replaced by shrimp in the years since, the Bangladesh Rice Research Institute recently introduced a hybrid rice that can be produced alongside shrimp in brackish water. Farmers of freshwater shrimp thus often practise dual-cultivation (shrimp and paddy farming) and sometimes even tri-cultivation (shrimp-paddy-fish farming). Farmers, in fact, are more concerned about viruses than about environmental effects, with some blaming NGOs for intentionally fabricating stories about the environmental and social damage caused by commercial shrimp farming to secure funding from various agencies. Farmers, in general, are also paying more attention to sanitary regulations. One respondent to the author's survey remarked that, "[a]fter harvesting shrimp, we used to keep them in the *chatal* [yard], which did not have any roof; now it is a government regulation that we need to have a house, mosaic floor, and six-foot tall wall and there must be a roof. There has to be a steel table in the house, and only arsenic-free water should be used to clean the shrimp before they go to the processing factories. There must be a *paka* [concrete] sanitary latrine around the shrimp ponds to avoid contamination. We all are following these regulations. We no longer use baskets made of bamboo, but use only the plastic ones as required by the HACCP manual."

Despite new government regulations aimed at wooing buyers and consumers, however, most small farmers cannot afford to follow them. In many cases, the implementation of environmental and sanitary regulations has been slow, and environmental externalities continue to affect local communities. Sometimes, the issues involved are highly complex in nature, with many associated factors requiring consideration at the same time. Several years ago, for example, the government, under pressure from environmental groups, banned the collection of fry from the sea because it was disturbing the biodiversity of the Sundarbans, but fry collection is still going on, albeit on a lesser scale. One reason is that hatcheries in Bangladesh are insufficient to meet the demand for shrimp fry. Another is that many rural people, especially women, who earn their livelihood from collecting fry have no alternative means of survival, making it difficult for the government to enforce the ban, although a number of NGOs are encouraging fry collectors to adopt alternative means of subsistence, such as tailoring, horticulture, and fishing. In addition, many farmers believe that shrimp fry collected from the sea is more resistant to viruses and other diseases than that from hatcheries. In short, the priorities of local people are sometimes quite different than those of environmental NGOs. Most stakeholders in shrimp farming do not believe, for example, that the industry is contributing to increased salinity, soil degradation, and mangrove destruction, although they concede that it is creating waterlogging, which, however, they consider a small price to pay compared with the economic gain and job creation.

Conclusion

Many elements of the former rice economy remain in Bangladesh, but the new shrimp production regime has generated many changes in the country's rural landscape. The introduction of the new regime has not been peaceful, and the industry has faced resistance and criticism from local and international environmental NGOs that have been adept at articulating, if not always providing convincing evidence of, its environmental and social problems. Over time, however, with the introduction and implementation of environmental and social regulations, the nature of the resistance and criticism has changed. The industry now is in a stage of "normalization," whereby the politics of resistance have been displaced and emasculated through the anti-politics of development (see Ferguson 1990). Local communities now accept the industry more widely, but the focus of the debate about its environmental and social legacy has shifted to the desire for short-term economic opportunities and benefits, in line with the agenda of the neoliberal globalization project, rather than long-term social and ecological sustainability.

Indeed, it is remarkable how thoroughly the rhetoric of environmentally sound shrimp aquaculture has insinuated itself into the official environmental discourse in Bangladesh. The practices of "scores of social actors and institutions [that have helped] generate a new development regime" (Goldman 2004, 167) are creating and administering the industry through a variety of knowledge-making apparatuses (see also Agrawal 2003; Brosius 1999; Escobar 1995). These actors and institutions are working through what Darier (1996) calls "environmental citizenship" at the level of "bio-power" (Foucault 1998), which has had the effect of disciplining many NGOs and others concerned about shrimp farming and turning them into subjected individuals.

"Better management practices" and regulations and institutions devised by governments of the global South and supported by donor agencies have led to a high degree of managerialism and a complex web of networks among bureaucrats and shrimp farm owners. Within these networks, the benefits flow primarily to the influential few with access to information. The new institutions, moreover, preclude other forms of engagements; according to Brosius (1999, 50), they are "both enabling and limiting. Defining themselves as filling particular spaces of discourse and praxis, they in effect define (or redefine) the space of action; they privilege some forms of action and limit others; they create spaces for some actors and dissolve spaces for others." In short, the new regime tends to marginalize small players and local communities, a situation upon which I elaborate in the following chapters.

5 International Environmental Regulation Regimes

The troubled social and environmental legacy of industrial aquaculture is partly responsible for generating a variety of environmental regulation and governance regimes. In response to growing public awareness of the negative effects of aquaculture development, increasing numbers of market-oriented certification schemes for aquaculture products are being developed and established. For example, the Hazard Analysis Critical Control Point (HACCP) regime, implemented by governments of the global South, is now more than a decade old, while the rise of private, third-party certifiers (TPCs) is a relatively new addition. Traditionally, government agencies have been responsible for monitoring food safety standards and other food quality attributes, but the emergence of certification is shifting responsibility for this task increasingly to TPCs.[1] This transformation, which Busch and Bain (2004, 337) call "the private regulation of the public," is shaping industrial aquaculture to a significant degree.

Although the basic concept underlying such product-labelling schemes is to provide economic incentives to producers and the industry to adopt more sustainable production practices while safeguarding or enhancing access to consumer markets (WWF 2007), these regimes have generated both winners and losers. In this chapter, I examine the evolution of the various standards and regimes that govern industrial aquaculture and their potential far-reaching implications for, among others, states, the industry, and farming communities. These certification schemes, despite offering alternative practices to promote environmentally and socially sustainable aquaculture, have tended to create a highly technical regime that precludes participation by many players, including local communities.

The HACCP Regime

Most countries of the global South have long had quality control mechanisms of one kind or another to ensure food quality and safety, but pressure from buyers and environmental groups is shifting regulation from public to private. Buyers in the European Union, for example, imposed a ban on shrimp exports from Bangladesh in 1997 because of what they called "sub-standard product," while other big buyers, such as the United States and Japan, pressured producers in the global South to adopt the private HACCP regime of regulations to maintain shrimp freshness and quality (Pokrant and Reeves 2003).

The HACCP system has a long history of development and evolution. The current global food safety system (see Table 5.1) began in 1945 with the establishment of the United Nations Food and Agriculture Organization. The General Agreement on Tariffs and Trade, concluded in 1947, included provisions for countries to apply measures necessary to protect human, animal, and plant life or health, but stipulated that such measures must not unjustifiably discriminate against countries in which similar conditions prevail or act as disguised restrictions on international trade (Sperber 2005). The HACCP system then began its long path of evolution until, in 1997, the Codex Document on HACCP Principles and Application" was achieved. Although the early HACCP system was quite simple, consisting of only three principles, the modern system is built upon seven principles (see Table 5.2); indeed, the EU ban on commercial shrimp products from Bangladesh was lifted only when government agencies in that country succeeded in satisfying buyers that they were applying the seven HACCP principles.

Table 5.1. The Regulatory Evolution of the Global Food System

Year	Organization Created
1945	Food and Agriculture Organization (FAO)
1947	General Agreement on Tariffs and Trade
1948	World Health Organization (WHO)
1963	FAO/WHO Codex Alimentarius Commission
1994	Agreement on Application of Sanitary and Phytosanitary Measures
1995	World Trade Organization
1997	Codex Document on HACCP Principles and Application

Source: Sperber (2005, 506).

Table 5.2. The Evolution of HACCP Principles

HACCP Principles, 1972	HACCP Principles, 1997
1. Conduct hazard analysis 2. Determine critical control points 3. Establish monitoring procedures	1. Conduct hazard analysis 2. Determine critical control points 3. Establish critical limits 4. Establish monitoring procedures 5. Establish corrective actions 6. Establish verification procedures 7. Establish recordkeeping procedures

Source: Sperber (2005, 506).

The emergence of the HACCP regime led to a massive restructuring of industrial aquaculture across the global South. In Bangladesh, for instance, many shrimp factory owners had to renovate their facilities and convert them into modern plants. The new regime also prompted the Bangladesh government to establish a Fish Inspection and Quality Control institution (FIQC) within the Department of Fisheries in the Ministry of Fisheries and Livestock. The FIQC now has three stations equipped with modern laboratory facilities and staffed with technical personnel. The activities and restructuring measures undertaken by the Bangladesh government to meet the requirements of the HACCP system include the following (summarized from Chowdhury and Islam 2000).

• The Fish and Fish Products (Inspection and Quality Control) Rules of 1989 were amended in 1997 on the basis of the HACCP system required by major buyers.
• More than 24,000 field-level personnel have been trained in post-harvest handling, transportation, hygiene, and sanitation.
• Suppliers of raw materials for processing plants have been brought into a compulsory registration scheme.
• Follow-up training programs on the HACCP system have been introduced for personnel of fish-processing plants.
• The quality of the water and ice used in fish-processing plants has been standardized.
• The infrastructure of fish-processing plants has been renovated and modified in accordance with the HACCP system.
• The authorities concerned have been strengthened and given proper laboratory facilities and other logistical support.

- A supervisory audit team has been formed to monitor the work of the competent authorities.
- The quality of fish and shrimp raw materials has been improved through monitoring and motivational work on post-harvest handling and transport.
- Reasonable assurance is now provided that fish and shrimp used as raw materials are free from chemical contaminants, environmental pollutants, and toxins through frequent monitoring.
- Appropriate steps are now taken for quality assurance by implementing a quality management program based on HACCP principles, including plant and process inspections, the provision of certificates for exportable lots after physical and microbiological tests of products, and the maintenance of a high standard of quality in all activities related to laboratory work and field inspection.

By 2000, fifty-eight licensed factories in Bangladesh had developed HACCP-based quality assurance protection manuals, and factory personnel had begun to implement the HACCP system in their respective plants by following sanitation standard operating procedures and good manufacturing practice (Chowdhury and Islam 2000).

The implementation of these measures involved a significant cost that, however, was not borne by buyers. Cato and Subasinge (2003) estimate that, by 1997, the Bangladesh shrimp-processing industry had invested US$17.6 million in plant upgrades.

Third-Party Certification Regimes

Although the HACCP regulations were developed by the private sector on the buyer side of the commodity chain, government agencies remain central in implementing, subsidizing, and organizing compliance with these private standards. The introduction of third-party certification regimes, however, has precipitated a shift in governance from public to private (see Hatanaka, Bain, and Busch 2005; Islam 2010). Growing public concern over harmful and unsustainable aquaculture practices has led non-governmental organizations (NGOs), civil society organizations, and the aquaculture industry to develop and implement numerous certification systems for "better management practices" that focus on sustainable production by minimizing the negative effects of aquaculture operations on natural resources and local communities while increasing product acceptance on international markets.

The certification programs available to the aquaculture industry focus on the issues of food safety; food quality; the environment; social responsibility; and animal welfare (WWF 2007). Several government and NGO entities have addressed the issue of sustainable aquaculture development by defining a conditional framework, as well as practices and procedures aimed at more environmentally sound and socially responsible aquaculture operations. The resulting guidance frameworks are often summarized and referred to as codes of conduct, good aquaculture practices, or better management practices (see Table 5.3).

Table 5.3. Aquaculture Principles and Codes of Conduct

Title	Description
Code of Conduct for Responsible Fisheries	Adopted by the FAO in 1995 and considered to be the international fundamental framework for the development of sustainable aquaculture standards.
Code of Good Practice	Developed in 1999 by the Global Aquaculture Alliance on the basis of the FAO Code of Conduct and further developed in recent years; today serves as the basis for the Good Aquaculture Practices certification scheme of the Aquaculture Certification Council.
Code of Conduct for European Aquaculture	Developed by the Federation of European Aquaculture Producers, with the primary goal of promoting the responsible development and management of a viable European aquaculture sector to assure a high standard of quality food production while respecting environmental considerations and consumers' demands.
International Principles for Responsible Shrimp Farming	Developed by the Shrimp Farming and the Environment Consortium (consisting of the FAO, the Network of Aquaculture Centers in Asia-Pacific, the United Nations Environmental Program, the World Bank, and the World Wildlife Fund) to provide guidance on the implementation of the FAO Code of Conduct for Responsible Fisheries in the shrimp aquaculture sector.
Code of Good Environmental Practices	Developed and issued by Fundación Chile in 2003 to provide a framework for the sustainable development of salmonid farming in Chile.
Code of Practice for Australian Prawn Farmers	Prepared by the Australian Prawn Farmers Association and developed with the input of Australian prawn farmers based on their current practices for the environmentally sound production of shrimp in Australia; its proposed use of both settlement and recirculation systems has been adopted by the majority of the industry; the code serves as an internal guideline for all Australian prawn farmers, but is not propagated as a standard on the market.

Source: WWF (2007, 16).

There is also increasing interest in the certification of aquaculture products, as well as an increasing number of schemes covering eco-labelling, organic certification, and, more recently, fair trade. Although the growing number of certification programs, and possible competition among certification schemes, could result in confusion among buyers and consumers, third-party certification is becoming a powerful means of demonstrating to customers and governments a commitment to the environmentally responsible production of safe, high-quality seafood products. Hemlock and Baldomir (2008) report that Walmart, the world's largest retailer, set 2012 as the target date for selling only certified fish, while fast-food giant McDonald's has switched from threatened species to the more plentiful pollock for its fish sandwiches. Currently, some thirty-six certification schemes and eight key international agreements exist that are relevant to aquaculture. At least another nine initiatives address sustainability issues and create a framework for differentiating sources of aquatic products in this respect (FAO 2007; Resolve 2012). The main schemes are collated in the Appendix, and Table 5.4 summarizes schemes on the basis of promoters. The thirty-six aquaculture certification schemes certify slightly more than 1.3 million metric tons of products, but only three – Best Aquaculture Practices (BAP), Friend of the Sea, and GLOBALG.A.P. – have volumes greater than 10,000 tons each. Thus less than 3 per cent of total aquaculture production is certified, although the percentage is greater for internationally traded products and especially for certain species, such as marine shrimp. GLOBALG.A.P. appears to have gained the greatest market penetration in Europe, with commitments to purchase products so certified by large retailers such as Tesco, Rewe, Edeka Group, Metro Group, Auchan, ALDI, and E. Leclerc, while US retailers such as Walmart, Kroger, SUPERVALU, and Ahold USA prefer to sell BAP-certified products. Aquaculture certification schemes have gained relatively little traction in Japan (Resolve 2012).

A new scheme called the Aquaculture Stewardship Council (ASC) began certifying aquatic products in 2012 (ASC 2012a). The ASC likely will draw considerable attention, since it will be implementing long-awaited standards being developed by the Aquaculture Dialogues of the World Wildlife Fund (WWF). In total eight standards, covering twelve species, have been formulated by these Dialogues. Five standards (for abalone, bivalves, pangasius, tilapia, and salmon) have already been finalized; standard for shrimp, is expected at the end of 2013 and standards for seriola/cobia will follow later (ASC 2012b). NGOs

Table 5.4. The Main Certification Schemes Relevant to Aquaculture

Schemes Promoted by Retailers	
GLOBALG.A.P.	www.GLOBALGAP.org/uk_en/
Safe Quality Food	www.sqfi.com & www.fmi.org
Carrefour	www.carrefour.com
Schemes Promoted by the Aquaculture Industry	
Global Aquaculture Alliance & Aquaculture Certification Council	www.gaalliance.org; www.aquaculturecertification.org
Shrimp Seal of Quality	
SIGES – SalmonChile	www.salmonchile.cl/frontend/index.asp; www.salmonchile.cl
Scottish Salmon Producers' Organisation Code of Good Practice	www.scottishsalmon.co.uk
Schemes Promoted by Governments	
Thai Quality Shrimp	www.thaiqualityshrimp.com
Certification schemes in China	Safety agri-food certification; ChinaGAP*; Green food standard
Vietnam Good Aquaculture Practices and Code of Conduct program Hong Kong Accredited Fish Farm Scheme	www.hkaffs.org/en/
Schemes Promoted by NGOs	
Marine Aquarium Council	www.aquariumcouncil.org
International Standards Organization	www.iso.org/iso/home.html
Organic Schemes	
International Federation of Organic Agriculture Movements	www.ifoam.org
Naturland	www.naturland.de
Soil Association	www.soilassociation.org
BioGro New Zealand	www.bio-gro.co.nz/index.php/
Bio Suisse	www.bio-suisse.ch/en/home.php
KRAV	www.krav.se
Fair Trade Schemes	
Alter-Trade Japan	www.altertrade.co.jp/english/index-e.html
Ethical Trading Initiative	www.ethicaltrade.org
Fairtrade Labelling Organizations International	www.fairtrade.org.uk
Animal Welfare and "Free-range" Schemes	
Freedom food	www.rspca.org.uk/home
Label rouge	Adapted from http://agriculture.gouv.fr/le-label-rouge,10506
Other Relevant Organizations and Schemes	
World Wildlife Fund aquaculture dialogues and standards	http://worldwildlife.org/cci/aquaculture.cfm
Marine Stewardship Council	www.msc.org

(Continued)

Table 5.4. *(Continued)*

Other Relevant Organizations and Schemes	
Seafood Watch of the Monterey Bay Aquarium	www.montereybayaquarium.org/wt_track. asp?k=u_sfw1
Environmental Justice Foundation	www.ejfoundation.org
Federation of European Aquaculture Producers	www.FEAP.info
International Fair Trade Association	www.products-and-services.com
Swiss Import Promotion Programme	http://importers.sippo.ch

* ChinaGAP is benchmarked against GLOBALG.A.P. standards and receives its support, but also receives strong support from the Chinese government.
Source: FAO (2007, 11).

critical of the ASC, however, focus on its lack of attention to social issues and claim that it will deal only minimally with negative environmental effects. One should also note that organic certification for aquaculture is a specialized market and not considered viable for most products, although it will continue to grow in importance as a niche component for many retailers (Resolve 2012).

Implications of Third-Party Certification

The proliferation of various third-party certification schemes in the global aquaculture sector has generated both optimism and tension. Although such schemes provide some legitimacy for neoliberal capitalism's accumulation, scholars have delineated far-reaching implications of their use. In one sense, such certification can be understood as a new regulatory regime (Hatanaka, Bain, and Busch 2005; Mutersbaugh 2002), which Cashore and colleagues (Cashore 2002; Cashore, Auld, and Newsom 2003) refer to as a "non-state market-driven" governance regime, and Vandergeest (2007) terms "environmental regulatory networks," in which environmental attributes are significant. Whatever it is called, the new regime is a way of imposing new labour demands on local producers and producer institutions, and it often serves to transform local politics (Beulens et al. 2005; Boselie, Henson, and Weatherspoon 2003; Henson and Loader 2001). Although the new regime reflects the growing power of TPCs to regulate the global agri-food system, and offers opportunities to create alternative practices that are more socially and environmentally sustainable (Hatanaka, Bain, and Busch 2005), it also tends to marginalize and exclude certain players.

Busch and Bain (2004, 341) argue that certification standards are "not merely objective technical or economic devices"; rather, the new regime is "producing both winners and losers, as actors who are unable to meet the new and more rigorous retail standards are excluded from the market." In the words of Hatanaka, Bain, and Busch (2005, 334), the regime is playing a fundamental role in "reconfiguring social, political, and economic relations throughout the contemporary agrifood system." In other words, certification often has the effect of marginalizing producers who cannot afford to participate or who lack the cultural, social, and technical knowledge to do so. The subsequent result is industry consolidation through the elimination of small players.[2]

Certification institutions often mandate local consultation, but seldom provide a substantial role for local communities and workers (see Certifying the Uncertifiable 2003; Vandergeest 2007). A key reason for their failure to do so is that such regimes tend to adopt immutable technical standards (Campbell and Stuart 2005), which, as Vandergeest (2007, 1155) points out, "circulate internationally, but are not open to community-based understandings of what constitutes sustainability." In other words, certification in the global agrifood system tends to marginalize the communities that it claims to protect. Social movements are therefore regrouping to contest the certification regime. A case in point is the international pressure being brought to bear against the WWF's "shoddy" shrimp certification standards (see, for example, Climate Connections 2011; Mangrove Action Project 2011). .

In May 2011 activists from more than forty organizations, including Asia Solidarity against Industrial Aquaculture (ASIA), COD-DEFFAGOLF Honduras, and Mangrove Action Project released an open letter signed by "The Conscientious Objectors" (COs) and addressed to committee members of the WWF's Aquaculture Dialogues. Calling its new ASC standards "a crude attempt ... [to perpetuate] unsustainable production systems," the COs dismiss the WWF's claim that the standards were developed in consultation with local communities and indigenous peoples who are affected by aquaculture farms. They allege, rather, that the WWF's plans to certify the export-oriented, industrial production of such species as shrimp, pangasius, and salmon were developed specifically to promote the interests of the aquaculture industry. They also point out that the standards were being diluted under pressure from the industry to ensure that 20 per cent of existing shrimp producers could be certified immediately after the standards were released.

The WWF's Aquaculture Dialogues were in part funded by the seafood industry, and the individual employed by the WWF to run the process was previously employed as a regional vice-president for a controversial aquaculture multinational that has been widely accused of labour violations and environmental destruction. "WWF is wrong to claim their standards include inputs from local 'stakeholders' when the main body of those stakeholders – the local resource users, who are directly affected by the industry – did not have any voice in determining these 'standards'," says Natasha Ahmad of ASIA. Riza Damanik of KIARA, a network of Indonesian fisher groups, agrees: "We saw the WWF Aquaculture Dialogue in Jakarta and protested at the venue ... 99 per cent of those in attendance were from the shrimp industry and the government. WWF's claim that communities were involved is a joke – they organized their so-called dialogue with affected local communities in a posh city venue." Another critic, Alfredo Quarto of Mangrove Action Project, charges that "[t]hese ... standards are just one more 'pie-in-the-sky' attempt to justify and expand the profits of an unsustainable and destructive industry, resulting in further loss of mangrove forests and displacement of local communities." According to Gudrun Hubendick of the Stockholm Shrimp Action Group, "WWF continues to ignore the risk that their shrimp certification scheme may result in actually increasing demand for shrimp, thus increasing the expansion of the bad practices that certification was supposedly trying to address through these standards."

The open letter's signatories work on an astonishingly diverse spectrum of issues, including human rights, consumers' rights, indigenous peoples' rights, land and water use, agriculture, environmental law and conservation, labour rights, marine and coastal ecology, soil science, social science, and fisheries. The COs claim that export-oriented industrial aquaculture has had a devastating impact on all these sectors. More precisely, the COs oppose the WWF's Shrimp Aquaculture Dialogue (ShAD) for the following reasons.

- There has never been involvement or representation in the so-called dialogue process for the majority of stakeholders or, more aptly, for local resource users who are most adversely affected by the shrimp industry in producer nations. ShAD's "stakeholders" are overwhelmingly those invested in the growth of the shrimp export industry.

- With each revision to the draft, the standards and their evaluation criteria have been progressively and deliberately diluted by the ShAD General Steering Committee (GSC) to ensure that at least 20 per cent of the existing shrimp industry can be certified immediately after the standards are released. The process clearly demonstrates the bias of the ShAD GSC.
- The ShAD GSC has resolutely refrained from undertaking or commissioning serious research to collect meaningful and verifiable inputs and feedback from local resource users in the manner prescribed by The Economics of Ecosystems and Biodiversity (see http://www.teebweb.org).
- The GSC's selection of its board members has not been fair from the beginning and is not representative of a transparent and democratic process. As such, the standards overwhelmingly represent industry interests – for example, the whole of Africa is "represented" on the ShAD GSC by shrimp industry nominees from Madagascar.
- Continued lack of proper legislation and enforcement in producer nations makes adherence to any certification standard unfeasible.
- The ShAD puts too much trust in the industry to monitor and regulate itself. The certification program depends upon an untried and untested auditing system. Other critical aspects of the process also require a "leap of faith" that previously disastrous practices miraculously will reverse their effects once the ShAD standards are released.
- The ShAD standards continue to perpetuate unsustainable and destructive open-throughput systems of aquaculture – with a legacy of 400,000 hectares (and counting) of abandoned ponds in producer nations. The standards also promote bad practices relating to "mitigation of the effects of mangrove loss."
- The process conveniently ignores widespread community displacement, human rights violations, and environmental damage to many thousands of hectares of land by the shrimp industry prior to 1999. Under current standards, ponds in these regions could be certified, and trends indicate that they will. The ASC becomes, therefore, a confessional for the shrimp industry, willing to grant indulgences in the form of certification.
- Export-oriented tropical shrimp production does not contribute to food security. Food security should not be measured by the weight of export production or the profit curve of the industry, but by the

availability of healthy and sustainable means of local food production for local consumption.

- There remains a great risk that WWF-ShAD certification, by plac-
  ing a green stamp on tropical shrimp, will expand the demand
  for farmed tropical shrimp – both certified and uncertified – thus
  promoting the continued (and possibly more rapid) expansion of
  unsustainable practices.
- Feed issues are still not satisfactorily resolved, and there is still no
  effective plan to meet increasing feed demands. The projected reliance on genetically modified soy and palm oil is of great concern.
- The COs requested, but did not receive, a breakdown of development time spent by ShAD in developing their social, environment,
  and technical standards.
- The ShAD GSC and their offspring in the ASC still have not taken
  any direct and effective actions to influence consumers in the
  importing nations to reduce shrimp consumption – extremely
  pertinent to the intent and purposes to any attempt at designing a
  certification program for shrimp.

Conclusion

The emergence of a third-party certification regime for industrial aquaculture appears to be a positive development in creating awareness
of environmental regulations, food safety issues, methods of achieving greater productivity, and the importance of a proper and timely
response to international market demands. At the same time, however,
it raises some fundamental questions with regard to the role of government, the participation of the communities in which shrimp farms are
located, and the fate of small farmers who cannot afford to participate
in such a highly technical regime. One can discern three conspicuous
shifts or trends in the wake of the imposition of third-party certification
in industrial aquaculture: the shift in the role of government from regulator to regulated; the marginalization of communities; and industry
consolidation.

Industrial aquaculture across the global South is now on the brink
of what Busch and Bain (2004, 337) term the "private regulation of the
public." Private TPCs are competing to take over the key certification
and managerial roles played by government, and although tension persists between parties and there is reluctance and scepticism on the part

of governments and some traders and/or exporters, there is abundant evidence to show that most have no option but to cooperate eventually with the emerging regime. Vandergeest (2007, 1163) argues that "producers who are able to obtain certification by the most important schemes secure privileged market access." What, then, are the broader implications for the global agri-food system?

The dilemma is that the certification regime has emerged with a promise to protect communities affected by environmental externalities and to ensure protection of human rights and community participation. As its technical measures move towards industry consolidation, however, in practical terms it leaves almost no space for community participation. The new regime, in fact, might further isolate communities. Still, it must work with communities, local civil administrations, and NGOs to achieve its goals and objectives. There is a model for community involvement, called "community-based natural resource management," that is supposed to enhance the role of communities in development projects or environmental regulations. As Vandergeest (2007) finds, however, the model tends to emerge where resources are less valuable and are not used to produce commodities for wealthier buyers – that is, in places where certification regimes are unlikely to succeed. Rather, certification regimes tend to emerge around highly contested products, such as shrimp, that have significant value.

Although private regulation is gradually displacing government agencies' domination in managing environment and natural resources, governments are left with some responsibilities that entail a paradox of power. In the new regime, consolidation of a government's power is tied to continuous consolidation of its cooperation with, and subordination to, market demands, orchestrated by what Gereffi et al. (2001) call the "NGO-industrial complex." In other words, the more a government works with the market, the more power it gains. The paradox is that, once a country produces a global commodity for wealthy buyers, its government has to surrender its key roles in managing the environment and monitoring food safety standards and food quality attributes to powerful market players, but, again, the same government's power emanates from its continuous and shifting collaboration with market demands (Islam 2008a).

As Thompson and Cowan (2000) point out, most of the literature on commodity chains in the global agri-food system is dominated by a discussion of the process of local or regional integration into the global economy, rather than by an examination of the reorganization and reconstitution of local and regional production-consumption relations and concomitant changes in gender and labour patterns and in environmental and agrarian landscapes. Twin-driven commodity chain analysis (discussed in Chapter 2) potentially provides a powerful tool and framework for analysing and understanding the key players and the roles they play in the chain. Who sets the parameters? Why? From what point of view and to what effect? Who is privileged, and who is marginalized? These are the questions that remain for future research.

6 Agrarian Transformation and Local Regulations

Since the era of colonization, a great deal of agrarian restructuring – along with a new agrarian division of labour – has taken place in the global South, albeit with substantial variances (see Friedmann 2005; Goodman and Redclift 1982; McMichael 1994; Singh 1998). After the end of the Second World War, local pre-capitalist estate agricultures began to converge slowly but surely towards very large-scale capitalist agriculture (Buttel 2001), which precipitated a shift from agri-colonialism to agri-industrialism (McMichael 1998, 2008).

One general impact of this transition has been what Araghi (1995) calls "global depeasantization," which is characterized by, among other factors, the dominance of private and/or foreign capital (Goodman and Watts 1997b); a high degree of concentration in export-oriented production, processing, and marketing (Heffernan and Constance 1994); the prominence of contract production and/or vertical integration in linking farm-level production and downstream processing and trade (Watts 1996); and major effects on rural populations as a consequence of restructuring processes that are simultaneously undermining existing agrarian livelihoods and reinforcing rural job insecurity and the political and economic marginality of rural workers (Raynolds 1997). In this chapter, I delineate the kind of agrarian transformation that has been generated by regulations governing commercial shrimp farming and other aspects of rural life whose goals are to manage the new production regime and mitigate rural tensions.

Agrarian Structure and Change: The Case of Bangladesh

"Agrarian structure" is conventionally understood as "the subset of institutions governing the distribution of rights in agricultural means of production, notably land" (Boyce 1987, 37). More specifically, it refers to the distribution of landholdings and to the organization of labour in agricultural production (Ito 2002); Singh (1998) adds a third component: the consumption pattern. Further expanding upon the concept in the case of the global South (see Rogaly 1999) and drawing insights from the synthesis of agrarian political economy and global restructuring perspectives, I describe five components of the agrarian structure in Bangladesh: the local supply chain, the ownership of land and tenancy agreements, the organization of labour, local rural regulations for managing rural tensions and conflicts, and the cultural and consumption patterns generated by the new production regime.

The Local Supply Chain and Its Beneficiaries

Shrimp production in Bangladesh involves a complex system of supply chains in which at least three major groups – shrimp farmers, local depot owners, and processing factories – are in action, with middlemen present at every stage. The process actually starts in the sea. Fry collectors, many of them women, sell their catch to local middlemen who in turn sell the collected fry to shrimp farmers. The Department of Fisheries estimates that about half a million fry collectors were working in the coastal zones of Bangladesh in the middle of the last decade (Bangladesh 2005). Although the government banned the collection of fry from the sea after an exerted campaign by environmental groups who argued that the practice destroys other species and disturbs the biodiversity of areas such as the Sundarbans, fry collection sea still goes on, albeit on a lesser scale, for compelling reasons outlined in Chapter 5.

Indeed, farmers prefer to use fry collected from the sea rather than grown in hatcheries. Middlemen, however, now pay collectors less, while farmers have to pay three times as much for sea-collected fry. Yet most small- and some medium-scale farmers face regular financial crises, and are unable to buy shrimp larvae without borrowing money from middlemen, who lend to farmers – mostly at no interest – on condition that the farmers then sell them shrimp at less than the actual market price. These middlemen, who are both *farias* (intermediaries who buy and sell products) and *aratdars* (commission agents), thus play a pivotal role in injecting credit into the supply chain and exerting control over sale prices and margins (see, for example, USAID Bangladesh 2006). Such price fixing is ensured by the conditions imposed upon the *dadon* (loan). *Farias* pay farmers as little as possible for their shrimp to maximize profits when subsequently selling to *aratdars*. Moreover, *farias* and *aratdars* employ relatively fewer grades than those prevailing in the export market – a tactic that tends to depress prices in the exchange. Other individuals, known locally as *dadondar* (loan providers or "loan sharks") and *mahajon* (the great people) – euphemistic terms for those who play exploitive roles – also provide *dadon* at high rates of interest.

Some farmers thus are caught in the vicious nexus of dependency and exploitation perpetuated by the middlemen. As one farmer interviewed for this book lamented, "[w]e take loans from [a] *mahajon* for shrimp cultivation. After we sell shrimp, we pay him back with interest. The circle goes on in this way." Indeed, all of the farmers I interviewed in freshwater shrimp areas complained that they had to buy shrimp feed at a high price and that they felt exploited by the shrimp feed agents. One reported that a "vested interest group controls the technology and shrimp feed, and sets the price without taking our affordability into consideration. This both discourages and marginalizes the small farmers who eventually fail to take this risk. It has made many of us entrepreneurs, but marginalized some at the same time." Another farmer echoed this testimony: "We have no control over fry, feed, and other technology. The price is very high and getting higher day by day. I think vested interest groups are getting the main share out of it. The price now is beyond the capacity of the poor farmers. Hence, poor farmers very rarely venture into shrimp cultivation. For shrimp feed, for example, the company sets a price, but does not care whether the farmers will live or die [can afford it or not]."

Although district fisheries offices used to provide loans to new shrimp farmers, one respondent complained that these loans were limited and involved both interest and bribes. The DOF no longer provides loans, although a number of national banks and non-governmental organizations (NGOs) have set up branches in shrimp-farming areas to provide loans to needy farmers and new entrepreneurs. Farmers still complain, however, that the avenues for government loans through national banks remain limited and sometimes require bribes. Microcredit-based NGOs, such as the Grameen Bank, are helping needy farmers, but they charge very high interest rates, sometimes more than 30 per cent. It is clear that both farm and non-farm capital is involved in extracting surplus value from the production process, both directly and indirectly. Ultimately, it is primarily the vulnerable farmers who are exploited and marginalized.

The simple route from hatchery to factory is, in fact, a complicated and lengthy chain with a number of interlocking interests. Shrimp from the farmlands usually are transported by middlemen in vans to urban depots, mostly situated near processing factories. Many shrimp collectors or middlemen also accept loans from depot owners to lend to and buy from farmers, and they are then bound to sell shrimp to the particular depot owner in question. Some pre-processing activities, such as washing, beheading, icing, and packaging, are carried out at the depots before the shrimp are sent to the factories for final processing. When a depot receives shrimp from different collectors, it supplies them directly to the factories or delivers them to the moneylenders, who then take responsibility for supplying the shrimp to the factories. In either case, the depot owners are paid not by the factories but by the moneylenders. The supply chain also has a number of other players – including ice sellers, ice factory owners, plastic box and sheet manufacturers, van operators and owners, and truck drivers and owners – whose livelihoods depend on the sector. It is the farmer, however, who tends to lose out the most in the process, with the middlemen, even those not involved in the mainstream shrimp trade, receiving a higher dividend. Figure 6.1 shows the local supply chain as a complex web combined with financial flows.

Indeed, as Tables 6.1 and 6.2 show, although shrimp farming is a financially profitable industry, it does not reward everyone involved in it equally. Such stakeholders as fry collectors, hatchery workers, depot workers, ice van operators, and processing workers remain in poverty, with incomes insufficient to support their families, even though they are much better off than they were during the previous paddy regime. Hatchery owners, large-scale farm owners, depot owners, middlemen or traders, processing plant owners, ice factory owners, exporters, and the like, in contrast, are among the big beneficiaries.

Land Ownership and Tenancy Agreements

Land ownership is unevenly distributed in the coastal regions of Bangladesh. The brackish water zones are legally owned by the government (*khas* land), but inland agricultural plots have clearly demarcated private ownership, much of it in the hands of large landowners (Ali 2006; Ito 2002). During the era of resistance to the introduction of shrimp farming (see Chapter 4), a powerful few in the Satkhira district,

Figure 6.1. The Local Shrimp Supply Chain, Bangladesh

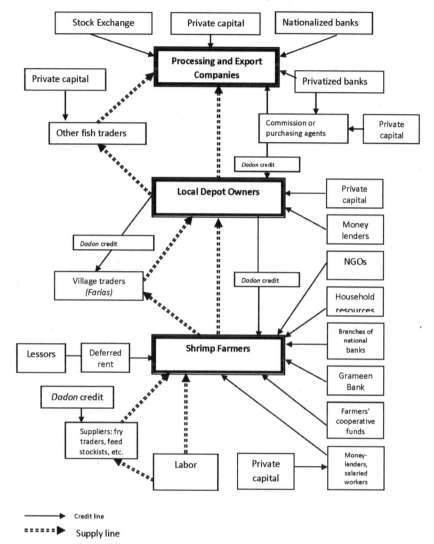

Source: Islam (2008a, 215); reprinted with permission from Elsevier.

Table 6.1. Annual Shrimp Industry Stakeholder Incomes by Income Source, Bangladesh, 2003

	Household Income		
	Shrimp-related Activities	Farm and Non-farm Activities	Total Household Income
Stakeholders	*(taka per year)**		
Shrimp farmers	670,180 (78.34)	185,270 (21.66)	855,450 (100)
Land lessors	32,890 (23.82)	105,185 (76.18)	138,075 (100)
Hatchery owners	870,135 (84.96)	153,985 (15.04)	1,024,120 (100)
Depot owners	126,600 (47.42)	140,400 (52.58)	267,000 (100)
Shrimp seed or fry collectors	13,550 (37.85)	22,250 (61.15)	38,800 (100)
Shrimp farm labourers	40,170 (75.00)	13,340 (25.00)	53,510 (100)
Processing plant workers	50,780 (51.33)	48,150 (48.67)	98,930 (100)
Hatchery workers	61,000 (70.67)	25,350 (29.36)	86,350 (100)
Feed mill workers	55,584 (78.41)	15,300 (21.59)	70,884 (100)
Depot workers	19,200 (36.20)	33,840 (63.80)	53,040 (100)
Shrimp traders (*faria*)	48,500 (65.63)	25,400 (34.37)	73,900 (100)

* The exchange rate in 2003 was US$1 = 67 taka.
Note: Figures in parentheses indicate percentage of total income.
Source: Islam, Talukder, and Miah (2004).

Table 6.2. Poverty Rankings and Economic Conditions in the Shrimp Supply Chain, Bangladesh

Stakeholder	Economic Situation	Wealth Rank (1–4)*
Fry collector	Owns no assets; involved in other occupations; employment irregular; subsistence living; no savings; female family members and children also involved in income-earning activities; education and health care beyond means; children also collect fry.	1
Hatchery owner	Owns production assets; shrimp is main source of income; earns a good income; employs workers; owns a house; children go to school; has limited ability to pay for medical care.	4

Table 6.2. *(Continued)*

Stakeholder	Economic Situation	Wealth Rank (1–4)*
Hatchery worker	Owns no assets; subsistence living; works as agricultural wage labourer during non-shrimp season; seasonal unemployment; other family members, including women, also work to maintain family; limited access to education and health care.	1
Farmer	Income varies; may be educated; takes loans from informal sources; shrimp is main source of income; can make other investments; children go to school; can afford health care; female family members also work in some cases.	3–4
Middleman or local trader	Lending money is main occupation; involved in other activities; buys fish at a low price and sells to processors; also sells a portion in the local market; children go to school; able to afford health care.	4
Depot owner	Employs workers; has other investments; takes loans from informal sources; shrimp processing major source of income; children go to school; able to afford health care.	4
Depot worker	No production assets; employment irregular, works as agricultural wage labourer during non-shrimp season; difficult to afford basic needs of life; other members of the family also work.	1
Processing plant owner	Rich; has made a big investment; takes loans from formal and informal sources; shrimp is the main source of income; enjoys good living conditions.	4
Processing worker (female)	No production assets; low wages; no alternative employment; seasonal unemployment; sometimes only earning member of the family; difficult to make a living on income.	1
Processing worker (male)	No production assets; low wages; employed in other activities during lean season; female and other members of the family also work; low standard of living.	1
Processing worker at landing centre	Seasonal employment; difficult to obtain alternate employment; subsistence living; other members of the family work; cannot afford basic facilities of life.	1
Ice van operator	May own van or be a paid van operator; seeks employment in other sectors during non-shrimp season; other members of the family also work; needs credit to buy van.	2

(Continued)

Table 6.2. *(Continued)*

Stakeholder	Economic Situation	Wealth Rank (1–4)*
Ice factory owner	Investment made; sells ice for various purposes, including shrimp; takes loans from formal and informal sources; employs van operators; sometimes also owns van; has other sources of income.	4
Procurement staff/processing plant agent	Fixed income paid by company; comfortable living; access to basic needs with no difficulty.	3
Exporter	Employs farmers and processing plant owners; makes a big investment; credit available from formal and informal sources; receives export incentives from the government; involved in other activities; high standard of living; female family members may or may not work.	4

*Note: 1 = Extremely poor; 2 = Poor; 3 = Moderately poor; 4 = Not poor.
Source: Khatun (2004, 43–4).

thanks to their close links to government officials and political leaders, obtained licences for shrimp cultivation and expropriated a great deal of *khas* and some privately owned land. As the political economy perspective predicted (Chapter 2), a polarizing trajectory in farm-size structure appeared in which fewer but larger farms dominated, and medium-sized farms were the least able to resist the economic pressure towards marginalization. There is no sign yet, however, that rich shrimp lords are appropriating land belonging to local farmers in freshwater regions such as Khulna and Bagherhat (see, for example, Ito 2002; Kendrick 1994; Rutherford 1994). On the contrary, increasing numbers of small peasant farmers in these localities are actively participating in shrimp farming, and shrimp is no longer viewed as the "business of outsiders." As well, some landless farmers have either taken up shrimp-related jobs in the new regime or managed to lease land from others to begin shrimp farming.

Local farmers in the freshwater zones of Bangladesh have remained the main actors in shrimp farming for several reasons. First, the clearly demarcated private ownership of inland agricultural plots makes it difficult for outsiders to obtain large tracts of land to convert into large-scale prawn farms, as, to do so, they would be forced to negotiate separately with a large number of small peasant farmers; Vandergeest, Flaherty, and Miller (1999) found a similar scenario in Thailand. Second, the controversies in coastal areas have raised local peasant farmers' awareness of the importance of land rights; consequently, they are determined not to let outsiders gain control of their property. Third, as we saw in Chapter 4, even in the coastal regions a peasant movement facilitated by local NGOs emerged to oppose land expropriation and the forceful exploitation of natural resources such as lakes and forests. This movement was strengthened, and turned violent, when outside shrimp lords attempted to use hired thugs to crush the resistance, with incidents of rape and murder reported. As a result, the government banned the licensing system, and many peasants managed to get back their lost land.

At the same time, land prices have skyrocketed due to the shrimp pond revolution, as Table 6.3 shows. Interviews I conducted for this study confirm Ito's (2002) suggestion that, despite the availability of new labour opportunities, old forms of contractual labour have become less common. The institutions of sharecropping and mortgages have virtually disappeared from shrimp farming (although not from rice farming). In their place, leasing has become the most common form of tenancy. Sharecropping arrangements vary in different areas, but in general a landowner receives one-third of the harvest and the remaining two-thirds is taken by the sharecropping tenant, who also supplies the production inputs. Again confirming Ito (2002), I find that

Table 6.3. Land and Lease Prices, Selected Regions of Bangladesh, 2001–10

Region	2001		2005		2010	
	Land Price	Lease Price	Land Price	Lease Price	Land Price	Lease Price
	(current US$ per hectare)					
Khulna	3,500–4,000	230–250	9,300–10,500	580–600	29,000–35,000	600–650
Bagherhat	1,800–2,300	115–230	8,100–9,500	460–480	21,000–26,000	460–500
Satkhira	2,900–3,400	115–150	8,100–9,500	350–370	23,000–30,000	400–450

Note: Land suitable for dual cultivation (prawn/shrimp and paddy) is more precious than that for single cultivation.
Source: Author's investigation.

the institution of sharecropping did not take off in shrimp farming for two reasons in particular, both connected to the reduced capacity of owners to exercise control over the shrimp labour process. The first is that – unlike paddy cultivation – landowners were unable to check on the growth of shrimp swimming underwater. The second reason is that – again unlike paddy cultivation, in which harvesting takes place in a single operation – individual shrimp can be caught and sold throughout the shrimp season without landowners' knowledge.

In addition to those noted above, other significant differences exist between the freshwater prawn regions (mainland Khulna and Bagherhat), where what are known locally as *golda* (*Macrobrachium rosenbergii*) are cultivated, and the brackish-water shrimp regions (the coastal areas of Satkhira), where *bagda* (*Penaeus monodon*) are cultivated. First, land expropriation, the commoditization of government-owned *khas* land and forests, farmer displacement, and the occupation of *ghers* (ponds) took place primarily in the brackish-water regions, and farmer resistance therefore generally took place there.

Second, most of the land used to cultivate brackish-water shrimp was reclaimed from forests, from barren land with little or no previous rice production, and from *khas* land. Further, the main entrepreneurs involved were outsiders. In the freshwater regions, in contrast, all of the land currently used for *golda* cultivation traditionally has been under private ownership and previously was used for paddy and vegetable farming. The farmers in these regions have not abandoned paddy production entirely, but have adopted dual or triple cultivation, combining paddy and/or freshwater fish farming with shrimp farming. Hence, the shrimp regime has not replaced the paddy regime entirely; rather, the two cohabit. The purchase and lease prices of land in the freshwater regions are therefore higher than those in the brackish-water regions.

Third, although – because of the aforementioned dual and triple cultivation that takes place in the freshwater regions – the economic turnover there could be expected to exceed that in the brackish-water regions, costs of shrimp production are much higher in the former than in the latter, for three main reasons. First, the hatcheries cannot meet the demand for *golda* fry, and therefore farmers in the freshwater regions have to rely on fry collected from rivers, which are more expensive. Second, unlike farmers in the brackish-water regions, those in the freshwater regions have to buy shrimp feed – both snails and factory-processed Saudi-Bangladeshi shrimp feed – on a regular basis. Third, the conversion of shrimp ponds to paddy fields and vice versa, as well as the necessary water arrangements, involve additional costs for farmers in the freshwater region. Water arrangements in the brackish-water regions, on the other hand, largely depend on natural tidal waves of rivers and estuaries. Recent evidence shows that, due to the high cost of production and increasing vulnerability to cyclones, theft, flood, and market fluctuations, among other things, farmers in both regions increasingly reluctant to continue shrimp/prawn cultivation. Instead, they are more willing to lease out their lands.

The Organization of Labour

Commercial shrimp farming has generated great changes in labour contracts. Landless farmers used to work as day labourers in paddy farms and could sell their labour only during the irrigation season. Today, they have new jobs as guards or caretakers, for example, which last for a fixed term ranging from six months to a year. Guards are employed by wealthy landlords, who contract out the work involved in shrimp farming (including winter rice cultivation on the land after the shrimp are harvested). The wages and exact employment arrangements for such jobs differ from case to case, but, according my interviews in the field in 2003, a caretaker working on a contract basis typically earned US$23–27) per month with food and US$30–38 per month without food. The pay rates for those on long-term contracts were lower than the daily wage rates, which varied between US$0.90 and $1.50, provided that such casual labourers could find work on most days of the month.

Similar forms of annual labour contracts exist throughout rural Bangladesh. The common arrangement is for the labourer to live in a wealthy farmer's household and undertake all kinds of work, domestic as well as agricultural. Respondents to my survey revealed that both wage rates and the availability of wage labour were lower in the previous paddy regime, which resulted in many day labourers going to the big cities of Dhaka and Chittagong to pull rickshaws. They also reported that the new regime did not change their economic conditions that much, and poverty remains a conspicuous condition for these day labourers. Many of them reported to be "sheer losers," as they are unable even to graze domestic animals that once gave them some level of sustenance.

Other shrimp-related jobs are also available, mostly on a daily basis, but on a smaller scale, including pond making, pond repairing, canal making, and shrimp catching. A few landless individuals trade in snail meat, which is used for shrimp feed in the freshwater regions; others have become drivers who transport shrimp, feed, fry, and the ice cubes needed for shrimp culture. "Before the pond revolution, the poor landless people of Satkhira used to go to Dhaka to pull rickshaws, as they did not have any work when the irrigation season was over," the district fisheries officer of Satkhira claimed. "Now, no rickshaw puller in Dhaka is from Satkhira," he added.

Ito (2002, 2004) shows that shrimp farming in the Bagherhat region has attracted migrant labour from other districts. The landless poor, if they are enterprising, can even lease ponds with loans from government banks and NGOs. My own survey reveals that many local farmers have also become businesspeople. As well, landless individuals who used to work in paddy fields as day labourers have adapted to the new production regime and taken up a variety of shrimp-related jobs. "Previously, we used to work for six months in the paddy fields, and did not have work in the off-season," one villager reported. "But now we have work all the year round." Many small farmers now lease out their own land and work either on someone else's shrimp farm or in another sector. Although this finding indicates the emergence of a wage-labour regime in which farmers are freed from their means of production (the land) and sell their labour in the open market to obtain a wage – an inherent characteristic of the capitalist mode of production – it is not clear whether these farmers enjoy greater bargaining power today. Rigg and Nattapoolwat (2001, 945) find a similar situation in Thailand: "Rural households are dividing their time between farm and non-farm activities, constructing livelihoods that are increasingly hybrid, both spatially and sectorally. Many of the new opportunities also have global elements." These new opportunities are accompanied, however, by widespread tensions and vulnerabilities.

Although the new production regime has opened up new opportunities for many to earn an income, the recent tendency among global buyers towards opting for linkages with fewer and larger suppliers to ensure traceability could have an impact on the farm structure. Many small farmers are already concerned that they are likely to lose out in the competitive commodity market. Therefore, although still in a nascent stage, the departure of small- and medium-scale farmers from their land and their transition to a subsistence mode based on wage labour is an emerging trend in the new export-oriented commodity regime; as Rigg (2006, 180) notes, "[l]ives and livelihoods ... are becoming increasingly divorced from farming and, therefore, from the land."

Changes have also taken with respect to the respective roles of men and women. The previous irrigation (paddy) regime was characterized by a clear-cut gendered division of labour, with only men hired as labourers in the paddy fields, while their wives performed housework. Although the shrimp regime has not broken completely with this gender division, a greater number of women now find work opportunities outside the home and earn an income. As one female labourer remarked during the course of my survey, "[o]nly males used to work in the paddy fields, and our family had a very limited income. Now I can contribute to the family income, as I clean shrimp ponds and earn money." Although women's participation in the workforce remains low and is concentrated in lower-paid jobs, they are finding work in a variety of sectors, including snail collection, shrimp feed preparation, the construction and cleaning of shrimp ponds, and shrimp cleaning. Men also work in these sectors, but earn higher wages than women, as Table 6.4 shows – which is one reason employers prefer to hire women.

Many women have internalized this wage difference as falling into the normal scheme of things. In the words of one, "[t]hey are males [*purush*] and we are females [*mohila*], and that's why they deserve to get more than what we're getting," Employers in the farming vicinities arbitrarily set differential wages for men and women, with practically no resistance from the latter. When these employers were challenged about the wage difference, one of them responded: "Equal wages for both male and female workers for the same job with same amount of labour is obviously an ideal [situation], but we continue this practice as nobody has told us not to, and the female workers are okay with it."

Table 6.4. Daily Wages by Type of Worker, Selected Regions of Bangladesh, 2006

	Adult Permanent		Adult Seasonal		Child Permanent		Child Seasonal	
	Male	Female	Male	Female	Male	Female	Male	Female
Region				*(US$ per day)*				
Khulna	1.23	0.92	1.23	0.92	0.78	0.62	0.62	0.54
Bagerhat	1.26	0.95	1.23	0.92	0.92	0.78	0.65	0.54
Satkhira	1.07	0.92	1.07	0.85	0.92	0.78	0.92	0.69
Average	1.19	0.93	1.18	0.90	0.87	0.72	0.73	0.59

Source: Author's investigation.

Yet, not all women are happy with these new jobs in the production sites. As one remarked during my survey, "[w]e're forced to work in shrimp ponds since we can no longer graze and look after our domestic animals ... All grazing lands have been eaten up by shrimp ponds. If I could have some cows, I would not work here [in shrimp ponds]. My [economic] return would have been even better." Chapter 7 examines these issues in more depth.

Local Rural Governance

Export-oriented industrial aquaculture across the global South has passed through what Peluso and Watts (2001) call "violent environments," and some "better practices" have emerged over time due to the multilevel hybrid form of environmental governance promoted by various actors. The conflict and violence surrounding shrimp farming in Bangladesh has not disappeared completely, however. Natural disasters, shrimp diseases, and theft are among the common risks and tensions associated with shrimp farming today. Ito (2002) finds that such problems vary according to the power relations among village households. Many wealthy, well-connected peasant households are obviously in a better position to survive man-made risks. For example, as thieves are likely to be afraid to steal from them, better-off peasant farmers are less likely to become victims of shrimp or prawn theft. Although this power differential is still in place in many areas, my own findings study suggest that, in the freshwater regions, villagers – both small- and large-scale farmers working together – have found alternative measures to stop shrimp or prawn theft and to maintain a form of local governance.

Apart from theft, many farmers are also concerned about the high price of shrimp feed and fry and the government's lack of support in terms of the provision of loans, training, and policing. The lack of available loans has given rise to the aforementioned exploitative institution of *dadon* (money lending). The water arrangements in the Bagherhat and Satkhira regions, and the failure to pay lease money in all regions, including Khulna, are the principal sources of tension and conflict. Salt intrusion into irrigated land, the unplanned and random construction of shrimp ponds and the resultant lack of drainage channels and irrigation canals between ponds, and the poor construction and inadequate maintenance of sluice gates are among the main reasons for the water arrangement problems. Moreover, the powerful get priority access to the water supply. The government is considering introducing a zoning system to resolve some of these rural conflicts, but locals in the fresh-water regions have also come forward with their own innovations, local knowledge, and institutions to manage tension, as outlined in the following example.

LATHIAL BAHINI

To promote self-governance and, because the government is unable to provide sufficient security, to protect their shrimp from theft and other problems, such as the bypassing of safety regulations, villagers in the Khulna region have formed *Lathial Bahini*, associations made up of selected members from each household who take turns guarding the village ponds against theft, which normally takes place at night. *Lathial Bahini* members also look after such issues as the water supply, government regulations, and the shrimp market. When guarding shrimp ponds, all members hold *lathi* (bamboo sticks) to defend themselves and scare off potential thieves, thus giving these associations their name. Any thief caught red handed is beaten with *lathi* and then taken before a village community hearing.

TEA STALLS

Many villages have tea stalls that, in addition to selling tea, show movies, mostly Hindi-language movies from Bollywood, which are more popular than local Bengali movies in rural Bangladesh. The tea stalls normally remain open all night, and customers – mostly members of *Lathial Bahini* – regularly frequent them to drink tea, gossip, and enjoy the entertainment on offer during the nighttime. The tea stalls thus work to protect the shrimp ponds, as the villagers' presence prevents thieves from carrying out their intended activities.

COMMUNITY HEARINGS

Landowners who lease out their land are insufficiently powerful to ensure they receive their rent in a timely fashion. The lease contracts in villages are generally oral rather than written in nature. The powerful shrimp lords who lease land from small farmers sometimes ignore these contracts and fail to make the agreed lease-payments, which obviously creates tension. To deal with such situations, many villages hold *salish* or *bichar* (community hearings) to resolve disputes and punish those held responsible. The *Morol* (community head) and union council chairman play considerable roles along with the *Thana* (local government council). If this village-level institution fails to resolve the problem, then locals go to the local fisheries officer or to court.

In the *salish*, however, the wealthy are often privileged. In my survey, one union council member, who is also a shrimp farmer, had this to say about the success of rural governance in managing conflict and tension:

> Sometimes people who have leased out their lands for shrimp cultiva-
> tion to powerful shrimp lords face troubles in getting their lease money.
> These poor people then come to me. As an elected member of the union
> council, I have some power to resolve these disputes. If I fail to resolve
> problems with my own power, we have to call for a *grammo salish* [village
> hearing]. We announce it in the village bazaar. Other influential people in
> my village also join in the *salish*. We make a verdict based on the hearing.
> Sometimes we impose certain sanctions such as a social boycott if [the]
> money is not paid on time. Sometimes a family member or a relative of
> the convicted takes the responsibility to pay the lease money. If we fail to
> resolve issues of concern through a village hearing, we then refer the issue
> to the chairman of the union council. If he fails, we complain to the local
> fisheries officer. If the local fisheries officer cannot collect the lease money,
> we then finally make a case to the local legal court. So far we have resolved
> our problems and we have not gone to the courts.

FARMERS' COOPERATIVE ASSOCIATIONS

In some areas, shrimp farmers have formed farmers' associations, whose members deposit a certain amount of money each month and run various facets of their operations. One objective of these associations is to provide loans to their members to render them less dependent on government and NGO loans, which are quite difficult to obtain and sometimes require a bribe. The secretary of one farmers' association, who is also a shrimp farmer, reported that "[e]very member of our association has a savings account and deposits 100 taka [US$1.50] per month. We have a plan to provide loans to our members within the next two years. For any loan to a shrimp farmer, the government banks take 8 per cent interest. Some cooperative NGOs charge even higher [interest]. We will try to see whether we can give loans to our members at less than 4 per cent interest. Self-sufficiency is our goal."

MOBILE COURTS AND OTHER INSTITUTIONS

Local governments employ sanctions and mobile courts to enforce the Hazard Analysis and Critical Control Point (HACCP) regulations at the farming level, such as the use of plastic rather than bamboo buckets, and to resolve rural tensions. The government's presence is weak, however, as reported to me by two respondents. "The government becomes very active when a foreign delegation is scheduled to inspect," a farmer said. A local government fisheries officer confirmed that, prior to an EU team visit in November 2005, "[w]e were working day and night to make sure everything is in order." In addition to the influence of local actors and the local civil administration, both the source and resolution of local tensions come from such actors as processing factory delegates, NGOs, local journalists (both print and broadcast), feed agents, and industry extension agents, as well as from such transnational agents as the EU delegates noted above. Although locals have an extraordinary capacity for self-governance, their freedom is largely constrained and reshaped by such non-local factors and actors. As noted in Chapter 2, the concept of environmental governance is based largely on important insights gleaned from authors such as Hatanaka, Bain, and Busch (2006); Lemos and Agrawal (2006); Ponte (2002a, 2002b); Raynolds (2004); Vandergeest (2007); and Wilkinson (2006), as well as from the ongoing debates surrounding chain governance. Clearly, however, governance is not unilinear, but multilayered, and is not always imposed from the top. Rather, as the community-based natural resource management model indicates, rural people can be the best managers of their own resources if they are given a fair chance to do so.

Changing Patterns of Consumption and Culture

The new production regime has also changed consumption patterns in rural Bangladesh. Commercial shrimp is generally not consumed locally because of its high price and because of the availability of lower-priced freshwater fish. As the local economy has been integrated into the global shrimp commodity chain, the flow of cash into the local economy has generated great change in the cultural and social landscape. Brick houses (mud houses were previously the norm), cell phones, gas-powered vehicles (especially motorbikes, which have replaced animal-powered vehicles), a shift from a traditional, predominantly vegetable-based diet to a more meat-based diet, higher levels of education, and a television in almost every household are some of the visible changes generated by the commercial shrimp regime. "Many people are *lale-lal* (red and colourful)," runs a local metaphor for locals' greater affluence. Indeed, a middle class, although still a minority, is emerging in rural Bangladesh. The traditional power structure, in which big landowners and village heads enjoyed power and privilege over everyone else, is now in decline. Some young entrepreneurs have managed to reap the harvest of the new production regime, although it is also true that other individuals have lost out.

Other cultural changes are also evident. Local people now have new forms of entertainment; films from Bollywood and sometimes even Hollywood are replacing rural *jatra* (stage drama). Soccer and cricket have replaced almost all of the traditional games played in rural Bangladesh. Increased exposure to various forms of mass media has also made rural Bangladeshis more aware of global politics – for example, during my own fieldwork, I found the Iraq War to be among the hot topics of discussion in rural areas. It is important to note that these changes cannot be attributed solely to shrimp culture, as many other factors are also contributing to the transformation of the rural landscape. However, changes in the shrimp-farming areas are quite abrupt and substantial compared with those in other rural areas of Bangladesh. Through shrimp cultivation, farmers are engaging in regular interactions with local political leaders, outside parties, local NGOs, government officers, and shrimp feed agents. Their traditional attachment to the land has now moved beyond the land – Rigg (2001) conceptualizes it, albeit in a positive vein, as "more than the soil" – turning them into conscious citizens and gradually linking them to urban culture while they remain in a rural setting. The rural-urban dichotomy is blurring day by day. As people in the region become increasingly linked to the global commodity network and exposed to global culture, the imagination of many has been captured by the Western lifestyle. The tension between traditional culture and Western consumer culture is increasingly obvious. As shrimp generates cash flows in the local economy, other economic activities have also emerged. Traditionally, economic transactions in Bangladesh's villages were carried out primarily in a weekly *haat* (market or bazaar); now, shrimp aquaculture has brought suburban-style bazaars or markets, open seven days a week, to almost every village. These bazaars comprise shrimp depots, cell phone stores, electronics stores, grocery stores, vans, tailors, libraries, stationers, schools, mosques, tea stalls, and other new attractions. For some people, economic prosperity has also stimulated the desire for higher levels of education. As a village elder said, "[p]reviously, we never thought of going to high school; now our kids are going to university."

Some villagers, however, express concern over the ongoing changes. "Kids have less respect for the elders, as they have money in their pockets," complained a village shopkeeper, adding, "wine and brothels have also spoiled many of them." In rural Bangladesh, drinking wine and having sex outside marriage are taboo. Although these taboos remain in place, the new generation has a greater tendency to break them. In my survey, I noted a paradox in a rural Bangladesh that has been transformed by shrimp production: previously, people had less money, but life was stable; now, they have more money, but life is highly vulnerable and unsettled. Older norms are in constant opposition to and negotiation with emerging rules, laws, and regulations. The situation is akin to what Raynolds (1997, 119) found in the Caribbean: "Restructuring is revealed to be a highly political process contested by a range of social actors where negotiated outcomes are far from certain. In the major arenas of agrarian transformation, domestic and international forces intersect, together configuring the parameters of change." Table 6.5 illustrates the older views that prevailed in rural Bangladesh (when it was dominated by the rice production regime) and the emerging views generated by shrimp aquaculture.

Table 6.5. Traditional versus Emerging Views in Rural Bangladesh

Themes	Traditional Views	Emerging Views
Livelihood and natural resource management	Linked mainly to land and rice production; grazing land, forests, and fisheries (lakes) are common natural resources (mainly government-owned (khas).	Multiple users, complex and diverse livelihood systems; common natural resources now owned by a powerful few with close links to government and political leaders; as natural resources and species are commoditized, the idea of common natural resources is becoming a thing of the past.
Community	Local, specific user groups.	Multiple locations, diffuse, heterogeneous, diverse, multiple social identities; rural people interact with diverse actors, including Western buyers, via the commodity chain.
Land rights	Coastal areas mainly in government ownership and other rural areas in private ownership, with no external pressures; clear boundaries of rights.	Movement against land expropriation; government banned licensing system to avoid land expropriation and paved the way for small farmers to enter the shrimp production regime; new regime characterized by overlapping rights and responsibilities, ambiguity, inconsistency, and flexibility.

(Continued)

Table 6.5. *(Continued)*

Themes	Traditional Views	Emerging Views
Legal systems	Fewer formal laws; social norms the basis of legal system; disputes resolved mainly by village head or union council chairman.	Formal laws in place apart from village head or union council chairman; national and transnational laws and regulations implemented; different systems and laws now coexist.
Institutions	Dadon (money-lending), sharecropping, mortgage, mayender (bondage or indentured labour).	Although a revived form of dadon remains, additional institutions such as national banks, cooperative guilds, huri (leasing arrangements), and micro-credit are more common today.
Power and control	Vertical power structure with elites, big land owners, community leaders at the top, middle-scale farmers in the middle, and poor landless farmers at the bottom.	Differentiated actors, conflict, bargaining, negotiation, and power relations are central to current social structure; power and control are more diverse, plural and horizontal, but individuals who control resources and technology – key to shrimp farming – have more power.
Governance	Separate levels: national, local government, union council, village heads, clan leaders (micro-level focus).	Multilevel governance approaches, fuzzy or messy interactions; local and global interconnections.

Source: Author's investigation.

Conclusion

Drawing insights from an analytic framework derived from a theoretical synthesis of the agrarian political economy and industrial restructuring and regulation approaches (discussed in Chapter 2), in this chapter I have explicated the dynamic and multifaceted nature of the agrarian transformations brought about by the shrimp production regime in rural Bangladesh. Although the new regime has altered the rural landscape and foreign cash has flowed into the local economy, not all social strata have benefited equally. Some stakeholders who have benefited less, however, are slightly better off in the current commodity regime than they were in the earlier rice regime. Whereas some farmers and young entrepreneurs have managed to reap a handsome harvest from the shrimp regime, many fry catchers, farmers, and even some traders are caught in a vicious cycle of dependency, exploitation, and vulnerability due to the presence of middlemen at every stage of the local supply chain. Although they enjoy different levels of affluence, most small- and even some medium-scale farmers – who together constitute around 70 per cent of the farming community in rural Bangladesh – remain trapped in this vicious cycle, as illustrated in Figure 6.2.

Although many NGOs are helping local communities in a variety of ways, others are using non-farm credits to extract benefits from the production regime. During the introduction of commercial shrimp farming, locals were sometimes displaced; as the local economy has gradually become connected to the global commodity chain, however, many rice farmers have switched to shrimp cultivation. Some farmers have been able to cope well with the new production regime, but many small- and medium-scale farmers eventually will lose out in the commodity market as buyers increasingly opt for linkages to fewer

Figure 6.2. Farmers' Vicious Cycle of Dependency, Bangladesh

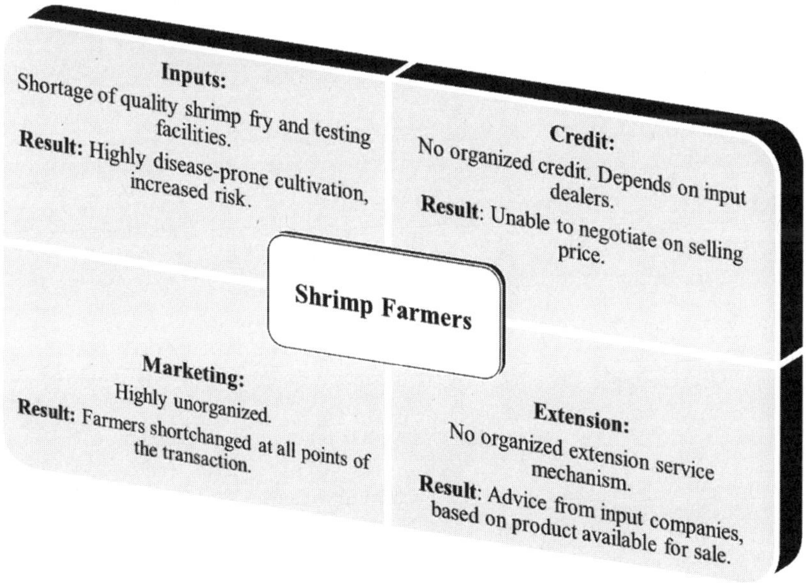

Inputs:
Shortage of quality shrimp fry and testing facilities.
Result: Highly disease-prone cultivation, increased risk.

Credit:
No organized credit. Depends on input dealers.
Result: Unable to negotiate on selling price.

Shrimp Farmers

Marketing:
Highly unorganized.
Result: Farmers shortchanged at all points of the transaction.

Extension:
No organized extension service mechanism.
Result: Advice from input companies, based on product available for sale.

Source: Author's investigation.

and larger producers. Indeed, the new regime has already transformed some small- and medium-scale farmers into wage labour. Many farmers are deeply concerned that they are producing something (shrimp) that they do not consume, while having abandoned something (rice) that they continue to consume as their staple food. This scenario, coupled with market competition and fluctuation, as well as the threat of viruses, makes them feel vulnerable. Moreover, many farmers in Bangladesh are living a paradox: they have access to foreign cash, but they have lost their self-sufficiency.

7 Gender and Employment Relations

In this chapter I explore how the twofold pressures transmitted from lead firms and environmental groups, as well as local social and ecological conditions, have created new forms of employment in the industrial aquaculture of the global South – particularly in the Bangladesh shrimp sector, which engenders both risks and opportunities for workers. Because of the high level of female participation in the workforce, a quite new phenomenon in the context of the global South, I highlight the gender issues that have arisen in the production and processing segments of the global commodity chain.

The chapter is organized into four sections. Following this introduction, I describe the privatization of labour and gender regulations, focusing on national and international standards and their incorporation into the certification agencies involved in this sector, including the Aquaculture Certification Council and the Shrimp Seal of Quality. I then explore the way in which the requirements of buyers, environmental non-governmental organizations (NGOs), and non-profit and/or development groups, as well as local social and ecological conditions, have transformed the nature of the commercial shrimp industry in Bangladesh and other countries of the global South. I also describe the characteristics of the workforce that these factors have engendered. In the fourth section I examine the working conditions of females in the processing centres, focusing on the paradoxical relationship between the ideal codes of conduct in the global commodity chain and the working conditions that currently persist in shrimp aquaculture in Bangladesh. In the final section I discuss the sociological implications of work in the shrimp commodity chain.

The Privatization of Labour and Gender Regulations

The Emergence of Private Regulation

As elaborated in Chapter 5, one of the most significant trends in the global agri-food system in recent years has been, to quote du Toit and Ewert (2002, 80), "not only the attempt to *de*regulate and liberalize international trade in agri-commodities, but also the proliferation of new forms of *re*regulation" [emphasis added]. Reregulation has emerged largely in response to the concerns of consumers in the wealthy nations of the global North (Marsden 1997). It has occurred partly at the governmental and intergovernmental levels – for example, in the deliberations of the Codex Alimentarius – but there has also been a marked increase in the number of private regulatory schemes (Blowfield 1999; du Toit and Ewert 2002). Aquaculture, in recent years, has witnessed increasing interest in certification, largely based on private regulations that apply to aquaculture products, as well as an increasing number of schemes covering eco-labelling, organic certification, and, recently, fair trade. The growing number of certification programs, and possible competition among certification schemes, could result in confusion among buyers and consumers (Fiorillo 2006; NACA 2007). As quality becomes the basis upon which the certification agencies compete with one another (Busch and Bain 2004), issues of labour and gender are currently incorporated in certification codes. Yet, although such issues are significant components of private regulation, the global agri-food literature has paid little attention to them.

Although scholars have used different terminologies or phrases to describe the current governance and regulatory trend in the agri-food system, including the "private regulation of the public" (Bush and Bain 2004, 337), "non-state market-driven governance" (Cashore 2002; Cashore, Auld, and Newsom 2003), and "environmental regulatory networks" (Vandergeest 2007), a common theme among them is the shift in the role of government from regulator to regulated. Traditional government regulations governing food safety and labour and gender relations have not only been replaced or complemented by private "quality metasystems" (Caswell, Bredahl, and Hooker 1998, 548), but government's pivotal role in maintaining safety and quality standards has also been replaced by private regulatory agencies, widely known as third-party certifiers (TPCs).[1]

At the core of this shift is the rise of what du Toit and Ewert (2002, 80) call "a complex new politics of consumption," due partly to the development of a consumer sector with a high level of disposable income and good access to the media and partly to the campaigning of NGOs and pressure groups in both the global South and North (du Toit and Ewert 2002; Vandergeest 2007). Consumer concerns have centred around long-established issues such as food safety and environmental degradation, and have also begun to include questions of labour exploitation and gender disparity in food-producing countries.

Labour and gender regulations sometimes are based on consultations with a wide range of stakeholders, including the International Labour Organization (ILO) and similar international organizations, and governmental regulatory agencies. Regulations – mostly private – are usually backed by independent monitoring, auditing, and certification schemes, and are increasingly focused on highly integrated processes of "farm to fork" chain management and documentation (Busch and Bain 2004; du Toit and Ewert 2002). Examples include the Euro-Retailer Produce Working Group protocol on Good Agricultural Practices (EurepGAP), the Forest Stewardship Council's scheme for the certification of sustainably managed forest products, the Ethical Trading Initiative's (ETI) Base Code on Worker Welfare in the United Kingdom, and the Marine Stewardship Council's (MSC's) environmentally responsible fisheries management program.[2]

Labour and Gender Regulations in Certification Schemes

Different certification agencies have incorporated labour issues differently. Some have clear and separate codes on labour, some merge the issue with social principles, and others, such as the MSC, mention social principles without indicating labour issues. The World Wildlife Fund (WWF), with the help of Unilever, formed the MSC in the late 1990s, ushering in the modern era of eco-labelling for wild fish. Based on the United Nations Food and Agriculture Organization's (FAO's) Code of Conduct for Responsible Fisheries, the MSC claims to "reward environmentally responsible fisheries management and practices with [a] distinctive blue product label" (MSC 2007a). Although the MSC is now recognized as "the undisputed leader in seafood eco-labeling" (Fiorillo 2006), focusing more on environmental management for local ecology and ecological communities, its social principles specify only "compliance with relevant local and national laws and standards and international understandings and agreements" (MSC 2007b, 1). Although the MSC principles include no section on labour or gender, the organization's commitment to managing and operating fisheries in a "responsible manner, in conformity with local, national and international laws and regulations" (MSC 2007b, 2) can be taken broadly to encompass issues of labour and gender. The MSC's first principle is: "A fishery must be conducted in a manner that does not lead to overfishing or depletion of the exploited populations and, for those populations that are depleted; the fishery must be conducted in a manner that demonstrably leads to their recovery" (MSC 2007b, 3).

Another pioneer in and leader of private sea food certification is the Aquaculture Certification Council (ACC), a certification body operated under the auspices of the Global Aquaculture Alliance (GAA). The recent commitments by Walmart, Darden Restaurants, and Lyons Seafood to buy only ACC-certified seafood (Islam 2010; Walmart 2005, 2006) have turned the ACC into a major global regulator. The GAA sets "Best Aquaculture Practices" – standards that address the social, environmental, and food safety issues surrounding shrimp aquaculture, while the ACC certifies shrimp hatcheries, farms, and processors based on GAA standards (ACC 2007a; NACA 2007). Unlike the MSC, the ACC has clear principles on labour standards. Its second standard, "Community," contains a subsection on "Worker Safety and Employee Relations" that clearly states: "Processing plants shall comply with local and national labor laws to assure worker safety and adequate compensation." The ACC recognizes (all quotes in this paragraph are from ACC 2007b) that "processing work is potentially dangerous because of the types of machinery needed and the use of potentially hazardous materials, especially coolants. Workers are usually not highly educated, and safety instruction may not be adequate. An uncaring employer may not provide safe and healthy working conditions." The ACC has also recognized that, in tropical countries, processing workers' "pay scales are low and wage or other labor laws may not be consistently enforced," and therefore processing factories "should maintain a good working relationship with not only employees but the communities in which they operate." To receive ACC certification, processing-plant management must show both compliance with labour laws and a commitment to worker safety. Certified processing plants are required to provide legal wages and a safe working environment, and should attempt to exceed these minimum requirements. In addition, the ACC requires that workers be given adequate initial training, as well as regular refresher training, on safety in all areas of plant operation. Workers should also be trained in the first aid of electrical shock, profuse bleeding, and other possible medical emergencies. In some locations plants must provide wholesome meals for workers, with food storage and preparation done in a responsible manner. Safe drinking water must be available at all times to employees working at the facility. During facility inspection, the ACC auditor evaluates whether conditions comply with labour laws. The auditor also interviews a random sample of workers to obtain their opinions about wages and safety conditions (ACC 2007b).

The aim of the Shrimp Seal of Quality (SSOQ) is to certify farmed shrimp in Bangladesh using certification standards based on the ACC's codes of conduct. The SSOQ certification process is voluntary, with certification implying that the operator is deemed to have met the minimum requirements for food safety and quality assurance, traceability, environmental sustainability, labour practices, and social responsibility. The SSOQ has a quite detailed set of regulations on labour. Its fourth principle, entitled "Labor Practices," has the following subpoints on labour regulations (SSOQ 2004, 3):

- Employers shall not use bonded or forced labour.
- Employers shall compensate workers in compliance with laws in force in Bangladesh.
- Employers shall ensure that working conditions comply with laws in force in Bangladesh. Employers shall evaluate health and safety hazards and take reasonable steps to eliminate or control risks to workers posed by these hazards, and educate the workers on these risks.
- Employers shall not require workers to work for more than the regular hours prescribed by laws in force in Bangladesh. Workers shall be entitled to at least one day off in every seven-day period without jeopardizing their employment. All overtime hours must be worked voluntarily.
- Employers shall not discriminate in employment based on gender, age, or religion.
- Employers shall ensure that no worker is subjected to any physical, sexual, psychological, or verbal harassment, abuse, withholding of earned wages, or other form of intimidation.
- Where children are employed, employers shall comply with the relevant provisions of laws in force in Bangladesh.[3] Where feasible, employers shall make accommodations to provide working children

access to educational opportunities. Employers shall not employ children under the age of 14.

- Employers shall comply with the relevant provisions of laws in force in Bangladesh relating to the welfare of female workers who are pregnant, breast-feeding, or on maternity leave.
- Labor shall be allowed to associate, organize, bargain collectively, and execute their rights as prescribed by laws in force in Bangladesh.

Apart from these extensive labour regulations, the SSOQ also has a number of social principles on landowners' legal rights and privileges; local communities' legal rights to access the common property resources that they depend on for their survival and livelihood, including, but not limited to, fishing grounds, rivers, and canals; the rights of neighbouring farmers and communities; and obligations to pay respect to the religious, cultural, and traditional beliefs and practices of the local community (SSOQ 2004). SSOQ currently remains non-functional in Bangladesh because of, among other reasons, tensions with the government.

Organic certification, although still a niche market, works as a kind of gold standard and is thus worth examining. The International Federation of Organic Agriculture Movements (IFOAM) is a global umbrella body for organic food and farming (NACA 2007). IFOAM's goal is the worldwide adoption of ecologically, socially, and economically sound systems based on the four principles of organic agriculture: health, ecology, fairness, and care (IFOAM 2007). With regard to the principle of fairness, IFOAM stipulates that "Organic Agriculture should build on relationships that ensure fairness with regard to the common environment and life opportunities" (2007, 3). Although the IFOAM principles contain no separate labour code section, the principle of fairness can be broadly applied to labour issues: "Fairness is characterized by equity, respect, justice and stewardship of the shared world, both among people and in their relations to other living beings. This principle emphasizes that those involved in organic agriculture should conduct human relationships in a manner that ensures fairness at all levels and to all parties – farmers, workers, processors, distributors, traders and consumers. Organic agriculture should provide everyone involved with a good quality of life, and contribute to food sovereignty and reduction of poverty. It aims to produce a sufficient supply of good quality food and other products" (3). IFOAM's Organic Guarantee System is designed to facilitate the development of organic standards and third-party certification. IFOAM certification bodies are accredited by International Organic Accreditation Services Inc. on a contract base (NACA 2007).

Probably the most active of the organic certifiers in the shrimp arena is Naturland. Naturland has developed standards on several aquaculture commodities, and issued its standards on organic shrimp production at the end of 1999. In addition to its own standards, Naturland is also accredited by IFOAM (NACA 2007; Naturland 2006). Its twelve broad principles focus mainly on farm management to ensure freshness and quality, and none addresses labour specifically. However, its last principle, "Social Aspects," touches upon the issue: "The operator of the farm has responsibility as well for the housing and living conditions of employees living permanently or temporarily on the farm area. The respective regulations concerning industrial law shall be adhered to" (Naturland 2006, 12).

The Aquaculture Stewardship Council (ASC), a newcomer in the market, has detailed regulations on "social responsibility," including with respect to labour. Although the ASC's proposed regulations and potential outcomes are quite lucrative and ambitious, doubt remains whether they can actually be implemented.

Other certification organizations or schemes that either set standards, regulations, or codes or that certify shrimp and other aquaculture farming and processors include the Accredited Fish Farm Scheme of Hong Kong; Alter-Trade Japan; BioGro New Zealand; Bio Suisse and the Swiss Import Promotion Programme; Carrefour (Europe); the FAO's CODEX Alimentarius Commission; the Conseil des appellations agroalimentaires du Québec (Canada); Fairtrade Labelling Organizations (FLO) International; the International Standards Organization – particularly ISO 14001, 9001, 22000, and, recently, ISO/TC 234; the International Social and Environmental Accreditation and Labelling Alliance; KRAV (Sweden); the Marine Aquarium Council; the Office International des Épizooties; Safe Quality Food; Seafood Watch; the Soil Association; Thai Quality Shrimp; and Quality Approved Scottish Salmon (Clapp 1998, Clapp and Fuchs 2009; NACA 2007).

Although some of these agencies, such as Thai Quality Shrimp, are operated by state agencies, they include various private standards required by buyers. A review of these certification schemes and their codes suggests that codes of conduct vary from agency to agency and from product to product. In comparison with other certification agencies, the FLO places greater emphasis on the issues surrounding labour, although the FLO mainly certifies agri-food products such as coffee, cocoa, vegetables, fruit, honey, and herbs and spices. In most of the aquaculture certification agencies, farm management and natural quality are strongly emphasized, with very few or no specific guidelines or regulations on labour, although their social principles often can be extended to labour issues. Strikingly, despite a number of vibrant social movements surrounding gender issues, none of the certifying agencies, with the exception of the SSOQ, has any clear-cut codes on gender regulations. In fact, they appear to be collectively silent on the issue.

Workforce Characteristics of Industrial Aquaculture

Women account for a significant proportion of the industrial aquaculture workforce across the global South; however, they are generally located at either the lower or upper end of the local supply chain – that is, either in the sea or rivers (fry collection) or processing factories (peeling, de-heading, and cleaning), respectively. Hence, female workers have lower prestige, power, and control than their male counterparts. In Bangladesh, for instance, women are self-employed in shrimp fry collection, and none is involved in fry trading, as Table 7.1 shows. The workforce in the processing factories of the global South is highly feminized, poorly paid, informal in nature, and lacking in employment contracts. This situation allows producers to further shift the costs and risks of production (those arising from adverse conditions or market fluctuations) to the workers, which has given rise to a phenomenon that Kritzinger, Barrientos, and Rossouw (2004, 17) refer to as the "externalization of farm labor": direct employment is on the decline, with an increasing number of workers now employed in the sector on an indirect contract basis.

Several factors are behind the externalization of farm labour in the global South. First, over the past decade, the nature of export-oriented production has been transformed, largely through buyers' tightening grip on the global commodity chain, linking the sector to its main EU and North American markets. Large supermarket buyers such as Walmart, restaurant chains such as Red Lobster and its parent company Darden Restaurants, and wholesalers such as Lyons Seafood – influenced by environmental groups and consumer movements – now dominate much of the trade, and thus can determine the specifications of supply on a pre-programmed basis to meet their own requirements.

Table 7.1. The Role of Women in Shrimp Aquaculture, Bangladesh

Activity	Female Workforce (%)
Collection of shrimp fry from the sea	70
Labour in shrimp ponds (for example, embankment, weeding)	40
Management in processing centres	1
Casual jobs in processing factories (for example, de-heading, counting, peeling)	80
Food processing, snail collection, snail breaking in freshwater shrimp	80
Shrimp pond owners and/or farmers	1–2
Business of shrimp (for example, trading, contractors, middlemen)	3–4

Source: Islam (2008b, 222).

They insist on stringent technical, environmental, and employment standards, but ultimately provide little guarantee of purchase and allow market conditions to govern prices. Processing factories operate at the point in the chain where the risks are most acute and where downstream and upstream pressures converge. Processors and exporters bear the risk of supply failure, which can be precipitated by adverse weather conditions, weak infrastructure, or political instability, all of which are more common in the global South. At the same time, they need to meet the complex demands of buyers, thus absorbing the costs and risks of production, standards compliance, transportation, and innovation. Processors and exporters ultimately pass these pressures on to the labour force. The situation is akin to that Dolan (2004, 123) finds in African horticulture: "While not entirely captive, most exporters have a high stake in the [world] market, having made substantial capital investments in sophisticated machinery and processing systems and requiring the margins of the supermarket trade to recoup their investments. It is exporters, therefore, that mediate pressures external and internal to the chain. They, in turn, deflect these pressures onto the labor force through organizational flexibility and the elasticity of labor." Second, globalization has led to the intensification of competition in the global shrimp and other aquaculture commodity markets, which is reflected in rising supply from the global South and downward pressure on the price producers receive. At the same time, governments of many countries in the global South, including Bangladesh, have liberalized the shrimp sector by abolishing internal monopolies – via such means as banning the licensing system – giving rise to increased internal competition. This fiercer competition has led processors and exporters to exploit the low-wage labour force through organizational flexibility and labour elasticity (Islam 2008b).

Finally, shrimp production is highly dependent on local ecology. Shrimp is harvested only during peak seasons, and is dependent on the lunar cycle. Harvesting takes place about twice a month during these seasons (for a total of about two weeks per month). Hence, a large labour supply is required for approximately two weeks a month during the peak seasons, with very little or no work available during the other two weeks of the month or during non-peak seasons. Because of tropical weather conditions, shrimp and other aquatic commodities are highly susceptible to bacteria, so rapidity in harvesting, delivering, and processing during the peak seasons is essential to ensure the freshness and quality buyers require.

All these factors affect the linkages through which shrimp producers access the global economy (Halim 2004). The combined pressures, operating through the global market and government channels, also affect the employment strategies of producers. Although the responses of shrimp farmers, traders, and managers and/or owners of processing factories vary, a dominant trend has been to move away from a permanent labour force towards increased reliance on various categories of flexible labour, especially contract labour supplied by third-party contractors. The use of contract labourers in processing factories confers significant advantages upon producers. It allows them to reduce labour costs; avoid the effects of more stringent labour legislation; and, most important, vary their labour requirements on short notice to meet the flexible but tight production schedules set by global buyers and the monthly harvesting cycle. There is, however, also a downside: producers are less able to control the skills, commitment, and employment conditions of workers to meet the quality standards demanded by buyers and environmental and other non-profit groups. Ironically, the advantages of flexibility for one agent in the chain often come at the expense of others, thus creating a paradox for the chain as a whole. Global integration, coupled with market deregulation and state legislation, appears to underlie the move by Bangladeshi shrimp producers, especially those in the processing factories, to downsize their permanent workforce to a core while increasing their use of flexible labour. Once these casual, flexible workers are hired for work in the processing factories, however, they must follow rigid rules and regulations with regard to hygiene, work time, and other quality requirements. These rules and regulations are largely orchestrated by buyers and influenced by environmental and social justice groups. The net result is that employment is characterized by *flexibility* in one sense but *rigidity* in another (Islam 2008b).

Human mobility is a salient feature of the new labour force, and it strongly conditions the composition of worker households (Dolan 2004). All nodes of shrimp aquaculture in the Global South hire workers from the locally available and abundant labour force. The women working in the processing factories, which are located primarily in urban and semi-urban areas, come from landless, marginalized socioeconomic backgrounds. For these women, employment in a processing factory marks a step towards proletarianization; their condition before such employment was even worse.

Box 7.1: Labour Conditions in Industrial Aquaculture

According to the Environmental Justice Foundation, "[w]omen are the preferred employees of shrimp processing factories ... For these workers, conditions are often less than ideal. Among the numerous abuses reported from these factories are physical violence and sexual assault, confinement, unsanitary conditions, illegal working hours and illegally low wages" (EJF 2003a, 22).

CASE STUDY: THAILAND

Some shrimp-processing factories in Thailand are reported to employ largely women, who stand all day and must ask permission to visit the toilet. There are no unions, overtime is compulsory, all hiring is casual, and there are no employment guarantees. It has been alleged that, in southern Thailand, there are factories where Burmese workers are housed in locked-in conditions – unable to leave the premises twenty-four hours a day – where average wages are half the legal minimum and strike activity has been met with violence and harassment. Shifts for Burmese workers can be as long as twenty hours in the high season. The Monland Restoration Council reported that, in November 2001, two Burmese migrant workers (Nai Myo Win, a thirty-seven-year-old man, and

Mi Tin Shwe, a forty-six-year-old woman) were beaten to death in front of co-workers at the Wat Jed shrimp-processing factory, apparently having been accused of stealing prawns.

CASE STUDY: ECUADOR

In Muisne and Cojimíes, former *concheras* (collectors of shellfish) accept temporary employment during the harvesting and packaging of shrimp. In mid-2000 their wages stood at US$2 for eight hours, with 20 cents more for each extra hour. The Ecuadorian NGO, FUNDECOL, reported *concheras* working for eighteen hours daily, standing up, and exposed to very low temperatures and disinfectant chemicals, including chlorine.

CASE STUDY: INDIA

Many female workers in Indian shrimp-peeling factories are reportedly held virtually captive by the factory owners, sleeping above the process-ing units where the inhalation of fish odours and ammonia refrigerants is unavoidable. A health report on these women found that they had skin problems and backache from standing for prolonged periods and urinary tract infections that were linked to inadequate toilet facilities. Handling ice-cold food for long hours has also been linked to arthritis. In 2000 it was reported that, in many processing units, half of workers' monthly US$30 salary was deducted to pay for their daily meal of thin gruel. Many of these workers are migrants from the southern state of Kerala. The Centre for Education and Communication reported in 1997 that such migrant women are often used as sex workers and that on-site abortions are not uncommon. A report published in 2002 stated that the female workforce in such factories is not allowed to form unions and is denied compensation for occupational hazards. In anonymous letter to activists from Bharatiya Mahila Federation, a worker charged that "[t]he company made us [sign] a paper and we don't know what was written on it. They call us in the morning at 3.30 or 4.00 a.m. and we have to work until 8.00 or 9.00 p.m." (EJF 2003a, 22).

BURMA'S SHRIMP SLAVES

A 1998 report by the US Department of Labor described forced labour in Burma, often for commercial ventures, including shrimp farming, to the benefit of military officers as follows: "As many as 13,000 Karens [an ethnic minority] were reportedly forced in 1995 to work without pay on a large rubber plantation, and in the construction of a dike for shrimp farming operations." In a 2000 update it was reported that, almost every day, especially during the rainy season, the Na Sa Ka [border police] collected men and children and forced them to work on black tiger shrimp farms. A 1998 ILO report includes testimonies of minority villagers who had been forced to work without payment on shrimp farms, some since they were children; one witness reported being beaten with a wooden stick on at least six occasions when he took a rest, while another said he knew of villagers who had been tortured for refusing to work. In October 2000, following ILO sanctions, the Burmese Ministry of Home Affairs ordered military and administrative units to cease conscription of forced labour, yet by May 2001 the practice had not entirely stopped. In December 2001 it was reported that the border police in the town of Maungdaw, near the Bangladesh border, would swoop down on Muslim minority youths and force them to work without pay in military-owned shrimp farms. In January 2002 it was reported that all villagers in Rakhine State were told they had to report for "voluntary service," which involved working for the military on shrimp farms.

Sources: EJF (2003a, 2003b); Goss (2000); Hindu Business Line (2000); ILO (1998); Jain and Chakraborty (2002); United States (1998).

Women in the Processing Factories: The Case of Bangladesh

As of 2006, there were 130 processing factories located in different urban and semi-urban areas of Bangladesh. USAID Bangladesh (2006) estimates that, in that year, more than 20,000 women were employed in these factories, representing 60 per cent of their labour force. Figure 7.1 shows the main activities of the processing factories.

The Gendered Division of Labour

Certain jobs in the shrimp-processing factories of Bangladesh – mostly irregular and poorly paid jobs in the production department and peeling section – are highly feminized. In the production department, for example, women's jobs involve, among other tasks, washing, de-heading, and chilling the shrimp. The administrative, managerial, technical,

Figure 7.1. Activities in Shrimp-Processing Factories, Bangladesh

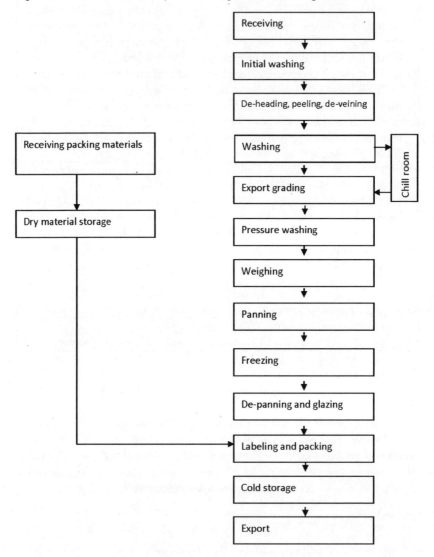

trade, and security departments are the domain of men, with little or no involvement by women. Women are rarely hired for management or commercial jobs in these factories because, as the chief executive officer of one factory claimed, they have "little aptitude for management and commerce." He added that the nature of administrative and managerial jobs "requires ... duties sometimes in the daytime, and sometimes the whole night, which is absolutely unsuitable for women." Despite this patriarchal bias and a number of cultural barriers, some factories have begun to hire women for administrative and management positions because "women workers can best be managed by a woman manager," as one factory owner opined. Although, in some cases, factory managers and/or owners were reluctant to reveal their treatment of their workers, they expressed the foregoing "rationales" for their treatment of women quite vociferously. Table 7.2 illustrates the gendered division of labour in the Bangladeshi processing factories.

As alluded to in Islam (2008b, 223), a gendered construction of culture is in place to dominate the hiring process in these factories and to become a precondition to the differential treatment of men and women. The processing workers, who are typically female and young, are viewed as cheap, dependent on their families, docile, exploitable, and easy to organize, whereas their male counterparts are seen as "masters of the household" and so, collectively, are "inflexible" (read, strongly unionized) in demanding lifetime employment and a "family wage." The irregular and lower-paid jobs "require huge patience, as the workers have to work in an odorous, cold room, standing up for a long time, which the males can hardly endure" because "they are less patient than the females," was the explanation one manager gave for hiring more women for certain lower-paid, although onerous, jobs. Another manager told me that "[w]e are doing a great favour to these women by giving them jobs, because they are illiterate, lower-caste women living in the slums, and some are even prostitutes." On top of that, he asserted, "women here are very easy to manage; we can get more women for a lower salary, while the men demand more."

The Casualization of Work and Its Legal Parameters

The majority of workers in the processing factories of Bangladesh are employed through contractors as casual labour, and thus do not fall within the legal definition of "worker," as stipulated in section 2 of the

Table 7.2. Distribution of Workers by Gender in Four Shrimp-Processing Centres, Bangladesh

Employment Section	Factory 1		Factory 2		Factory 3		Factory 4	
	Male	Female	Male	Female	Male	Female	Male	Female
	(number)							
Administration	5	0	3	1	4	0	20	2
Accounts	3	0	2	0	2	1	5	2
Commercial	2	0	2	0	2	0	7	0
Management	2	0	2	1	2	0	5	1
Procurement	3	0	2	0	2	2	8	0
Quality assurance	3	1	4	1	3	2	14	2
Production	24	50	12	26	23	56	40	85
Cold storage	6	0	2	0	4	2	16	0
Export	2	0	3	0	2	0	10	0
Sanitary	4	0	2	0	3	0	12	0
Mechanical	12	0	11	0	10	0	20	2
General	16	0	12	2	10	0	26	0
Security	9	0	6	0	6	0	17	0
Peeling	0	100	0	48	0	78	15	215
Other	4	2	3	3	5	2	8	9
Total	95	153	66	82	78	143	223	318

Note: For ethical reasons, the names of the factories cannot be revealed.
Source: Islam (2008b, 224).

Industrial Relations Ordinance Act of 1969: "a person who enters into a contract of service under the management and does not include a person who works under the control and supervision of the contractor." Further, inspectors from the Department of Labour bear no legal responsibility with regard to these casual labourers other than to check their cleanliness and look for health hazards. In the interviews I carried out for this study, some of these workers told me that they are sometimes laid off by the contractors without any compensation in the middle of their expected employment period. The country's 1965 Factory Law (sections 8–9) stipulates that compensation is to be paid only to those workers whose names are on the muster rolls of a shop or commercial or industrial establishment. Thus, casual workers have no legal right to compensation.

Wages and Benefits

Casual workers, including women, are not paid directly by the factory owners, but by contractors, who themselves are paid by the production unit. The contractors are responsible for the workers' attendance and discipline, and they hire and fire workers with no involvement from the factory management. Casual workers are unaware of the amount of money the factory owners pay the contractors for their labour, and the factory owners are unaware of the contractors' salary system. In many cases, the contractors not only pay a low salary; they also delay payment to workers. Wages vary, depending on the nature of the work in the different sections. Female casual workers "get 4 taka [US$0.06] for de-heading a bucket containing eight kilos of shrimp, and 5 taka [US$0.07] for ten kilos of shrimp," one such worker reported. They also have to work very long hours (an average of twelve hours per day) to earn this small amount: "For de-heading ten kilos, we need to work for an hour but get only 5 taka [US$ 0.07 cents]." The contractors pay child workers significantly less. One teenage girl stated: "If you ask our contractor about our situation, he will say a lot of good things – sufficient salary, proper medication, optimum care and so on, but all are just lies. Sometimes, he delays payment, and we starve. We cannot say anything for fear of losing our jobs. And if we lose this little job, we have no ... alternative avenue [of survival]" (Islam 2008b, 226).

The permanent female labour force in the production and peeling sections gets between 1,500 and 2,400 taka (US$23–$37) per month. Both casual and permanent workers reported that their wages are not enough for survival. The former said that the most they can make in one month if they work twelve-hour days is 1,800 taka (US$28). "Everything is very costly in the market, and this money is not sufficient for even food, let alone clothing or housing," said one worker. The dissatisfaction with the wages and the misery of family conditions are reflected in the statement of another respondent (Islam 2008b, 226): "I have six children. My husband is physically disabled now. He used to work in the shrimp factory before; now he cannot work. I and my two daughters are working for our survival. We do not have work every week or every day, as it depends on the peak season. Last week, we worked for only two days and earned 150 taka [US$2.3] only. We need to buy medicine for our affected hands before going to work. The income of these three members is not even sufficient to feed our family. You see, we're desperately in need of repairing our house, but we do not have any financial ability."

This flexible and informal work is accompanied by rigid factory rules. A young girl complained: "We have a break for one hour for lunch and dinner, depending on shifts, but we are not paid for this break. The factory does not provide us any food. We have to undergo verbal abuse if we are a little late in finishing our food." During the peak seasons, these women said they usually work continuously for twelve to thirteen hours. However, one factory manager argued: "Our workers are in a better condition than the garment workers. We provide salaries in different scales, 2,000 to 20,000 taka [US$30–$308], depending on education, qualifications, and the level of jobs they are doing, while in garment factories, one gets only 900 taka [US$14] per month, which is nothing in Dhaka City. With 2,000 taka, one can survive in Khulna City, but not in Dhaka City." Factories have to rely heavily on casual workers because, according to another factory manager, "during the peak season, a lot of shrimp need to be processed quickly." However, he continued, "although we do not get enough shrimp for processing every day, we still have permanent labourers, and we're giving them regular salaries" (Islam 2008b, 227).

Vulnerability and Exploitative Work Relations

Women accept low wages simply to survive. They accept the working conditions for two basic reasons. First, the supply of female workers is higher than the demand for them, giving employers an opportunity to exploit a relatively cheap source of labour. Second, the absence of alternative income-generating activities compels women to work in the shrimp-processing factories. For these two reasons, the vulnerability of one person becomes the capital of another. One fourteen-year-old worker complained: "If we told our politicians that without meeting our demands, we would not vote for them, then they would not allow us to walk in the streets. Nobody is with us, but everybody is around us to exploit our vulnerabilities." Their vulnerability makes them reluctant to speak out against exploitative working relations. If a worker complains, she is certain to be fired. One woman explained her situation (Islam 2008b, 228):

Our condition is so vulnerable that our hiring and firing depends on the will of the contractor. If he knows that we talk to factory management regarding our salary or benefits, the possibility is that we will be fired immediately. If we mobilized, it would not work, as the contractor would find other workers. We do not, therefore, dare to lose what we have. Our vulnerability becomes their property. The factory management deals ... with the contractor in everything, and not with us. The factory wants work, not the welfare of the workers. We work for twelve hours but often get paid for ten hours. Six taka per hour is nothing compared to the hardship we undergo in the factory.

Given the fierce competition for wage employment, the shrimp factory workers, irrespective of their sex, tend to abide by the factories' existing rules, practices, and regulations to avoid confrontations with management. Female workers want appreciation for their work, a fair salary, proper treatment of work-related diseases, protective equipment such as gloves and gumboots, and a one-hour break with pay. Such desires, however, represent a dilemma for the factories. Although factory managers I interviewed admitted that some contractors engage in shoddy employment practices, they continue to deal with them for a number of reasons. First, the factories could give casual workers permanent positions but only if a regular supply of shrimp were available. Second, the factories would go bankrupt if they employed all the casual workers permanently and paid them a salary when there was no work. "I did not get shrimp in two peak seasons, and I lost 1,000,000 taka [US$15,385]. I tried but failed," said one factory owner. Some factories, however, are putting pressure on contractors to stop exploiting casual workers: "If our workers are exploited, the factories will be the ultimate losers," opined a factory manager. In short, if Bangladesh had a complete, intensive aquaculture system and if factories had an adequate daily supply of shrimp, these problems would cease (Islam 2008b, 228–9).

The Health Situation

Female workers in the processing factories suffer from a variety of illnesses, such as fungal infections on their hands that can be so severe that they are unable to use their hands to eat, colds, severe muscle strain, back pain, eye irritation, diarrhea and other stomach-related diseases, and cuts and bruises. Factory management claim they designate local doctors to treat both permanent staff and casual workers, but workers claim supervisors give them ointment only for fungal infections on their hands. The Department of Labour is responsible for checking the health situation of female workers, and yet the Khulna division of the department admitted to me that it had no doctors to assist in this process.

Moreover, there is no regulation of occupational health and safety in the shrimp factories, and workers are often forced to toil in unhygienic conditions. In the case of work-related accidents, women are not covered by insurance policies, but rely on the mercy of their employers; on very rare occasions, they are compensated with a one-off payment for a workplace accident. There is also no provision for sick or maternity leave. Most employers operate on the basis of "no work, no pay" (Halim 2004; Islam 2008b).

The Hazard Analysis Critical Control Point (HACCP) training modules recommend the use of gloves (as elaborated in Islam 2008b, 229–30), yet I observed workers being given gloves only during the final stage of packaging. Managers noted that female workers are reluctant to wear gloves because it slows down their work, although one worker reported otherwise: "We want gloves, but they are not provided to us, as wearing them slows down the work and involves a little cost for them." The Marie Stopes Clinic Society, an NGO, provides periodic medical checkups for permanent workers, with the help of their employers, in ten out of twenty-nine EU-certified factories in the Khulna district; this medical treatment, however, is given to casual workers. One woman reported: "After working non-stop for ... twelve to thirteen hours, we become tired, sick, and exhausted." As the shrimp buckets are extremely cold, she added, "our hands get frozen, and we have to drag those down to the packing room. We all have fungal infections."

Female workers are better than their male counterparts at peeling, cleaning, counting, and boxing shrimp, but they get little sympathy from the factory management. A young worker, just fifteen years of age, reiterated the dire conditions in which these women work: "The factory management never thinks of the extreme hard work that we do, and of providing gloves to keep our hands normal and free from fungal infection so that with the same good hands we can work for them. The permanent workers get medical treatment, but we don't. They treat us like we are subhuman. Our hands become severely infected; we cannot care for them, cannot use them for eating, and cannot show them to others. We feel tired, exhausted, traumatized, and sick, but do not get any treatment. We want medicine, but the management does not care about anything." It must be noted, however, that some large factories do provide their female workers with better facilities than the small-scale factories, at least in terms of toilet facilities and break rooms.

Workers' Awareness

Female workers are conscious of their poor working conditions, the implications of the health problems they suffer, and the various forms of harassment and exploitation they encounter at work, but they have no platform from which to express their grievances in public. Those I interviewed expressed their views on the problems they face in social, economic, and political terms. Shrimp factory workers have no trade unions or other organizations that work for their collective welfare. The managers of the factories I visited said they have a collective bargaining agent who meets with management yearly and negotiates salaries and other benefits, such as leave, festival and production bonuses, and so on, but casual workers have no representation in these discussions. Female respondents opined that job opportunities would increase if there were women's associations (Islam 2008b).

Despite their poor working conditions, the female workers I interviewed were generally unaware of their rights and obligations as workers. Very few were aware of the procedures regarding the formation of trade unions, and those who were aware of them were generally worried about possible harassment by management. In addition, the abundant supply of female labour for the shrimp factories means that any women who participate in such activities can be easily replaced. Some workers nevertheless have attempted to form independent workers' committees, but with no notable result.

Box 7.2: Service Providers

A number of NGOs provide services to the workers of processing factories workers, as well as to other individuals in the vicinity. Among those I identified were the Integrated Development Foundation, Young Power in Social Action, and the Community Development Centre, which provide services to marginalized communities, including the poor stakeholders in shrimp farming, mainly in the Chittagong region, but also in other areas of Bangladesh. The following NGOs, in particular, work in the Khulna region.

UNNAYAN

Established in 1983 as the result of an institutional initiative by Women for Women, Unnayan works in the Khulna, Satkhira, Narail, and Jessore districts, and has approximately 35,000 members. It supports women and other distressed and underprivileged people. Unnayan claims to offer a number of services and to be involved in a range of projects, including: operational skills development for income-generating activities; micro finance for poverty reduction; training for increased capacity and competence; non-formal education; low-cost housing; action research on waste recycling; comprehensive reproductive health care; a Khulna-Jessore drainage rehabilitation project; a Sundarban biodiversity conservation project; the Fourth Fisheries project; an arsenic mitigation project; social forestry; sanitation and safe drinking water provision; and an NGO support service for organizational development.

It is important to note that Unnayan is a female-managed NGO. All members of its executive committee, and about 70 per cent of those engaged in its management, are women. Its project and field staff, however, are divided equally between the sexes. Every training module addresses the rights and responsibilities of women, as well as the social problems and constraints they encounter. Unnayan is also involved in promoting women's rights in the shrimp sector. It is currently working at the production level, not at the processing level. It is one of the active partner NGOs in the Fourth Fisheries Project implemented by the Ministry of Fisheries.

RUPANTAR

Established in 1992, Rupantar is currently one of the largest local NGOs in the Khulna region, working in the southwestern coastal area covering the Khulna, Bagerhat, Satkhira, Narail, Jessore, Pirojpur, and Barguna districts. Rupantar offers a range of programs from environmental to cultural development, with major themes including organizational development at the grassroots level; conservation of the environment and biodiversity; conservation of the Sundarban forests; women's empowerment at the Union Parishad level; prevention of violence against women; gender issues; local leadership capacity building; and awareness raising through song, folk drama, and popular publications.

Rupantar organizes a variety of training programs for different target groups. The main focuses of these training programs, the organization reports, are gender and development, development communication, staff skills development, female leadership, local government and union council leadership, and disaster management and preparedness. Rupantar is not directly involved in the shrimp sector.

THE MARIE STOPES CLINIC SOCIETY (MSCS)

The MSCS is a non-profit organization working in twenty-three districts in Bangladesh that mainly provides reproductive health services. In Khulna, the MSCS has extended its operations to the shrimp-processing factories, where it treats fungal infections and other health complaints in the permanent female workforce. The factory owners pay the MSCS 25 taka (US$0.33) per month per worker to provide the service. The organization was the only services provider allowed to provide health services to permanent workers; it does not cover casual workers. MSCS staff members pointed out, however, that they believed casual workers should also be provided with medical services, because they are greater in number and more directly involved in shrimp-processing activities. Of the processing factories currently in operation in Khulna City, the MSCS provides services to just eleven.

COOPERATIVE FOR ASSISTANCE AND RELIEF EVERYWHERE (CARE)

CARE is an international NGO that has been working in Bangladesh since the late 1980s. It currently operates in a number of districts, including Khulna, Jessore, Satkhira, Narail, Gopalgonj, and Bagerhat. CARE has undertaken various types of development programs, including rural infrastructure development (roads, bridges, and culverts), capacity building for union councils and local NGOs, revolving loan funds for destitute men and women, and awareness raising (for example, about HIV/AIDS and climate change). CARE has a separate training division, the purpose of which is to provide training facilities to its various target groups. The main focus of its training is the skills development of both project staff and beneficiaries. Gender awareness is the overarching theme of the various training modules. CARE Bangladesh runs the Golda Project, which deals specifically with the freshwater prawn sector. The project has investigated women's participation in shrimp culture and highlighted the multiple impacts, both positive and negative. It has also helped destitute women improve their livelihoods through the provision of income-generating opportunities. CARE was not found to be very active among factory workers.

Source: Author's investigation.

Conclusion

The study of shrimp workers in Bangladesh is important for at least two reasons. First, it gives consumers in the global North, whose vision tends not to stray too far beyond their own intellectual shores, a significant example of the highly exploitative operation of the current form of capitalism that is euphemistically called "globalization." Second, it rightly places female workers – hundreds of thousands of whom labour in appalling conditions at the head and tail ends of a local supply chain that sees shrimp harvested and processed in Bangladesh for markets in Europe, Japan, and the United States – at the centre of this process (Islam 2008b).

Three main sets of forces are at work. The first and most forceful are those that come from international buyers such as supermarkets; the least forceful are those that come from the workers and their unions. Environmental and social justice groups comprise the middle-range influence, with their attempts to better the conditions of workers via regulations that ensure the production processes are hygienic and the end product is safe for Europeans, Japanese, and Americans to eat.

Female workers, unsurprisingly, are located at the lower ends of the occupational hierarchy. It is predominantly women who gather the shrimp larvae from the sea and who, in the processing plants, clean the shrimp, cut off their heads, and get them ready for shipping. Women are also the most vulnerable in terms of employment security and are the lowest paid. To make matters worse, they often suffer from fungal infections from handling shrimp without the protection of gloves, which the contractors who employ them refuse to provide and which they cannot afford to buy themselves.

This gendered division of labour is promoted by employers and accepted by male and female workers alike. Such acceptance does not mean, however, that the appalling conditions of their work go unacknowledged by the female workers. Their oral testimony makes it abundantly evident that these women have a clear understanding of the way in which they are being exploited. The difficulty in Bangladesh, as in countless other locales in the global South, is that the resources for successful resistance – unions, worker solidarity, widespread public support – are too weak or the female workers are too unwilling to draw upon them. These women are thus left with little opportunity to protest, particularly as they are necessarily preoccupied with their day-to-day struggle for subsistence and even survival. The dull compulsion of the economic, to use one of Karl Marx's more memorable phrases, is nowhere more applicable than here (Islam 2008b).

The globalization of the agri-food system has given Bangladeshi women an opportunity to participate in the shrimp sector, although this opportunity has been accompanied by a variety of risks and vulnerabilities that their male counterparts do not necessarily face. Global commodity chain analysis facilitates identification of both the nature of the power relationships among the agents in the chain and the nodes at which risks and vulnerabilities are experienced most keenly. The power of lead firms – coupled with pressure from environmental and social justice groups and local ecology – influence the outcomes of production and processing for the workers of Bangladesh and other countries in the global South.

The paradox is that both buyers and environmental and social justice groups exert pressure on factories to enforce high and continuously shifting technical and employment standards, but that same pressure, when combined with local conditions, creates flexible and vulnerable working conditions. The situation has also led some processing factories to engage in corrupt practices. For instance, factories sometimes maintain fake paperwork to show to buyers and environmental groups (when delegations come for an inspection) to suggest they are following prescribed labour standards even though they are engaged in significant malpractice in this regard. How certification regimes can pinpoint these problems and broadly address the sector's labour issues is a subject for further study.

Similar to the situation that Dolan (2004) has observed in African horticulture, flexibility has become pivotal to the shrimp farms' competitive strategy to innovate and develop new products, respond rapidly to changes in demand, and capitalize on new market opportunities. Yet the advantages of flexibility for one agent in the chain often result in considerable disadvantages for others. These disadvantages, moreover, are disproportionately shouldered by the female workers who predominate in unprotected job categories situated mainly at the lower end of the shrimp production chain. As well, although the factories transfer the risks downstream, they are not borne uniformly by the labour force. Workers' experience of employment is, as Dolan (2004, 123) finds, "contingent upon the nature of their insertion into the chain, the type of task they perform, the institutional and social contexts in which they live, as well as a range of social factors such as age, gender, and marital status, all of which determine how and to what extent they can restructure their lives to fulfill the flexibility that companies seek." Therefore, young, single, and unencumbered women are the most positive about their employment situation, citing the social relationships they formed during their long hours at the factory, the opportunity the job gave them to live on their own, and the ability to exercise freedoms that are generally restricted for rural women. In contrast, women who migrated to the factory regions with their children are less positive about their employment, because their capacity to fulfil their domestic responsibilities is made all the more taxing by the factories' flexible labour strategies. Hence, gendered social relations intersect with the shrimp commodity chain, creating varying outcomes for workers and their families (Islam 2008b).

Although the industry has increased labour demand and created employment opportunities that are often superior to the local alternatives available, these gains have been realized through what Dolan (2004, 124) calls "the comparative advantage of women's disadvantage," which also marks other global commodity chains. How can the structure of the value chain allow companies to maintain the flexibility and low labour costs they require to maintain international competitiveness while ensuring more equitable and empowering labour market outcomes for workers, particularly women? The real challenge is to identify the policies and practices that Bangladesh can undertake to reap the benefits of the globalization of the agri-food system while protecting its workers, particularly its non-formal ones (Islam 2008b).

In this chapter, I have highlighted the apparent gap between the labour standards in the private regulatory regimes and actual labour practices. As local labour practices are largely influenced by local ecological (monthly harvesting cycles) and social (the abundance of cheap labour) conditions, fundamental questions arise as to whether and how private certification schemes or regimes can address the labour and gender issues involved, and who is setting standards for whom and with what effects (Islam 2008b). Do they consult with local stakeholders regarding labour standards that are consistent with local ecological and social conditions?

8 Conclusion: Industrial Aquaculture, Future Trends, and Sustainability

Since time immemorial, food has played a pivotal role not only in human health and well-being but also in economics, culture, and politics. Whereas early hunter-gatherer societies depended on food sources within their tribal territories, most contemporary peoples in relatively rich countries consume food from all over the globe. As Oosterveer (2006, 467) observes, "the physical distance between the places of production and places of consumption is growing fast while the time gap between producing and consuming a food is closing rapidly." With the globalization of the agri-food system, developing nations are orienting their products to meet global market demands. Consequently, many local agriculture systems in those countries are becoming linked to global commodity chains (GCCs) or networks, generating complex intersections and sometimes tensions between the local and the global (see Busch and Bain 2004; Gale and Haward 2011; Hatanaka, Bain, and Busch 2005; Islam 2008a). These networks involve diverse actors, including some influential ones situated outside them, with diverse power relations.

Over the past thirty years, the extensive body of literature on the global agri-food system has tended to place too much emphasis on the industrialization and standardization of food production and processing and on the process of local or regional integration into global markets. Although this trend still prevails in the literature, a number of more recent studies show the dynamics of local and regional changes and the transformations generated by global commodity networks. Drawing on an analytic framework composed of GCCs, environmental governance, agrarian transformation, and gender relations, I have combined these two broad aspects of the global agri-food system to explore not only how food products and processes have been industrialized and standardized on a global scale, but also how the processes of industrialization and standardization have generated significant changes in local rural settings in the global South, such as changes in environmental movements, work patterns, gender relations, and agrarian transformations. My study of the Blue Revolution, with its particular focus on the industrial farming of shrimp – a controversial commodity largely produced in the global South but a highly lucrative seafood item for wealthy consumers in the global North – provides crucial insights into how the global agri-food system is being restructured in the age of neoliberal globalization.

I have shown how global processes and local dynamics intersect, thereby defining the parameters of change in local settings. Significant changes in the environmental and agrarian landscapes, gender relations, and environmental politics of the global South can be attributed to the Blue Revolution. Although some positive changes have taken place – albeit in terms of economic gains harvested by a fortunate few – the Blue Revolution has made complex intersections and created tensions between the local and the global. In the context of neoliberal globalization, countries in the global South are under pressure to participate in the world market by integrating themselves into the GCC, often sidelining local priorities in the process. This pressure, coupled with the economic logic of environmental sustainability as a common state ideology, has led many countries in the global South to embrace the Blue Revolution as a "development project," despite its known environmental and social costs. At the same time, the powerful rhetoric of "feeding the hungry" has allowed global managers to deploy their regime of control and governance over the global South. Distant terrains, watersheds, coastal areas, mangrove forests, and wetlands thus have become a significant landscape for capitalist accumulation.

At the same time, the Blue Revolution, as a "development project" for the countries in the global South, has generated millions of jobs. Improvements in recent years in the form of, for example, "better management practices" have normalized the aquaculture industry, making it acceptable and profitable to many. Indeed, such a strategy seems to dominate the discourse that argues that, rather than revert to an earlier production regime, it is better to find ways to maximize gains through environmental and social sustainability, and minimize pains through, for example, environmental and food justice. Such an approach, as Alkon and Agyeman (2011, 332) suggest, is "not merely to better understand the effects of industrial racism and economic in-equality on the food system, but also to ... create a broad, multiracial, and multiclass movement that can challenge the dominance of indus-trial agriculture [aquaculture in this case] and ... to create something more sustainable and just." It is critical, however, that low-income and marginalized communities in this new production regime have a means of expressing their concerns for their rights and wider social justice. Thus, the industry as a whole, including development planners and third-party certifiers (TPCs), should incorporate, among other things, community-based natural resource management, with the aim of im-proving social and environmental conditions in the global South. For industrial aquaculture's current realities, future trends, and prospects for sustainability, previous chapters offer some crucial insights that I highlight below.

Moving beyond the Traditional Dichotomy in GCC Governance

Today's global marketplace constitutes what McMichael (2008, 6) calls "a tapestry of networks of commodity exchanges" that "bind produc-ers and consumers across the world." Although these networks are highly complex and dynamic, and vary in nature and organization from commodity to commodity, scholars have used the GCC approach quite successfully over the past three decades to discern the multiple trajectories and structures of governance in the agri-food system. Al-though the GCC approach is able to grasp this recent transformation quite well, I suggest that we need to move beyond Gereffi's (1994, 1999) buyer-driven versus producer-driven dichotomy.

Environmental governance is another conceptual thread that can elu-cidate the ways in which the GCC uses its power to manage natural resources, and the environmental and social effects of the use of those resources. This approach encompasses the activities of governments, as well as those of other actors, including business, non-governmental organizations (NGOs), and networks or communities of those affected and concerned, each with competing claims to authority over particu-lar issues. Governance, which is also at the analytical core of GCC anal-ysis, involves numerous social structures and processes that influence how decisions are made, rules enforced, conflicts resolved, and projects funded, monitored, and evaluated.

The combination of conceptual threads I have employed in this book makes a robust analytical framework that is needed to comprehend

fully the complex dynamics at work in the social and political landscapes of the global South. It has allowed me, particularly in the context
of Bangladesh, to examine why and how private regulation or certification regimes have emerged and been implemented; to explore the
various ways in which shrimp production is regulated and driven by
various human and non-human agents and actors; to look into the current engagement of certification and its future effects on shrimp aquaculture; to examine the environmental and agrarian changes that have
taken place; and to investigate gender and employment relations.

In agri-food studies, the GCC approach has been used mainly to explore production-consumption networks, and thus traditionally has
privileged analyses of buyers and, secondarily, suppliers, although recent studies have extended GCC analysis to explore local labour relations and gender issues. In this book, the GCC approach has enabled
me to explore the production-consumption networks in which the
producers of commercial aquaculture are linked to buyers in the European Union, the United States, Japan, and other countries of the global
North. That linkage, as well as governance within the chain, has helped
me to elucidate not only the ways in which food products and processes have been industrialized and standardized on a global scale, but
also the ways in which the processes of industrialization and standardization have generated significant changes in local settings. Moving
beyond the traditional buyer-driven and producer-driven dichotomy,
a new analytical core – the twin-driven commodity chain – makes a
valuable contribution to the value-chain literature and highlights some
of the key issues of power and governance within these chains. Encom-
passing environmental and social certification programs that recognize
and reward individual firms that operate according to pre-established
rules, the twin-driven commodity chain model is important because its
growth in the global aquaculture sector has led stakeholders to promote
it to address a range of other key global policy problems, including
fisheries depletion, mining destruction, the environmental and social
deterioration associated with coffee production, the effect of tourism on
ecologically sensitive areas, and sweatshop labour practices.

Governing Industrial Aquaculture: Trends and Trajectories

Local communities have their own particular ways of regulating the
environment, but as natural resources, such as the Sundarbans and
government-owned lands in Bangladesh, have become increasingly

commoditized in the wake of industrial aquaculture, new environmental and social problems have emerged. Environmental groups, both local and global, and TPCs are bringing these problems and the issues associated with them to the world's attention, not only raising concerns, but also suggesting and formulating a variety of environmental and social regulations. Feeling the heat of the environmental and social justice movement, powerful players in the commodity chain, such as the World Bank and wealthy buyers in the European Union and the United States, now are exerting pressure on the producing countries of the global South to implement such regulations. Indeed, most of the formal environmental and social regulations currently in place are the result of complex local and global dynamics and factors, of which one can discern at least four that are conjoined with neoliberal global governance: the transnational environmental and social justice movement; information technology and consumer awareness; quality as the basis for competition; and the view of states as lacking the capacity to implement food safety and quality regulations.

Because of the bureaucratic complexity, political problems, corruption, and inefficiency that prevail in the region, many governments in the global South are viewed as lacking the proper management capacity to meet the shifting demands of buyers and environmental groups in the global shrimp market. These governments have been the primary agents in implementing Hazard Analysis Critical Control Point manuals in response to buyers' concerns about quality. Despite considerable success in this arena, however, we have also seen significant failure in meeting market demands, which, in combination with other factors, has paved the way for TPCs in the global South. Although the operation of such private certification schemes in the global South is still in its nascent stage, and although many schemes – the Aquaculture Stewardship Council, for example – are still in formation and engaged in campaigns and public relations to convince key stakeholders of their value, one can predict that third-party certification eventually will transcend all major barriers and become fully operational in the next few years. That powerful players such as Walmart have already committed to buying only privately certified seafood is a significant boost in this direction.

Most governments of the global South view these private undertakings as a paradigm shift in state power, with the state's moving from its traditional role as food safety regulator to its being regulated by neoliberal governance and market dictates over internal affairs. Some states argue, however, that sanitary regulations have to do with global human health and biological issues, rather than with power, and that they should be implementing them regardless of pressure from buyers (see, for example, Islam 2008a). At the beginning of the Blue Revolution, states in the global South appeared to serve as an interface between neoliberal governance and local natural resources, but as the centrality of neoliberal control and governance has become evident through, for example, private certification regimes in some locales, states have gradually come to feel disenfranchised and vulnerable in the face of transnational giants and shifting demands and regulations. The implication is a clear movement from neoliberal global governance to the generation of a new kind of global citizenship based on consumer choice and the cultural logic of eco-rationality, and the sidelining or even subversion of long-established nation-state citizenship.

My analysis of shrimp aquaculture in Bangladesh suggests a number of significant trajectories, with implications for other agri-food industries and global export-oriented industries. First, as issues of quality, environmental sustainability, traceability, and social responsibility have become an integral part of the global agri-food system – largely because of environmental movements ranging in scale from the local to the global – buyers are tightening their grip on the commodity chain. This situation creates a paradox: the actors closest to the buyers are often privileged, whereas others in the chain, including small producers, are likely to be excluded or marginalized. Although the key argued aim of the social responsibility principle currently underpinning various certification regimes is to ensure the rights of small players and ecological communities, the new certification regime's shift from social to technical forms of solutions has the potential to exclude marginalized communities still further.

Second, the GCC approach remains a viable theoretical way to examine and understand the complexity of and abruptly shifting transitions in the global agri-food system, including cultured shrimp in the global South. However, continuously shifting regulations – mainly the result of pressure from buyers, retailers, and environmental, social justice, and other non-profit groups – have influenced and subsequently modified the nature of the aquaculture commodity chain. We thus need to move beyond the traditional buyer-driven versus producer-driven commodity chain dichotomy postulated by Gereffi and his colleagues (1994). As noted earlier, the nature of power and governance in the current shrimp commodity chain can be characterized best as a twin-driven commodity chain, an approach that promises new insights into the study of the agri-food system, particularly the cultured food industries.

Third, in line with the findings of Humphrey and Schmitz (2001), the greater the extent to which a lead firm specifies non-standard parameters, the greater is the likelihood that the firm will also have to arrange for enforcement, whether it carries out such activities directly or contracts others to perform them. A clear indication of this tendency is the emergence of TPCs – part of what Busch and Bain (2004, 337) call the "private regulation of the public" – which increasingly will play a pivotal role in acting on buyers' behalf while, paradoxically, both sidelining and engaging with the governments of the global South.

Fourth, the emergence of TPCs, and the incentive for lead firms to shift parameter setting and enforcement from their own control to TPCs, shifts the burden from buyers to producers and local processors, as the costs of certification are normally borne by the latter. Hence, new certification regimes again will privilege buyers, leaving producers and local suppliers with new costs, responsibilities, and vulnerabilities. Industrial aquaculture is already vulnerable to this trend, partly because of its troubled environmental and social legacies; the emerging certification regime could render it even more vulnerable.

Fifth, researchers have argued that, as the competence of local suppliers increases, chain governance through buyers can be expected to loosen, provided the increased competence is accompanied by the emergence of local agents who can monitor and enforce compliance with general or buyer-specific standards (see, for example, Humphrey and Schmitz 2001). I argue, however, that shifting regulations and the emergence of TPCs in fact could diminish this possibility. Lead firms' growing tendency to opt for linkages to fewer and larger suppliers to ensure traceability heralds a significant shift in governance. We can expect lead firms actually to tighten their grip on, and direct control over, the commodity chain, albeit sometimes by leaving a significant portion of governance in the hands of private certifiers working on their behalf, if not at their behest. Communities, small farmers, and other actors who are not only closer to, but an integral part of, the chain are bound to be marginalized.

Finally, brands and labels are playing an increasingly important role in the strategies of many enterprises; as Humphrey and Schmitz (2001, 27) suggest, "branding and chain governance tend to go together." This is certainly true in the case of shrimp and other aquaculture commodities. The price of and demand for shrimp in the global market depend largely on the particular certification agency certifying it. In Bangladesh, for example, shrimp is still certified by the government – which has not yet gained the trust of consumers – and, therefore, fetches a lower price in the global market.

Despite important improvements over the past two decades, industrial aquaculture – shrimp, in particular – remains a contested industry because of its negative social and environmental legacies. Since its inception, shrimp aquaculture in the global South has faced resistance and criticism from local and international environmental NGOs. With the introduction and implementation of environmental and social regulations, however, mostly through the twin-driven commodity chain, the nature of this resistance and criticism has changed. The industry has gained wider acceptance in local communities – largely through the cultural logic of eco-rationality and development governmentality – yet concerns over environmental and social issues persist. I have found, however, that local producers are more concerned about viruses and emerging regulations than they are about environmental externalities.

As we have seen in the Bangladesh case study, although the new production regime is changing rural landscapes and foreign cash is flowing into local economies, it has not benefited all social strata equally. A variety of stakeholders – including casual workers in factories, fry collectors, ice-van pullers, day labourers in shrimp ponds, guards, and many small-scale farmers – are reaping few benefits, although admittedly many are better off than before. As well, some striking, and less positive, contours of the new regime can be discerned.

First, such institutions as the *dadon* [money lending] and other non-farm creditors continue to extract benefits from the regime, trapping most small- and some medium-scale farmers in a vicious cycle of dependency. Moreover, as large buyers in the global North opt for linkages with fewer but larger producers to ensure traceability, these farmers are likely to become marginalized even further. The regime is also moving slowly towards industry consolidation, and a polarizing trajectory in farm size is beginning to emerge in which fewer but larger farms dominate and medium-sized farms are the least able to resist the economic pressure towards marginalization.

Second, in its initial stage, commercial shrimp farming displaced many local residents in the brackish-water regions of Bangladesh. Currently, however, and as the political economy approach predicted, there is a reverse migration in a few areas as landless farmers from other districts and previously displaced locals seek employment – albeit poorly paid – in the shrimp production areas. This new wage labour class includes small- and medium-scale farmers who failed to cope with the new regime, and so the displacement they face is of a new kind.

Third, along with economic change, the new regime is also changing rural cultural, traditional, political, and consumption patterns, with inevitable winners and losers. Actors with access to global information and who have managed to locate themselves closer to wealthy buyers are reaping a more bountiful harvest than their smaller and more remote counterparts.

Fourth, the current financial benefits and affluence most farmers enjoy are accompanied by vulnerability and a loss of self-sufficiency. For example, farmers have no control over the shrimp market, price negotiations, or the shifting regulations governing the production regime, none of which is of their own making. As well, the regime is pushing farm businesses and farm households into dependency on non-farm goods and inputs purchased in the market, compelling them to produce shrimp as a commodity with an exchange value in order to obtain cash income. Furthermore, farmers are producing a commodity (shrimp) that they do not consume, while in large part being forced to abandon production of their staple food (rice), a situation that has exacerbated their feelings of insecurity and vulnerability. Finally, the continuous threat of viruses, theft, and natural disasters such as floods and cyclones keeps farmers worried. In sum, what is emerging is a commercial shrimp regime that is driven by a nexus of three Ps: profit, power, and policy.

Over the past twenty years, the participation of women in economic activities in the global South has expanded beyond family farm enterprises to the global market economy. As I have highlighted with respect to shrimp aquaculture in Bangladesh, however, a number of paradoxical trends are evident with regard to gender issues and the nature of employment in the global South. The linkage of local agriculture to the global commodity chain has created different opportunities for women and men. It has given women opportunities to earn a livelihood and has elevated their social status. Consequently, the traditional gendered division of labour, in which men were the sole breadwinners and women were responsible for housework, is changing. These new opportunities for women are accompanied, however, by challenges and tensions.

Traditionally, the division between formal and informal forms of work has been denoted by distinct formal and informal sectors (Barrientos, Dolan, and Tallontire 2004; Dolan 2004). The climate of deregulation has widened this division, however, with increasing numbers of both men and women now working in informal types of jobs as the share of secure, permanent, full-time jobs declines throughout the world (ILO 2002; Lund and Srinivas 2000). The bitter reality today, to quote Barrientos, Dolan, and Tallontire (2004, 1), is that "informal working arrangements are becoming the norm in many export sectors dominated by global value chains. Gender inequality arises because women are more likely to be concentrated in informal work, with few labor rights and little social protection."

Echoing the findings of Barrientos and Barrientos (2002), I discern a continuum emerging between formal and informal work in shrimp production. Towards the informal end of the continuum, workers lack employment security, have few employment rights, receive inadequate employment benefits or social protection, lack trade union organization, and bear a high level of risk and vulnerability in their jobs. This continuum is often replicated in GCCs, where more formal employment is found at certain prominent nodes in the chain, but, as the supply end becomes more fragmented, employment becomes more informal – for example, through the use of contract labour and casual workers. Gender inequality arises because, with few exceptions, men are more likely to be concentrated towards the formal end of the continuum and women towards the informal end. Work in the shrimp-processing factories of Bangladesh is therefore characterized by feminization and casualization. Women dominate certain sections of these processing factories, such as those where chilling, beheading, washing, counting, and the like take place. The work in these sections is both flexible (in terms of timing, the labour contract, and low pay) and rigid (in terms of the strict regulations that prevail in the work environment). Despite the feminization of the workforce in these factories, women have made few inroads into managerial jobs, which have formal labour rights and contracts.

It is obvious that the globalization of the agri-food system is exploiting women in the global South as a cheap source of labour. These women are deprived of proper wages, while the shrimp traders become increasingly powerful, although they too sometimes face vulnerability in the wake of shifting regulations. Moreover, most female workers are employed in the private sector without any government regulatory control, and their labour is exploited to bring foreign cash into the national economy. Women also encounter various forms of work-related discrimination and violence. Such discrimination exists not only because of discriminatory laws, but also because of the non-applicability of certain crucial laws to specific situations, such as the casual employment sector in which the vast majority of female shrimp workers toil. How private certification regimes should address this gender gap is an important question for further investigation. As I have shown, workers are clearly aware of the unfair labour practices they face, so it will be important for private regulatory agencies to give workers a say in the labour standards that apply to them.

Supporters of neoliberal governance argue, however, that employment in processing factories is not inherently negative for women, many of whom would otherwise be unemployed or working in the domestic economy. Accordingly, supporters suggest that the advantages and disadvantages of employment in the new production regime need to be weighed in relation not only to paid productive work, but also to the manner in which such work is balanced with and affects women's reproductive role. There could be advantages to organizing production in ways that fit in with women's other tasks. A nuanced analysis of the role of women in paid employment in the production of commodities such as shrimp is therefore needed, one that takes all of these factors into account. Only in this way will it be possible to examine the obstacles that prevent women from reaping the advantages that men enjoy from such work, the enhancement of gender equity in employment, and women's access to the rights and benefits associated with employment.

Of the various Blue Revolution commodities produced in the Global South, shrimp aquaculture in Bangladesh provides an appropriate site for delineating the current nature of the global agri-food system within global capitalism. The industry exhibits complex links between the global and the local, which are full of both opportunities and challenges and produce both winners and losers. What is apparent is that shifting regulations, driven by environmental groups and lead firms via the shrimp commodity chain, have sometimes inflicted pain and shock on the country's aquaculture industry as they drive the government and other stakeholders towards new practices regardless of whether local settings are prepared to accept these practices. Although regulations have rendered certain contentious issues, such as environmental protection, human rights, traceability, and quality, more acceptable in local politics – and thereby enhanced civic consciousness among the stakeholders involved – not all stakeholders are able to survive in the shifting production regime. Moreover, as noted, with the emergence of TPCs in shrimp aquaculture, the trend is towards greater consolidation, sidelining the state and marginalizing small players.

The contrasting opportunities and challenges in this era of neoliberal globalization raise at least three fundamental questions that merit further investigation. First, to what kind of policy regime should a country subscribe to overcome these challenges and, at the same time, to maximize national welfare by cooperating with market demands? Second, if a country decides to adopt a market-oriented policy, will this policy necessarily bear the economic and social fruit that market advocates promise – that is, economic growth beneficial to the incomes of the poor? Finally, how is globalization's enlarging economic pie being distributed among the masses and, more important, how is the growth generated by globalization being transfused into, and distributed among, the national socio-economic strata?

More precisely, the emergence of third-party certification regimes in the global South raises certain fundamental questions that I have attempted to highlight throughout this book: What is the role of the state in the wake of the full implementation of a private certification regime? How can states and private regimes move from tension to collaboration? As scepticism and concern prevail among the majority of stakeholders, who fear that TPCs will marginalize small players, how can the regime protect these players and transmit gains to all social strata? Will the regime move from civic democracy to consumer democracy, whereby the key players in the chain are accountable only to wealthy consumers, not to poor producers and their communities? How can communities participate meaningfully in the new regime? What new spaces can the regime create for communities and marginalized players, including women? Does the new regime signal the replacement of civic democracy with marketocracy and technological governmentality in the global South?

The real challenge lies in how countries in the global South can implement policies and practices that allow them to reap the benefits of globalization while protecting their people and the environment from social and environmental externalities. Taking a broader perspective, the instruments that the global South needs in the current precarious juncture of neoliberal globalization and the agri-food system are perhaps a combination of three "Gs": *good policies* that respect market decorum and environmental sustainability; *good governance* that ensures pro-poor growth and participation and entails market confidence; and a bit of *good luck* to ensure that the premium of growth and sustainability is not taken away by unfortunate global disruptions and is not enjoyed by only a fortunate few.

Appendix: Certification Schemes

This Appendix details some of the existing certification programs for aquaculture. No endorsement of or support for any particular certification system is intended or implied.

The *Accredited Fish Farm Scheme* is a government scheme developed by the Hong Kong Agriculture, Fisheries and Conservation Department (AFCD). The scheme's aim is to brand local products and increase consumer confidence in fish quality. The AFCD has published a series of Good Agricultural Practices (GAP), as well as practices on feed management, environmental management (both saltwater and freshwater), and animal health management with which registered farmers must comply. The scheme provides transparency of the production system via farm registration, fry registration, and a quality assurance system through regular monitoring at the farm level and pre-market product monitoring (Hong Kong 2011).

Alter-Trade Japan (ATJ) is a Japanese company involved in the fair trade of several commodities, including bananas, coffee, and shrimp. The company was established by consumers' cooperatives and groups to promote direct trade between producers and consumers. Products from extensive registered shrimp farms in Indonesia that follow ATJ's own standards are labelled "eco-shrimp," and they have been recognized by Naturland as organic shrimp since 2002. ATJ's local subsidiary in Indonesia initiated community-based activities to strengthen the social aspects of production in 2006 (ATJ 2011).

The *Aquaculture Certification Council* (ACC) is the certification body of the Global Aquaculture Alliance (GAA). The founders and board members of both the GAA and ACC are predominantly seafood and shrimp aquaculture industry representatives. GAA sets "best aquaculture practices" standards that address the social, environmental, and food safety of shrimp aquaculture. The ACC certifies shrimp hatcheries, farms, and processors on the basis of the GAA standards. As part of the scheme's vertically integrated approach, a three-star label is granted if products are from an ACC-certified hatchery, farm, and processor (ACC 2002).

The *Aquaculture Stewardship Council* (ASC) is an independent, non-profit organization founded in 2009 by the World Wildlife Fund (WWF) and the Dutch Sustainable Trade Initiative to manage global standards of responsible aquaculture, which are under development by the Aquaculture Dialogues, a program of roundtables initiated and coordinated by the WWF. Following a business development phase, the ASC has been fully operational since mid-2011. The ASC aims to become the world's leading certification and labelling program for responsibly farmed seafood by working with aquaculture producers, seafood processors, retail and food service companies, scientists, conservation groups, and the public to promote the best environmental and social seafood choices. Its ultimate goal is to certify about 20 per cent of all global aquaculture commodities (ASC 2011).

BioGro New Zealand is a non-profit organic producer and consumer organization that has been actively working to grow organic goods in New Zealand since 1983. BioGro's organic standards include an aquaculture section (fish, shellfish, and crustaceans), and its certification covers farms, processors, exporters, input manufacturers, distributors, and retailers (BioGro New Zealand 2011).

Bio Suisse is a private sector umbrella association of organic farming organizations and farms based in Switzerland; its members include the Research Institute of Organic Agriculture FiBL. According to its Web site, 11 per cent of Swiss farmland (more than 800 processing and trade companies) complies with BioSuisse standards, which apply to organic agriculture products designed for the Swiss market. Farmed freshwater finfish has been included in the standards since 2001, with species such as carp, char, trout, and perch gaining certification. Organic produce carrying its common label, the Bud (German, *Knospe*) has a market share in Switzerland of about 60 per cent (Bio Suisse 2011).

Carrefour is the number one retailer in Europe and the second largest in the world, after Walmart. The company sells Carrefour Quality Line (CQL) fair trade shrimp produced in Brazil, Madagascar, and Thailand. The intention of the CQL is to develop food products that are safe from farm to table and that comply with international food safety standards (Carrefour 2006).

The *CODEX Alimentarius Commission* was created in 1963 by the United Nations Food and Agriculture Organization (FAO) and the World Health Organization to develop food safety standards, guidelines, and related texts to protect consumer health, ensure fair trade practices in the food trade, and promote the coordination of all food standards work undertaken by international governmental organizations and non-governmental organizations (NGOs). The Codex Alimentarius system presents a unique opportunity for all countries to join the international community in formulating and harmonizing food standards and ensuring their global implementation (FAO and WHO 2011).

The *Ethical Trading Initiative* (ETI) is an alliance of companies, NGOs, and trade unions that aims to promote and improve the implementation of corporate codes of practice that cover supply chain working conditions. Its ultimate goal is to ensure that the conditions of workers producing for the UK market meet or exceed international labour standards. Underpinning all of its work is the ETI Base Code and accompanying Principles of Implementation. The Base Code contains nine clauses that reflect the most relevant international standards with respect to labour practices, whereas the Principles of Implementation set out the general principles governing implementation of the Base Code. The ETI focuses on helping to make international trade work better for poor and otherwise disadvantaged populations (ETI 2010).

The *Euro-Retailer Produce Working Group protocol on Good Agricultural Practices* (EurepGAP) was a private sector group of retailers that set voluntary standards for the certification of agricultural products. EurepGAP was a pre-farm-gate standard, so the label was not directly visible to consumers. Integrated Aquaculture Assurance (IAA), a EurepGAP subgroup, certifies aquacultured salmon in Scotland, and has established a technical committee to begin work on shrimp aquaculture products. EurepGAP also began working on catfish in Vietnam. In 2007, EurepGAP became GLOBALG.A.P., which sets voluntary standards for the certification of agricultural products around the globe. The GLOBALG.A.P. standards are designed primarily to reassure consumers about how food is produced on the farm by minimizing the detrimental environmental effects of farming operations, reducing the use of chemical inputs, and ensuring a responsible approach to worker health and safety and animal welfare. GLOBALG.A.P. serves as a practical manual for GAP anywhere in the world. Its basis is an equal partnership of agricultural producers and retailers that wish to establish efficient certification standards and procedures (GlobalG.A.P. 2011).

Fairtrade Labelling Organizations International (FLO) is the worldwide fairtrade standards-setting and certification organization. It permits more than 800,000 producers and their dependents in more than 40 countries to benefit from the Fairtrade label. FLO guarantees that products sold with the Fairtrade label anywhere in the world and marketed by a national initiative conform to Fairtrade standards and contribute positively to disadvantaged producers (FLO 2010).

Friend of the Sea is an eco-labelling scheme for marine capture fisheries and aquaculture products. According to its criteria, a certification body called Bureau Veritas audits products' chain of custody and fisheries conformance. The aquaculture products covered include salmon, halibut, and turbot (Friend of the Sea 2011).

The *Gold Standard for Sustainable Aquaculture Ecolabel Design* developed by the Environmental Law Institute and the Ocean Foundation is a certification scheme that seeks to surpass other existing schemes in standards and values. In its Technical Report, the Gold Standard claims that existing and planned labels focus on incremental improvements to production processes rather than on sustainability. In these labels, sustainability is more a buzzword than a guideline for implementation. Moreover, existing eco-labels lack credibility due in part to a lack of institutional controls and inadequate consideration of key impacts of production and processing. In addition, it is not clear that these efforts have resulted in improvements in environmental or social practices on the ground. By complying with the International Social and Environmental Accreditation and Labelling Alliance (ISEAL) Code of Practice (see below), the Gold Standard seeks to consider comprehensively the effects on the environment, society, human health, and animal welfare, scientific standards-setting, careful controls on certification decisions, transparent review and reporting on performance, and robust objections procedures (ELI 2008).

The *International Federation of Organic Agriculture Movements* (IFOAM) is a global umbrella body for organic food and farming. IFOAM's goal is the worldwide adoption of ecologically, socially, and economically sound systems based on the principles of organic agriculture. The organization's Organic Guarantee System is designed to facilitate the development of organic standards and third-party certification. IFOAM certification bodies are accredited by the International Organic Accreditation Service Inc. on a contract basis. IFOAM has 800 affiliates in over 115 countries. Its members farm more than 37 million hectares of organically managed land and sell US$55 billion worth of products (IFOAM 2011).

The *International Social and Environmental Accreditation and Labelling (ISEAL) Alliance* sets voluntary standards in sectors ranging from forestry and agriculture to fisheries, manufacturing, and textiles. It operates programs that reward producers for good social and environmental performance, and is backed by independent third-party certifiers, thus enabling supply chain companies and end consumers to make more sustainable purchasing decisions. The ISEAL Alliance developed, and complies with, the Code of Good Practice for Setting Social and Environmental Standards to strengthen the credibility of the standards-setting procedure. Full members of the ISEAL Alliance include the ASC, FLO, the Forest Stewardship Council (FSC), IFOAM, the Marine Aquarium Council, the Marine Stewardship Council, the Rainforest Alliance, and Social Accountability International. Collectively, ISEAL Alliance members represent over US$53 billion worth of certified products (ISEAL 2011).

The *International Standards Organization* (ISO) has an environmental management standard, ISO 14001:2004, intended to minimize shrimp farming's harmful effects on the environment. It also has a quality management systems standard, ISO 9001:2000, and a food safety management system, ISO 22000:2005, for processing and others facilities. ISO Technical Committee 234, Fisheries and Aquaculture, was established in February 2007 to achieve standardization in the fisheries and aquaculture field (ISO 2011).

KRAV, a Swedish organization, and its Norwegian counterpart, *Debio*, have developed organic standards for farmed salmonids (salmon, trout, rainbow trout, and char) produced in those two countries. KRAV is also engaged in the development of standards for sustainable capture fisheries in Scandinavian waters and has drafted standards for the eco-labelling of fish and fisheries (KRAV 2010).

The *Marine Aquarium Council* (MAC) is an international, non-profit organization that brings marine aquarium animal collectors, exporters, importers, and retailers together with aquarium keepers, public aquariums, conservation organizations, and government agencies. The MAC has developed standards for ecosystem and fishery management; collection, fishing, and holding; and handling, husbandry and transport.

It also recently developed a Mariculture and Aquaculture Management standard that covers all aquaculture segments – from brood stock management to the transport of cultured marine ornamentals. The MAC is among six pioneering non-profit organizations (the others are the FLO, FSC, IFOAM , the Marine Stewardship Council, and the Rainforest Alliance) that have reached the highest standards of credible behaviour in ethical trade by complying with the ISEAL Code of Good Practice (MAC 2009).

The *Marine Stewardship Council (MSC)* is an independent, global, non-profit organization that works towards environmentally responsible fisheries through certification programs. Based on the FAO's Code of Conduct for Responsible Fisheries, the MSC has developed an environmental standard for sustainable and well-managed fisheries, and rewards environmentally responsible fishery management and practices with a product label. An MSC-approved independent certification company undertakes assessments, taking into account the views of all stakeholders. The MSC scheme is currently limited to the products of capture fisheries (MSC 2011). Hemlock and Baldomir (2008) report that, since 2000, the MSC has certified more than 1,100 products in 36 countries, including at least 100, such as wild Alaskan salmon, in the United States. Walmart's announcement that it will buy MSC-certified seafood (wild-caught) has made the Council a world leader in certification.

Naturland has developed standards for several aquaculture commodities, and issued standards governing organic shrimp production at the end of 1999. The Naturland Standards for Organic Aquaculture (January 2005 version) include a section specifically on the pond culture of white shrimp. In addition to its own standards, Naturland is also one of the certification bodies authorized to certify products to IFOAM organic standards (Naturland 2011).

The *Office international des épizooties (OIE)* develops norms for disease reporting and health standards for trade in both terrestrial and aquatic animals. The OIE standards for the latter are published in the Aquatic Animal Health Code. The OIE is also currently working on aquatic animal welfare, which may be included in future in the Animal Health Code. The World Trade Organization's Sanitary and Phytosanitary Measures (SPS) Agreement encourages member countries to base their aquatic animal health regulations on the OIE's standards (OIE 2009).

Product Authentication International (PAI) is a leading approved certifier of food products, food authenticity, labelling claims, and food chain traceability in Europe. PAI claims to ensure that standards meet their intent in every way, are meaningful, and are effectively implemented. With its Technical Advisory Panels, PAI has developed a large range of food chain standards that are accepted as leading edge in terms of quality, safety, security, and environmental and animal welfare. PAI has three integrated divisions, Food, Farm, and Animal Feed, and a department that specializes in the development and provision of database-driven management solutions for the agri-food sector. This specialist department has developed the highly successful Pyramid supply chain management system now being used by manufacturers, suppliers, and retailers. PAI is accredited by the United Kingdom Accreditation Service for EN 45011 (Product Certification) and operates throughout Europe, the Far East, and South America from its UK base (PAI 2007).

Quality Approved Scottish Salmon is a code of practice for Scottish finfish aquaculture developed by two industry associations – Scottish Quality Salmon and the Shetland Salmon Farmers Association, recently renamed Shetland Aquaculture. The Scottish Quality Salmon mark is a voluntary industry certification scheme that is accredited by Food Certification Scotland (NACA 2007).

Quality Assurance International (QAI), founded in 1989, offers verification services to ensure preservation of the organic integrity of food and fibre products from seed to shelf. Headquartered in San Diego, California, QAI maintains operations in Japan, Canada, and Latin America, and has US satellite offices in Minnesota and Vermont. QAI offers innovative, comprehensive certification programs that allow producers, trading companies, manufacturers, private labellers, restaurants, and retail distributors to guarantee that their products meet the regulatory guidelines or standards applicable to their specific needs. In a nationwide independent shelf study, it was found that two out of three certified organic products on US store shelves use QAI's certification services. QAI claims to serve the organic industry with professional, cost-effective certification that provides international accessibility, global operations, fixed fees, and independent, third-party, on-site inspections that guarantee organic integrity (QAI 2011).

Safe Quality Food (SQF) is a program under the auspices of the Food Marketing Institute (FMI), which represents food retailers and wholesalers. The SQF1000 certification standard covers production, and SQF2000 is a processing plant certification system. SQF covers a wide range of products internationally, including a variety of aquaculture commodities such as fish, molluscs, and crustaceans (SQF 2011).

Seafood Watch is a program run by the Monterey Bay Aquarium and designed to raise consumer awareness, predominantly in the United States, about the importance of buying seafood from sustainable sources. The program has developed recommendation criteria for aquaculture species (MBA 2011).

The *Shrimp Seal of Quality* (SSOQ), developed by USAID Bangladesh, was a private, voluntary program for the certification of farmed shrimp in Bangladesh. The SSOQ certification standard targeted shrimp farmers and processors, and certified that the operator was deemed to have met the minimum requirements in the areas of food safety and quality assurance, traceability, environmental sustainability, labour practices, and social responsibility (SSOQ 2002, 2004). The scheme recently ceased operations, however, and the outlook for the future is unclear.

The *Soil Association* is the United Kingdom's leading independent charity and non-profit organization that campaigns for and certifies organic food and the organic farming system. It has prepared standards for the organic farming of salmon, trout, and shrimp. Soil Association Certification Ltd., a wholly owned subsidiary of the Soil Association, has been approved by the Advisory Committee on Organic Standards to offer organic certification to Soil Association standards (Soil Association 2011).

The *Swiss Import Promotion Programme (SIPPO)* is an import promotion and development agency with support from the State Secretariat for the Economy of the Swiss government. SIPPO published "International Standards for Organic Aquaculture Production of Shrimp" in conjunction with Naturland and the International Maritime Organization in 2002. It has also been coordinating with the Vietnamese Ministry of Fisheries to develop an organic certification scheme for black tiger shrimp farmed in the Ca Mau province of Vietnam (SIPPO 2011).

Thai Quality Shrimp is a certification system for shrimp aquaculture developed by Thailand's Department of Fisheries. Thai Quality Shrimp guidelines have been developed in accordance with CODEX, ISO14001 (EMS), and the FAO Code of Conduct for Responsible Fisheries. The certification system covers hatcheries, farms, processing plants, and distributors and promotes products under the Thai Quality Shrimp label (FAO 2007).

The *United Kingdom Accreditation Service* (UKAS) is the sole UK government-recognized national accreditation body authorized to assess, against internationally agreed standards, organizations that provide certification, testing, inspection, and calibration services. UKAS accreditation claims to demonstrate the competence, impartiality, and performance capability of these evaluators. UKAS is a non-profit-distributing company that is limited by guarantee, and it operates under the terms of a Memorandum of Understanding with the government through the Secretary of State for Innovation, Universities and Skills (UKAS 2009).

Canadian Certification Schemes

The *Canadian Aquaculture Industry Alliance* (CAIA) has developed a number of certification tools to ensure the international competitiveness of the Canadian seafood farming industry, including the National Code System for Responsible Aquaculture, and Brand Canada.

The *National Code System for Responsible Aquaculture* (NCSRA) provides a series of national standards based on the Hazard Analysis Critical Control Point (HACCP) system for food safety, environmental management, and product traceability for Canadian seafood farming operations, and addresses the same categories of risks as the SQF program. The NCSRA is available for use by all CAIA members, including producers, processors, and feed companies. SQF-certified companies are also recognized as meeting NCSRA standards (CAIA 2011).

Brand Canada is a logo developed by the Canadian seafood farming industry as a symbol of Canada's leadership in the environmentally responsible production of safe, high-quality aquaculture products. Any company that passes an SQF or NCSRA audit gains the right to affix the Brand Canada logo to its products (CAIA 2011).

The *Conseil des appellations agroalimentaires du Québec* (CAAQ) is a non-profit Canadian corporation under the auspices of the Quebec Companies Act. The CAAQ's mission is to develop standards, provide accreditation to certification bodies, and make recommendations to the Quebec government regarding recognition of designations. The Quebec Organic Reference Standard includes a section on aquaculture, covering fish, molluscs, and crustaceans (QAI 2009).

Notes

1. Introduction

1 Traditional or "extensive" aquaculture relies on tidal action for the provision of food and shrimp fry, and requires as inputs mainly the labour involved in impounding low-lying areas along bays and tidal rivers where the shrimp can be grown to market size. Modern shrimp farming is far more capital and input intensive. Semi-intensive ponds are stocked not by the tides but by trawler-caught post-larval shrimp or by hatcheries. Similarly, pumps replace tides as the source of water exchange, and feeds are artificial. Yields are much higher, ranging from 50 to 5000 kilograms per hectare, as against 50–500 kilogrms per hectare for extensive farming. Intensive aquaculture involves even closer management: the system uses small ponds (0.1–1.5 hectare) and is able to stock shrimp densely through a combination of heavy feed inputs, waste removal, and aeration; yields range from 5000 to 20,000 kilograms per hectare (Hall 2004, 316). Among various types of aquaculture commodities produced in the global South, two are prominent: brackish-water shrimp (*Penaeus monodon*) and freshwater prawns (*Macrobrachium rosenbergii*); I refer to both as industrial or commercial shrimp.

2 See, for example, Atkins and Bowler (2001); Bonanno et al. (1994); Busch and Bain (2004); Buttel and McMichael (2005); Chapman (2000); DeLind (2000); Dimitri and Richman (2000); Dolan and Humphrey (2000); Freidberg (2004); Gale and Haward (2011); Higgins and Lawrence (2005); Levy and Newell (2005); Marsden, Flynn, and Harrison (2000); Marsden and Little (1990); Marsden and Murdoch (2006); Maxwell and Slater (2004); McMichael (1994, 1995); Mutersbaugh (2002); Ponte (2002b); Raynolds (2004); Smyth and Phillips (2002); Stanford (2002); and Vandergeest (2007).

3 See Baird (2002); Barrientos and Dolan (2006); Bowles and Harriss (2010); Boychuk (1992); Boyd (1998); Friedmann (1978); IDRC (2005); Islam (2008b); Montalbano (1991); Peluso and Watts (2001); Shiva (2000); and Vandergeest, Flaherty, and Miller (1999).

4 See, for example, Blowfield et al. (1999); Fine, Heasman, and Wright (1996); Freidberg (1997, 2004); Goodman and Watts (1997b); Islam (2009); McMichael (1994, 1995); Raynolds (1997); and Shiva (2000).

5 See, for example, Bonanno et al. (1994); Clapp and Fuchs (2009); Goodman and Watts (1997b); Marsden and Murdoch (2006); and McMichael (1994, 1995).

6 See Friedland (1994); Gibbon, Ponte, and Lazaro (2010); Lockie, Lyons, and Lawrence (2000); and Stanford (2002).

7 Consumers are motivated to demand increasingly specific products, and they have information technology that enhances their ability to seek, identify, and procure these products.

8 Champions of these new mechanisms include former United Nations secretary general Kofi Annan, who in January 1999 exhorted world business leaders to "embrace and enact" the UN Global Compact, whose nine principles covering human rights, labour, and the environment "unite the powers of markets with the authority of universal ideals." An inventory produced by the Organisation for Economic Co-operation and Development listed 246 codes of corporate conduct, while the Global Reporting Initiative, an organization dedicated to standardizing corporate sustainability reporting, estimates that more than 2,000 companies voluntarily report their social, environmental, and economic practice and performance (Gereffi et al. 2001). Many more products are now coming under certification schemes.

9 See Clapp (2005); Clapp and Fuchs (2009); Gereffi et al. (2001); Raman and Lipschutz (2010); and Utting and Marques (2009).

10 These terms are sometimes used interchangeably, but useful distinctions can be made between them according to the purpose for which they are designed (Smyth and Philips 2002). Identity preservation systems offer "closed-loop" segregation of a product from seed to product, based on the willingness of a buyer to pay a premium for a particular quality product. Segregation schemes, by contrast, are designed to keep undesirable products out of supply chains (for example, to keep genetically modified soy out of supply chains destined for human consumption in European markets). Finally, traceability schemes are designed to give retailers the ability to trace food contamination to its source by keeping records of a product's movement throughout a supply chain.

11 Externality describes a situation in which the benefits or costs of an economic activity affect a third party. Pollution is clearly a negative externality.

12 See Boyd and Clay (1998); CAP (1995); Clay (1996, 2004); Philips, Lin, and Beveridge (1993); Scott (2000); Sernbo and Kloth (1996); Shiva (1995); Vandergeest (2004); and Vandergeest, Flaherty, and Miller (1999).

13 A worldwide association of industry stakeholders formed in 1997, the GAA has a vested interest in ensuring the safe production and delivery of shrimp worldwide. Its mission statement reads as follows: "The Global Aquaculture Alliance exists both to promote the aquaculture industry and to advance environmental and social responsibility throughout the process of raising, processing, and distributing aquaculture products" (http://www.gaalliance.org/).

14 Locals can range from local farmers and villagers to NGOs and even to national government groups. Globals, in contrast, can range from transnational environmental groups to international consumers. The local/global dichotomy is problematic, however, as the distinction between the local and the global is becoming increasingly blurred.

15 To form a unified private certification scheme – known as the Aquaculture Certification Council – to address social and ecological concerns about farmed aquaculture, the World Wildlife Fund has been organizing a series of dialogues around the world since 2007. The goal of the dialogues is to create measurable, performance-based global standards. The dialogues seek to follow international guidelines for standards-setting developed by the International Social and Environmental Accreditation and Labelling Alliance. As creating standards that address environmental as well as social effects is challenging and complex, the Shrimp Aquaculture Dialogue invited a large and diverse group of people involved in that industry to participate; see http://www.worldwildlife.org/what/globalmarkets/aquaculture/aquaculturedialogues.html.

2. The Analytical Framework

1 In many cases, the buyer specifies precisely how particular standards should be attained by requiring and perhaps helping to introduce particular production processes and monitoring procedures. When the buyer plays this role, it is referred to as the "lead firm" in the chain.

2 Many recent scholars have used the term "global value chain" (GVC) in lieu of the GCC, although one might question the difference between the two. Since Gereffi's seminal book chapter (1994) was published, however, transnational giants have changed quite dramatically, outsourcing many

activities, developing strategic alliances with competitors, and becoming less vertically integrated and more network oriented. Today, global-scale networks of legally independent firms no longer make simple items; they also make capital- and technology-intensive goods and services. The GVC framework, accordingly, specifies a more elaborate set of governance forms and provides a crucial way of explaining changes in governance patterns over time. See Gereffi, Humphrey, and Sturgeon (2005); see also Global Value Chains Initiative (2006).

3 In the computer industry, for example, the coordination of activities appears to be based on the combination of arm's-length market relations and network-style governance based upon a division of competences between firms (Sturgeon 2001).

4 Although price is usually treated as a variable determined by the market, it is frequently the case that major customers (particularly those competing more on price than, for example, on product quality) insist that their suppliers design products and processes to meet a particular target price. Moreover, there is a common tendency for buyers to look for cheap labour to allow them to buy at a lower price and realize greater profits in a competitive market (see Humphrey and Schmitz 2001, 21).

5 See, for example, Dolan and Humphrey (2000); Freidberg (2004); Gibbon (2001a, 2001b); Islam (2008a, 2008b); Ponte (2002a, 2002b); Raynolds (1994a, 1994b, 2002, 2004); and Talbot (2002).

6 Collins (2005, 5) provides a long list of approaches that have been combined with GCC analysis, such as the labour process approach, actor network theory, the political economy of development and of agriculture, world systems theory, network analysis, industrial upgrading, regulation theory, and social constructionism.

7 Although even the apparel and car industries can be said to involve non-human actants, such actants are more likely to be considered in the agri-food sector because of its ties to metabolic processes and the influence of scientific studies.

8 See, for example, Daviron and Gibbon (2002); Gale and Haward (2011); Muradian and Pelupessy (2005); Ponte (2002a, 2002b); Petit (2007); Raynolds (2002, 2004); and Wilkinson (2006).

9 By "global managers," McMichael (2008) is referring to the officials of multilateral institutions such as the International Monetary Fund and the World Bank, the political elites of the Group of Eight major industrialized economies, the executives of transnational corporations, and global bankers, as well as the bureaucratic elites who administer international free trade and environmental conservation agreements.

10 The Institute on Governance (IOG) (http://iog.ca) is a non-profit organization that explores, shares, and promotes the concept of "good governance"
in Canada and abroad, and helps governments, volunteer sectors, communities, and the private sector to put the concept into practice for the
well-being of citizens and society.

11 See Frank, Hironaka, and Schofer (2000); Mol and Sonnenfeld (2000);
Schofer, Ramirez, and Meyer (2000); and Spaargaren and Mol (1992).

12 See Bredahl, Holleran, and Zaibet (1994); Caswell, Bredahl, and Hooker
(1998); Caswell and Hooker (1996); Clapp (1998, 2005); Clapp and Fuchs
(2009); and Uzemeri (1997).

13 See, for example, Barrett et al. (2002); Busch and Bain (2004); Bredahl et al.
(2001); Hatanaka, Bain, and Busch (2005); Henson and Northen (1998);
Henson and Reardon (2005); Tanner (2000); Vandergeest (2007); and Zuckerman (1996).

14 See, for example, Hatanaka, Bain, and Busch (2006); Muradian and
Pelupessy (2005); Mutersbaugh (2002); Ponte (2002a); Raynolds (2004);
and Wilkinson (2006).

15 For reviews of this body of literature, see, for example, Atkins and Bowler
(2001); Bowler (1992); Goodman and Watts (1994); Marsden et al. (1986);
Vandergeest (1988); and Watts (1996).

16 For example, Busch and Bain (2004); Daviron and Gibbon (2002); Dolan
(2004); Goodman and DuPuis (2002); Ito (2004); Muradian and Pelupessy
(2005); Raynolds (2002); and Wilkinson (2002, 2006).

17 For example, Bair and Peters (2006); Barrientos, Kabeer, and Hossain
(2004); Gibbon (2003); Giuliani, Pietrobelli, and Rabellotti (2005); Joekes
(1995); Kabeer (2003); Lund and Srinivas (2000); Ong (1997); and Siddique
(2003).

18 See, for example, Barrientos and Barrientos (2002); Barrientos, Dolan,
and Tallontire (2003); Barrientos, Kabeer, and Hossain (2004); Başlevent
and Onaran (2004); Dolan (2004); Gammage et al. (2006); Halim (2004);
Kritzinger, Barrientos, and Rossouw (2004); Mehrotra and Biggeri (2005);
Pokrant and Reeves (2003); and Raynolds (2001).

3. Neoliberalism and the Emergence of the Blue Revolution in the Global South

1 For example, Boyd and Clay (1998); CAP (1995); Clay (1996, 2004); Fla-
herty, Vandergeest, and Miller (1999); Philips, Lin, and Beveridge (1993);
Scott (2000); Sernbo and Kloth (1996); Shiva (1995); and Vandergeest,
Flaherty, and Miller (1999).

2 See, for example, Adnan (1991); Ahmed (1996); Battacharya, Rahman, and Khatan (1999); Deb (1998); Islam (2009); Manju (1996); Nijera Kori (1996); and Rahman (1995).

3 When shrimp aquaculture began in Bangladesh, the government issued licences to different entrepreneurs to cultivate shrimp in the coastal regions. Most of these entrepreneurs were not residents of those regions, however, and were therefore viewed as outsiders by locals.

4 See Halim (2004); Islam (2008b); Pokrant and Reeves (2003); Siddique (2004); and USAID Bangladesh (2006).

4. The Blue Revolution and Environmental Dilemmas

1 See, for example, Ahmed (1996); Alam et al. (2005); Ali (2006); Battacharya, Rahman, and Khatan (1999); Boyd and Clay (1998); CAP (1995); Clay (1996, 2004); Deb (1998); Haque (2004); Islam (2002); Manju (1996); Metcalfe (2003); Nijera Kori (1996); Philips, Lin, and Beveridge (1993); Rahman (1995); Scott (2000); Sernbo and Kloth (1996); Shiva (1995); Vandergeest, Flaherty, and Miller (1999); and WWF (1997).

2 World Food Day was established by FAO member countries at the FAO's Twentieth General Conference in November 1979; the date chosen, 16 October, is the FAO's anniversary. See http://www.fao.org/wfd2007/what-is-wfd/about-wfd.html.

3 The NACA is an intergovernmental organization that receives financial support and technical assistance from a variety of multilateral and government agencies, and focuses on sustainable shrimp aquaculture. The NACA is also concerned with environmental issues surrounding shrimp production and food safety issues; see www.enaca.org.

4 The consortium has published numerous reports and case studies on shrimp aquaculture; see http://www.enaca.org/shrimp, under the Case Studies heading.

5 See the Web site of the GAA at http://www.gaallaince.org.

6 See Ahmed (1996); Alam et al. (2005); Ali (2006); Battacharya, Rahman, and Khatan (1999); Deb (1998); Haque (2004); Islam (2002); and Metcalfe (2003).

7 See World Bank (1999). Total project costs were US$60.8 million, of which the government of Bangladesh contributed US$9.3 million, the UK Department for International Development contributed US$15.5 million, and the Global Environmental Facility provided a US$5 million grant. A US$28 million-equivalent interest-free IDA credit was provided on standard IDA terms with 40 years to maturity and 10 years' grace. The beneficiaries also contributed US$3 million to the project costs.

8 The GEF is a financial mechanism that provides grant and concessional funding to recipient countries for projects and activities that address climate change, biological diversity, international waters, and depletion of the ozone layer. Thirty-one countries, thirteen of them recipients, pledged more than US$2 billion in grant resources to the GEF's Core Fund over the initial three-year period (1994–7). As of January 1996, 153 countries were participating in the GEF. The World Bank shares responsibility for implementing GEF activities with the United Nations Development Programme and the United Nations Environment Programme (World Bank Group 1999).

9 In 1975 India completed the Farakka Barrage, about eighteen kilometers from its border with Bangladesh, to divert 1,133 cubic meters per second of Ganges water into the Bhagirati-Hoogly River, with the ostensible purpose of flushing the accumulated silt from the riverbed, thereby improving navigability at Calcutta Port. The unilateral withdrawal of water from the Ganges during the low-flow months has caused both long- and short-term effects in Bangladesh.

10 See, for example, Ahmed (1996); Alam et al. (2005); Ali (2006); Battacharya et al. (1999); Deb (1998); Gammage et al. (2006); Haque (2004); Islam (2002); Manju (1996); Metcalfe (2003); Nijera Kori (1996); Rahman (1995); and USAID Bangladesh (2006).

11 As noted in Chapter 2, *quality* includes both experience characteristics, such as freshness or taste, that can be detected directly by consumers after purchase and credence or non-material characteristics such as the environmental and ethical conditions of production, which consumers cannot detect (see Vandergeest 2007).

5. International Environmental Regulation Regimes

1 See Barrett et al. (2002); Bredahl et al. (2001); Busch and Bain (2004); Golan et al. (2001); Hatanaka, Bain, and Busch (2005); Henson and Northen (1998); Henson and Reardon (2005); Tanner (2000); Vandergeest (2007); and Zuckerman (1996).

2 See Busch and Bain (2004); Deaton (2004); Mutersbaugh (2002); Tanaka and Busch (2003); Tanner (2000); and Vandergeest (2007).

7. Gender and Employment Relations

1 See Barrett et al. (2002); Bredahl et al. (2001); Busch and Bain (2004); Golan et al. (2001); Hatanaka, Bain, and Busch (2005); Henson and Northen

(1998); Henson and Reardon (2005); Tanner (2000); Vandergeest (2007); and Zuckerman (1996).
2 See Blowfield (1999); MSC (2007a); NACA (2007); Vandergeest (2007); and Zadek, Prudan, and Evans (1997).
3 Article 66 of the Factories Act, 1965, defines a child as a person under the age of seventeen.

References

ABN Newswire. 2007. "China is the world's largest producer and exporter of seafood, according to the latest Glitnir report." Available online at http://www.abnnewswire.net/press/en/44180/China_Is_The_Worlds_Largest_Producer_And_Exporter_Of_SeafoodAccording_To_The_Latest_Glitnir_Report.html; accessed 27 May 2013.

About Seafood. 2013. "Top 10 Consumed Seafood." Available online at http://www.aboutseafood.com/about/about-seafood/top-10-consumed-seafoods; accessed 7 February 2013.

ACC (Aquaculture Certification Council). 2002. "Aquaculture Certification Council." Available online at http://www.aquaculturecertification.org/; accessed 26 September 2011.

ACC. 2007a. *ACC Advances Cluster Farm Certification: Best Aquaculture Practices Certification of Production Processes for Seafood Buyers.* Available online at http://www.aquaculturecertification.org/; accessed 13 August 2007.

ACC. 2007b. *Guidelines for BAP Standards.* Available online at http://www.aquaculturecertification.org/index.php?option=com_content&task=view&id=57; accessed 13 August 2007.

Acker, J. 2006. *Class Questions: Feminist Answers.* Lanham, MD.: Rowman & Littlefield.

Adnan, S. 1991. "Minority View of Appraisal Mission for Phase III of DDP Regarding Project Policy towards Shrimp Culture: An Alternative Approach." Report prepared for the DDP Phase III Appraisal Mission. Dhaka, October.

Aftabuzzaman. 1996. "Swimming through Troubled Waters: Bangladesh Perspective." Paper prepared for Bangladesh Frozen Foods Exporters Association. Dhaka.

Aglietta, M. 1979. *A Theory of Capitalist Regulations.* London: New Left Books.

Agrawal, A. 2003. "Environmentality: Technologies of Government and the Making of Subjects." Presented at the Asian Environments Series Lectures, York Centre for Asian Research, York University, Toronto, 29 September.

Ahmed, F. 1996. *In Defense of Land and Livelihood*. Ottawa: Sierra Club.

Alam, S.M.N, C.K. Lin, A. Yakupitiyage, H. Demaine, and M.J. Phillips. 2005. "Compliance of Bangladesh Shrimp Culture with FAO Code of Conduct for Responsible Fisheries: A Development Challenge." *Ocean and Coastal Management* 48 (2): 177–88. Available online at http://dx.doi.org/10.1016/j. ocecoaman.2005.01.001.

Ali, A.M.S. 2006. "Rice to Shrimp: Land Use/Land Cover Changes and Soil Degradation in Southwestern Bangladesh." *Land Use Policy* 23 (4): 421–35. Available online at http://dx.doi.org/10.1016/j.landusepol.2005.02.001.

Alkon, A.H., and J. Agyeman. 2011. "Conclusion: Cultivating the Fertile Field of Food Justice." In *Cultivating Food Justice: Race, Class and Sustainability*, ed. A.H. Alkon and J. Agyeman. Cambridge, MA: MIT Press.

AquaNIC (Aquaculture Network Information Centre). 2003. "Shrimp farming report strong on attack, weak on facts." Available online at www.aquanic. org/news/2003/shrimp.htm; accessed 22 May 2007.

Araghi, F. 1995. "Global Depeasantization, 1945–1990." *Sociological Quarterly* 36 (2): 337–68. Available online at http://dx.doi.org/10.1111/ j.1533-8525.1995.tb00443.x.

Arce, A., and T. Marsden. 1993. "The Social Construction of International Food: A New Research Agenda." *Economic Geography* 69 (3): 293–311. Available online at http://dx.doi.org/10.2307/143452.

Asaduzzaman, M., and K.A. Toufique. 1998. "Rice and Fish: Environmental Dilemmas of Development in Bangladesh." In *Growth or Stagnation? A Review of Bangladesh's Development 1996*. Dhaka: Centre for Policy Dialogue, University Press.

ASC. 2011. "Aquaculture Stewardship Council." Available online at http:// www.ascaqua.org/; accessed 26 September 2011.

ASC. 2012a. "First Responsible Farmed Pangasius with ASC Label Now Available in the Netherlands." Available online at http://www.asc-aqua.org/ index.cfm?act=update.detail&uid=133&lng=1; accessed 30 October 2012.

ASC. 2012b. "Species and Planning." Available online at http://www. asc-aqua.org/index.cfm?act=tekst.item&iid=3&lng=1; accessed 30 October 2012.

ATJ (Alter-Trade Japan). 2011. "What Is Alter-Trade Japan?" Available online at http://www.altertrade.co.jp/english/01/01_01_e.html; accessed 26 September 2011.

Atkins, P., and I. Bowler. 2001. *Food in Society: Economy, Culture, Geography.* London: Arnold.

Bair, J., and E.D. Peters. 2006. "Global Commodity Chains and Endogenous Growth: Export Dynamism and Development in Mexico and Honduras." *World Development* 34 (2): 203–21. Available online at http://dx.doi.org/10.1016/j.worlddev.2005.09.004.

Baird, Vanessa. 2002. "Fear Eats the Soul." *New Internationalists*, October, 9–12.

Bangladesh. 1983. Ministry of Fisheries and Livestock. *The Marine Fisheries Ordinance.* Dhaka.

Bangladesh. 1992. Ministry of Environment and Forests. *Environmental Policy.* Dhaka.

Bangladesh. 1996. Ministry of Agriculture. *New Agricultural Extension Policy.* Dhaka.

Bangladesh. 1998. Ministry of Fisheries and Livestock. *National Fish Policy.* Dhaka.

Bangladesh. 1999. Ministry of Water Resources. *National Water Policy.* Dhaka.

Bangladesh. 2001. Ministry of Land. *National Land Policy.* Dhaka.

Bangladesh. 2002. Ministry of Fisheries and Livestock. Department of Fisheries. *Shrimp Aquaculture in Bangladesh: A Vision for the Future.* Dhaka.

Bangladesh. 2004a. Ministry of Fisheries and Livestock. *Brief on Department of Fisheries Bangladesh.* Dhaka.

Bangladesh. 2004b. Export Promotion Bureau. *Annual Report 2004.* Dhaka: Export Promotion Bureau.

Bangladesh. 2005. Ministry of Fisheries and Livestock. Department of Fisheries. *Department of Fisheries Annual Report 2005.* Dhaka.

Bangladesh. 2010. Ministry of Fisheries and Livestock. Department of Fisheries. *Fisheries Statistical Yearbook of Bangladesh 2008–2009.* Dhaka: Ministry of Fisheries and Livestock, Department of Fisheries, Fisheries Resources Survey System.

Barrett, H.R., A.W. Browne, P.J.C. Harris, and K. Cadoret. 2002. "Organic Certification and the UK Market, Organic Imports from Developing Countries." *Food Policy* 27 (4): 301–18. Available online at http://dx.doi.org/10.1016/S0306-9192(02)00036-2.

Barrientos, A., and S.W. Barrientos. 2002. *Extending Social Protection to Informal Workers in the Horticulture Global Value Chain.* Washington, DC: World Bank.

Barrientos, S., and Catherine Dolan, eds. 2006. *Ethical Sourcing in the Global Food System.* London: Earthscan.

Barrientos, S., C. Dolan, and A. Tallontire. 2003. "A Gendered Value Chain Approach to Codes of Conduct in African Horticulture." *World Development*

31 (9): 1511–26. Available online at http://dx.doi.org/10.1016/S0305-750X(03) 00110-4.

Barrientos, S., N. Kabeer, and N. Hossain. 2004. "Gender Dimensions of the Globalisation of Production." Working Paper 17. Geneva: International Labour Office.

Başlevent, C., and Ö. Onaran. 2004. "The Effects of Export-oriented Growth on Female Labour Market Outcomes in Turkey." *World Development* 32 (8): 1375–93. Available online at http://dx.doi.org/10.1016/j. worlddev.2004.02.008.

Battacharya, D., M. Rahman, and F.A. Khatun. 1999. *Environmental Impacts of Trade Liberalization and Policies for the Sustainable Management of Natural Resources A Case Study on Bangladesh's Shrimp Farming Industry.* Dhaka: Centre for Policy Dialogue.

Béné, C. 2005. "The Good, the Bad and the Ugly: Discourse, Policy Controversies and the Role of Science in the Politics of Shrimp Farming Development." *Development Policy Review* 23 (5): 585–614. Available online at http:// dx.doi.org/10.1111/j.1467-7679.2005.00304.x.

Bennett, S., D. Scott, A. Karim, I. Sobhan, A. Khan, and S.M.A. Rashid. 1995. *Specialist Study, Wetland Resources: Final Report.* Northeast Regional Water Management Plan, Bangladesh Flood Action Plan 6. Dhaka: Bangladesh Water Development Board, Flood Plan Coordination Organisation. Available online at http://bicn.com/wei/resources/nerp/wrs/index.htm; accessed 16 July 2013.

Beulens, A.J.M., D.F. Broens, P. Folstar, and G. Hofstede. 2005. "Food Safety and Transparency in Food Chains and Networks Relationships and Challenges." *Food Control* 16 (6): 481–6. Available online at http://dx.doi.org/ 10.1016/j.foodcont.2003.10.010.

Bio Suisse. 2011. "Who Is Bio Suisse." Available online at http://www. biosuisse.ch/en/whoisbiosuisse.php; accessed 26 September 2011.

BioGro New Zealand. 2011. "New Zealand's Leading Organic Certifier." Available online at http://bio-gro.co.nz/index.php; accessed 26 September 2011.

Blowfield, M. 1999. "Ethical Trade: A Review of Developments and Issues." *Third World Quarterly* 20 (4): 753–70. Available online at http://dx.doi. org/10.1080/01436599913541.

Blowfield, M., A. Malins, B. Maynard, and V. Nelson. 1999. *Ethical Trade and Sustainable Rural Livelihoods.* Chatham Maritime, Kent, UK: Natural Resources Institute, Natural Resources and Ethical Trade Programme.

Bonanno, A., L. Busch, W.H. Friedland, L. Gouveia, and E. Mingione, eds. 1994. *From Columbus to Congra: The Globalization of Agriculture and Food.* Lawrence: University Press of Kansas.

Boselie, D., S. Henson, and D. Weatherspoon. 2003. "Supermarket Procurement Practices in Developing Countries: Redefining the Roles of the Public and Private Sectors." *American Journal of Agricultural Economics* 85 (5): 1155–61. Available online at http://dx.doi.org/10.1111/j.0092-5853.2003.00522.x.

Bowler, I., ed. 1992. *The Geography of Agriculture in Developed Market Economies*. London: Longman.

Bowles, P., and J. Harriss, eds. 2010. *Globalization and Labour in China and India Impacts and Responses*. London: Palgrave Macmillan. Available online at http://dx.doi.org/10.1057/9780230297296.

Boyce, J.K. 1987. *Agrarian Impasse in Bengal: Institutional Constraints to Technological Change*. Oxford: Oxford University Press.

Boychuk, R. 1992. "The Blue Revolution." *New Internationalist* 234 (August). Available online at http://newint.org/features/1992/08/05/blue/; accessed 15 June 2007.

Boyd, C.E., and J. Clay. 1998. "Shrimp Aquaculture and the Environment." *Scientific American* 278 (6): 58–65. Available online at http://dx.doi.org/10.1038/scientificamerican0698-58.

Boyd, C.E., J.A. Hargreaves, and J. Clay. 2002. *Codes of Practice and Conduct for Marine Shrimp Aquaculture*. Bangkok: Network of Aquaculture Centres in Asia-Pacific. Available online at http://www.enaca.org/modules/health/index.php; accessed 9 December 2007.

Boyd, S. 1998. "Secrets and Lies." *New Internationalist* 303 (July).

Boyer, R. 1990. *The Regulation School: A Critical Introduction*. New York: Columbia University Press.

Bredahl, M.E., E. Holleran, and L. Zaibet. 1994. "ISO Certification in the European Food Sector." *European Report on Industry, Quality, and Standards* 2 (10): 25–6.

Bredahl, M.E., J.R. Northen, A. Boecker, and M. Normile. 2001. "Consumer Demand Sparks the Growth of Quality Assurance Schemes in the European Food Sector." In *Changing Structure of Global Food Consumption and Trade*, WRS-01–1. Washington, DC: Department of Agriculture, Economic Research Service.

Brosius, J.P. 1999. "Green Dots, Pink Hearts: Displacing Politics from the Malaysian Rain Forest." *American Anthropologist* 101 (1): 36–57. Available online at http://dx.doi.org/10.1525/aa.1999.101.1.36.

Brosius, J.P., A.L. Tsing, and C. Zerner. 1998. "Representing Communities: Histories and Politics of Community-Based Natural Resource Management." *Society & Natural Resources* 11 (2): 157–68. Available online at http://dx.doi.org/10.1080/08941929809381069.

Busch, L., and C. Bain. 2004. "New! Improved? The transformation of the global agrifood system." *Rural Sociology* 69 (3): 321–46. Available online at http://dx.doi.org/10.1526/0036011041730527.

Buttel, F.H. 2001. "Some Reflections on Late 20th Century Agrarian Political Economy." *Sociologia Ruralis* 41 (2): 165–81. Available online at http://
dx.doi.org/10.1111/1467-9523.00176.

Buttel, F.H., and P. McMichael, eds. 2005. *New Directions in the Sociology of
Global Development*. Research in Rural Sociology and Development 11. Bing-
ley, UK: Emerald Group Publishing.

Cadman, T. 2011. *Quality and Legitimacy of Global Governance: Case Lessons from
Forestry*. London: Palgrave Macmillan. Available online at http://dx.doi.
org/10.1057/9780230306462.

CAIA (Canadian Aquaculture Industry Alliance). 2011. "Farming Canadian
Waters with Care." Ottawa. Available online at http://www.aquaculture.
ca/; accessed 26 September 2011.

Callon, M. 1986. "Some Elements of Sociology of Translation." In *Power, Action
and Belief: A New Sociology of Knowledge*, ed. J. Law. London: Routledge and
Kegan Paul.

Campbell, H. 2005. "The Rise and Rise of EurepGAP: European (Re)invention
of Colonial Food Relations?" *International Journal of Sociology of Agriculture
and Food* 13 (2): 1–19.

Campbell, H., G. Lawrence, and K. Smith. 2006. "Audit Cultures and the
Antipodes: The Implications of EurepGAP for New Zealand and Austra-
lian Agri-food Industries." In *Between the Local and the Global: Confronting
Complexity in the Contemporary Agri-Food Sector*, ed. T. Marsden and J. Mur-
doch. New York: Elsevier. Available online at http://dx.doi.org/10.1016/
S1057-1922(06)12004-1.

Campbell, H., and A. Stuart. 2005. "Disciplining the Organic Commodity." In
Agricultural Governance: Globalization and the New Politics of Governance, ed.
V. Higgins and G. Lawrence. London; New York: Routledge.

CAP (Consumers Association of Penang). 1995. "Aquaculture: Problems and
Issues." Penang, Malaysia.

Carrefour. 2006. "Guaranteeing Product Safety and Quality." Available online
at http://www.carrefour.com/cdc/responsible-commerce/product-safety-
and-quality/; accessed 26 September 2011).

Cashore, B. 2002. "Legitimacy and the Privatization of Environmental Governance: How Non-state Market-driven (NSMD) Governance Systems Gain
Rule-making Authority." *Governance: An International Journal of Policy, Administration and Institutions* 15 (4): 503–29. Available online at http://dx.doi.
org/10.1111/1468-0491.00199.

Cashore, B., G. Auld, and D. Newsom. 2003. "The United States Race to
Certify Sustainable Forestry: Non-state Environmental Governance and
the Competition for Policy-making Authority." *Business and Politics* 5 (3):

219–59. Available online at http://dx.doi.org/10.1080/1369525042000 189393.

Caswell, Julie A., M.E. Bredahl, and N.H. Hooker. 1998. "How Quality Management Metasystems Are Affecting the Food Industry." *Review of Agricultural Economics* 20 (2): 547–57.

Caswell, J.A., and N.H. Hooker. 1996. "HACCP as an International Trade Standard." *American Journal of Agricultural Economics* 78 (3): 775–9. Available online at http://dx.doi.org/10.2307/1243303.

Cato, J.C., and S. Subasinge. 2003. "Food Safety in Food Security and Food Trade Case Study: The Shrimp Export Industry in Bangladesh." *2020 Vision for Food, Agriculture and the Environment*. Focus 10, Brief 9. 17 September.

Certifying the Uncertifiable. 2003. "FSC Certification of Tree Plantations in Thailand and Brazil." *World Rainforest Movement*. August 2003.

Chapman, N. 2000. "Food Standards Matter in the Global Market." *Prepared Foods* 169 (5): 38–41.

Chowdhury, S.N., and M.R. Islam. 2000. "HACCP Implementation and Quality Control in the Fish Processing Industry of Bangladesh." *Agribusiness Bulletin* 45 (25 January).

Clapp, J. 1998. "The Privatization of Global Environmental Governance: ISO 14000 and the Developing World." *Global Governance* 4 (3): 295–316.

Clapp, J. 2005. "Global Environmental Governance and Corporate Responsibility and Accountability." *Global Environmental Politics* 5 (3): 23–34. Available online at http://dx.doi.org/10.1162/1526380054794916.

Clapp, J., and D. Fuchs, eds. 2009. *Corporate Power in Global Agrifood Governance*. Cambridge, MA: MIT Press.

Clay, J.W. 1996. "Market Potentials for Redressing the Environmental Impact of Wild Cultured and Pond Produced Shrimp." Report prepared for the World Wildlife Fund. Geneva.

Clay, J.W. 2004. *World Agriculture and the Environment*. Washington, DC: Island Press.

Climate Connections. 2011. "Sign On: Open Letter Denounces Shoddy WWF Shrimp Certification Standards." Available online at http://climate-connections.org/2011/05/10/sign-on-open-letter-denounces-shoddy-wwf-shrimp-certification-standards/; accessed 16 September 2011.

Collins, L.J. 2005. "New Directions in the Commodity Chain Analysis of Global Development Process." In *New Directions in the Sociology of Global Development*, ed. F.H. Buttel and P. McMichael. New York: Elsevier.

Consortium Program. 2002. *Shrimp Farming and the Environment: Can Shrimp Farming Be Undertaken Sustainably?* Report prepared by the World Bank, the Network of Aquaculture Centres in Asia-Pacific, the World Wildlife Fund, and the UN Food and Agriculture Organization. Available online at www. worldwildlife.org/cci/aquaculture_pubs.cfm; accessed 16 April 2003.

Darier, É. 1996. "Environmental Governmentality: The Case of Canada's Green Plan." *Environmental Politics* 5 (4): 585–606. Available online at http://dx.doi.org/10.1080/09644019608414294.

Daviron, B., and P. Gibbon. 2002. "Global Commodity Chain and African Export Agriculture." *Journal of Agrarian Change* 2 (2): 137–61. Available online at http://dx.doi.org/10.1111/1471-0366.00028.

Davis, M. 2006. *Planet of Slums*. London: Verso.

Deaton, B.J. 2004. "A Theoretical Framework for Examining the Role of Third-party Certifiers." *Food Control* 15 (8): 615–9. Available online at http://dx.doi.org/10.1016/j.foodcont.2003.09.007.

Deb, A.K. 1998. "Fake Blue Revolution: Environmental and Socio-Economic Impacts of Shrimp Culture in the Coastal Areas of Bangladesh." *Ocean and Coastal Management* 41 (1): 63–88. Available online at http://dx.doi.org/10.1016/S0964-5691(98)00074-X.

Deere, C.D., and M. Leon. 2001. *Empowering Women: Land and Property Rights in Latin America*. Pittsburgh: University of Pittsburgh Press.

DeLind, L. 2000. "Transforming Organic Agriculture into Industrial Organic Products: Reconsidering National Organic Standards." *Human Organization* 59 (2): 198–208.

Dicken, P. 1998. *Global Shift: Transforming the World Economy*, 3rd ed. New York: Guilford Press.

Dimitri, C., and N. Richman. 2000. *Organic Food Markets in Transition*. Greenbelt, MD: Winrock International.

Dolan, C. 2004. "On Farm and Packhouse: Employment at the Bottom of a Global Value Chain." *Rural Sociology* 69 (1): 99–126. Available online at http://dx.doi.org/10.1526/003601104322919928.

Dolan, C., and J. Humphrey. 2000. "Governance and Trade in Fresh Vegetables: The Impact of UK Supermarkets on the African Horticulture Industry." *Journal of Development Studies* 37 (2): 147–76. Available online at http://dx.doi.org/10.1080/713600072.

Doty, R.L. 1996. *Imperial Encounters: The Politics of Representation in North-South Relations*. Minneapolis: University of Minnesota Press.

Duplisea, B. 1998. "What's Behind Shrimp Farming?" Available online at http://207.112.105.217/PEN/1998-10/duplisea.html; accessed 3 May 2001.

du Toit, A., and J. Ewert. 2002. "Myths of Globalisation: Private Regulation and Farm Worker Livelihoods on Western Cape Farms." *Transformation* 50 (1): 77–104. Available online at http://dx.doi.org/10.1353/trn.2003.0010.

Economist. 2003. "The Promise of a Blue Revolution: How Aquaculture Might Meet Most of the World's Demand for Fish without Ruining the

Environment." 7 April. Available online at http://www.economist.com/node/1974103; accessed 11 February 2012.

EJF (Environmental Justice Foundation). 2003a. *Smash and Grab*. London: Environmental Justice Foundation in Partnership with WildAid.

EJF. 2003b. "Dying for Your Dinner: Western Demand for Shrimp Promotes Human Rights Abuses in the Developing World." Available online at www.commondreams.org/news2003/0626-04.htm; accessed 22 May 2007.

ELI (Environmental Law Institute). 2008. *Gold Standard for Sustainable Aquaculture Ecolabel Design: Technical Report*. Washington, DC: Environmental Law Institute and the Ocean Foundation.

ESCAP and ADB (Economic and Social Commission for Asia and the Pacific and Asian Development Bank). 2000. *State of the Environment in Asia and the Pacific*. New York: United Nations.

Escobar, A. 1992. "Reflections on 'Development': Grassroots Approaches and Alternative Politics in the Third World." *Futures* 24 (5): 411–36. Available online at http://dx.doi.org/10.1016/0016-3287(92)90014-7.

Escobar, A. 1995. *Encountering Development: The Making and Unmaking of the Third World*. Princeton, NJ: Princeton University Press.

ETI (Ethical Trading Initiative). 2010. "Ethical Trading Initiative: Respect for Workers Worldwide." Available online at http://www.ethicaltrade.org/; accessed 26 September 2011.

FAO (Food and Agriculture Organization). 2007. "A Qualitative Assessment of Standards and Certification Schemes Applicable to Aquaculture in the Asia–Pacific Region." Rome. Available online at ftp://ftp.fao.org/docrep/fao/010/ai388e/ai388e00.pdf; accessed: 30 October 2012.

FAO. 2010. *The State of World Fisheries and Aquaculture*. Rome.

FAO. 2012. *The State of World Fisheries and Aquaculture*. Rome.

FAO, NACA, UNEP, WB, and WWF. 2006. *International Principles for Responsible Shrimp Farming*. Available online at http://www.enaca.org/uploads/international-shrimp-principles-06.pdf; accessed 24 August 2007.

FAO and WHO (World Health Organization). 2011. "CODEX Alimentarius." Available online at http://www.codexalimentarius.org; accessed 26 September 2011.

Ferguson, J. 1990. *The Anti-Politics Machine: 'Development,' Depoliticization, and Bureaucratic Power in Lesotho*. New York; London: Cambridge University Press.

Fine, B. 1994. "Towards a Political Economy of Food." *Review of International Political Economy* 1 (3): 519–45. Available online at http://dx.doi.org/10.1080/09692299408434297.

Fine, B., M. Heasman, and J. Wright. 1996. *Consumption in the Age of Affluence: The World of Food*. London; New York: Routledge.

Fiorillo, J. 2006. "WWF and GAA contend for label." *2005 IntraFish Media AS*, 2 October.

Flaherty, M., P. Vandergeest, and P. Miller. 1999. "Rice Paddy or Shrimp Pond: Tough Decision in Rural Thailand." *World Development* 27 (12): 2045–60. Available online at http://dx.doi.org/10.1016/S0305-750X(99)00100-X.

FLO (Fairtrade Labelling Organizations International). 2010. "Fair Trade International." Available online at http://www.fairtrade.net/; accessed 26 September 2011.

Fold, N. 2002. "Lead Firms and Competition in 'Bipolar' Commodity Chains: Grinders and Branders in the Global Cocoa-Chocolate Industry." *Journal of Agrarian Change* 2 (2): 228–47. Available online at http://dx.doi.org/10.1111/1471-0366.00032.

Foucault, M. 1979. "On Governmentality." *Ideology & Consciousness* 6: 5–21.

Foucault, M. 1984. "Space, Knowledge, and Power." In *The Foucault Reader*, ed. P. Rabinow. New York: Pantheon Books.

Foucault, M. 1991. "Governmentality." In *The Foucault Effect. Studies in Governmentality*, ed. G. Burchell, C. Gordon, and P. Miller. London: Harvester Wheatsheaf.

Foucault, M. 1998. *The History of Sexuality*, vol. 1, *The Will to Knowledge*. London: Penguin.

Foucault, M. 2000. *Power*, ed. J.D. Faubion; trans. R. Hurley. New York: Random House.

Frank, D.J., A. Hironaka, and E. Schofer. 2000. "The Nation State and the Natural Environment over the Twentieth Century." *American Sociological Review* 65 (1): 96–116. Available online at http://dx.doi.org/10.2307/2657291.

Freidberg, S. 1997. "Contacts, Contracts, and Green Bean Schemes: Liberalisation and Agri-entrepreneurship in Burkina Faso." *Journal of Modern African Studies* 35 (1): 101–28. Available online at http://dx.doi.org/10.1017/S0022278X97002358.

Freidberg, S. 2004. *French Beans and Food Scares: Culture and Commerce in an Anxious Age*. New York: Oxford University Press.

Friedland, W.H. 1984. "Commodity Systems Analysis: An Approach to the Sociology of Agriculture." In *Research in Rural Sociology and Development*, ed. H.K. Schwarzweller. Greenwich, CT: JAI Press Inc.

Friedland, W.H. 1994. "The New Globalization: The Case of Fresh Produce." In *From Columbus to ConAgra: The Globalization of Agriculture and Food*, ed. A. Bonanno, L. Busch, W.H. Friedland, L. Gouveia, and E. Mingione. Lawrence: University Press of Kansas.

Friedmann, H. 1978. "Simple Commodity Production and Wage Labour in the American Plains." *Journal of Peasant Studies* 6 (1): 71–100. http://dx.doi.org/10.1080/03066157808438066.

Friedmann, H. 1982. "The Political Economy of Food: The Rise and Fall of the Postwar International Food Order." *American Journal of Sociology* 88 (Supplement): S248–86. Available online at http://dx.doi.org/10.1086/649258.

Friedmann, H. 1986. "Family Enterprises in Agriculture: Structural Limits and Political Possibilities." In *Agriculture: People and Policies*, ed. G. Cox, P. Lowe, and M. Winter. London: Allen and Unwin. Available online at http://dx.doi.org/10.1007/978-94-011-5962-3_3.

Friedmann, H. 1993. "The International Political Economy of Food: A Global Crisis." *New Left Review* 197:29–57.

Friedmann, H. 2000. "What on Earth Is the Modern World-System? Foodgetting and Territory in the Modern Era and Beyond." *Journal of World-Systems Research* 6 (2): 480–515.

Friedmann, H. 2005. "From Colonialism to Green Capitalism: Social Movements and the Emergence of Food Regimes." In *New Directions in the Sociology of Development*, ed. P. McMichael and F.H. Buttel. Oxford: Elsevier.

Friedmann, H., and P. McMichael. 1989. "Agriculture and the State System: The Rise and Decline of National Agricultures, 1870 to the Present." *Sociologia Ruralis* 29 (2): 93–117. Available online at http://dx.doi.org/10.1111/j.1467-9523.1989.tb00360.x.

Friend of the Sea. 2011. "Friend of the Sea: Sustainable Seafood." Available online at http://www.friendofthesea.org/; accessed 26 September 2011.

Gale, F., and M. Haward, 2011. *Global Commodity Governance: State Responses to Sustainable Forest and Fisheries Certification.* London: Palgrave Macmillan.

Gammage, S., K. Swanburg, M. Khandkar, M.Z. Islam, M. Zobair and A.M. Muzareba. 2006. *A Gendered Analysis of the Shrimp Sector in Bangladesh.* Dhaka: Greater Access to Trade and Expansion, USAID.

Gereffi, G. 1994. "The Organization of Buyer-driven Global commodity Chains: How US Retailers Shape Overseas Production Networks." In *Commodity Chains and Global Capitalism*, ed. G. Gereffi and M. Korzeniewicz. Westport, CT: Praeger.

Gereffi, G. 1999. "International Trade and Industrial Upgrading in the Apparel Commodity Chain." *Journal of International Economics* 48 (1): 37–70. Available online at http://dx.doi.org/10.1016/S0022-1996(98)00075-0.

Gereffi, G., J. Humphrey, R. Kaplinsky, and T. Sturgeon. 2001. "Globalization, Value Chains and Development." *IDS Bulletin* 32 (3): 1–9. Available online at http://dx.doi.org/10.1111/j.1759-5436.2001.mp32003001.x.

Gereffi, G. J. Humphrey, and T. Sturgeon. 2005. "The Governance of Global Value Chains." *Review of International Political Economy* 12 (1): 78–104. Available online at http://dx.doi.org/10.1080/09692290500049805.

Gereffi, G., and M. Korzeniewicz, eds. 1994. *Commodity Chains and Global Capitalism.* Westport, CT: Praeger.

Gibbon, P. 2001a. "Agro-commodity Chains." *IDS Bulletin* 32 (3): 60–8. Available online at http://dx.doi.org/10.1111/j.1759-5436.2001.mp32003007.x.

Gibbon, P. 2001b. "Upgrading Primary Production: A Global Commodity Chain Approach." *World Development* 29 (2): 345–63. Available online at http://dx.doi.org/10.1016/S0305-750X(00)00093-0.

Gibbon, P. 2003. "The African Growth and Opportunity Act and the Global Commodity Chain for Clothing." *World Development* 31 (11): 1809–27. Available online at http://dx.doi.org/10.1016/j.worlddev.2003.06.002.

Gibbon, P., S. Ponte, and E. Lazaro, eds. 2010. *Global Agri-food Trade and Standards: Challenges for Africa*. London: Macmillan. Available online at http://dx.doi.org/10.1057/9780230281356.

Giuliani, E., C. Pietrobelli, and R. Rabellotti. 2005. "Upgrading in Global Value Chains: Lessons from Latin American Clusters." *World Development* 33 (4): 549–73. Available online at http://dx.doi.org/10.1016/j.worlddev.2005.01.002.

Glitnir Bank. 2007. *Glitnir: China Seafood Industry Report*. Reykjavik: Glitner Group. Available online at http://skjol.islandsbanki.is/servlet/file/store156/item49466/Glitnir%20%20China%20Seafood%20Industry%20Report%202007.pdf; accessed 27 May 2013.

Global Value Chains Initiative. 2006. "Global Value Chains: Concepts and Tools." Available online at http://www.globalvaluechains.org/concepts.html.

GlobalG.A.P. 2011. "Welcome to GLOBALG.A.P." Available online at http://www.globalgap.org/uk_en/; accessed 26 September 2011.

Golan, E., F. Kuchler, L. Mitchell, C. Greene, and A. Jessup. 2001. "Economics of Food Labeling." *Journal of Consumer Policy* 24 (2): 117–84. Available online at http://dx.doi.org/10.1023/A:1012272504846.

Goldman, M. 2004. "Eco-governmentality and other Transnational Practices of a 'Green' World Bank." In *Liberation Ecologies*, 2nd ed., *Environment, Development, Social Movement*, ed. R. Peet and M. Watts. London; New York: Routledge.

Goodman, D., and E.M. DuPuis. 2002. "Knowing Food and Growing Food: Beyond the Production- Consumption Debate in the Sociology of Agriculture." *Sociologia Ruralis* 42 (1): 5–22. Available online at http://dx.doi.org/10.1111/1467-9523.00199.

Goodman, D., and M. Redclift. 1982. *From Peasant to Proletarian: Capitalist Development and Agrarian Transitions*. New York: St Martin's Press.

Goodman, D., and M. Watts. 1994. "Reconfiguring the Rural or Fording the Divide?: Capitalist Restructuring and the Global Agri-food System." *Journal of Peasant Studies* 22 (1): 1–49. Available online at http://dx.doi.org/10.1080/03066159408438565.

Goodman, D., and M. Watts. 1997a. "Agrarian Questions, Global Appetite, Local Metabolism, Nature, Culture and Industry in fin-de-siecle Agri-food system." In *Globalising Food: Agrarian Questions and Global Restructuring*, ed. D. Goodman and M. Watts. London: Routledge.

Goodman, D., and M. Watts, eds. 1997b. *Globalising Food: Agrarian Questions and Global Restructuring*. London: Routledge. Available online at http://dx.doi.org/10.4324/9780203444894.

Goss, J. 2000. "Shrimp Farming Does Not Reduce Rural Poverty." *Third World Network*, November 2000. Available online at http://www.twnside.org.sg/title/2117.htm; accessed 16 July 2013.

Greenpeace. 1998. "Industrial Shrimp Aquaculture, Fast Track to a Dead End: Choluteca Declaration." Presentation to FAO Technical Consultation on Policies for Sustainable Shrimp Aquaculture, Bangkok, 8–11 December.

Gupta, A. 1998. *Postcolonial Developments: Agriculture in the Making of Modern India*. Durham, NC: Duke University Press.

Habib, E. 1998. "Legal Aspects of Shrimp Cultivation." Paper presented at the Workshop on Environmental Impact of Structural Adjustment Policies in Bangladesh, Dhaka, 17 May 1998.

Hagler, M. 1997. "Shrimp: The Devastating Delicacy." *Greenpeace Report*. Available online at http://www.greenpeace.org/raw/content/usa/press/reports/shrimp-the-devastating-delica.pdf; accessed 3 May 2007.

Halim, S. 2004. *Shrimp Processing in Bangladesh: Socio-Economic Overview*. Dhaka: International Labour Organization Regional Office.

Hall, D. 2004. "Explaining the Diversity of Southeast Asian Shrimp Aquaculture." *Journal of Agrarian Change* 4 (3): 315–35. Available online at http://dx.doi.org/10.1111/j.1471-0366.2004.00081.x.

Hamilton, R. 2004. "A Green Seal of Approval." *IDBAMERICA*, 26 January. Available online at www.iadb.org/idbamerica/index.cfm?thisid=2533; accessed 26 January 2004.

Hammersley, M., and P. Atkinson. 2003. *Ethnography: Principles in Practice*. London: Tavistock Institute.

Haque, A.K.E. 2004. *Sanitary and Phyto-Sanitary Barriers to Trade and Its Impact on Environment: The Case of Shrimp Aquaculture in Bangladesh*. Winnipeg: International Institute for Sustainable Development.

Harvey, D. 2003. *The New Imperialism*. Oxford: Oxford University Press.

Hatanaka, M., C. Bain, and L. Busch. 2005. "Third-Party Certification in the Global Agrifood System." *Food Policy* 30 (3): 354–69. Available online at http://dx.doi.org/10.1016/j.foodpol.2005.05.006.

Hatanaka, M., C. Bain, and L. Busch. 2006. "Differentiated Standardization, Standardized Differentiation: The Complexity of the Global Agri-food

System." In *Between the Local and the Global: Confronting Complexity in the Contemporary Agri-Food Sector*, ed. T. Marsden and J. Murdoch. New York: Elsevier.

Heffernan, W.D., and Constance, D.H. 1994. "Transnational Corporations and the Globalization of the Food System." In *From Columbus to ConAgra: The Globalization of Agriculture and Food*, ed. A. Bonanno, L. Busch, W.H. Friedland, L. Gouveia, and E. Mingione. Lawrence: University Press of Kansas.

Hemlock, D., and L. Baldomir. 2008. "Sustainable seas: environmental and industry groups help consumers pick healthy and eco-friendly seafood." *Sun Sentinel* (Ft Lauderdale, FL), 29 June. Available online at http://articles.sun-sentinel.com/2008-06-29/business/0806270469_1_fish-farms-seafood-ocean-science; accessed 29 May 2013.

Hempel, E., and U. Winther. 2002. "Shrimp Farming and the Environment: Can Shrimp Farming be Undertaken Sustainably?" Background report for the Consortium Programme on Shrimp Farming and the Environment. Washington, DC: World Bank.

Henderson, J.E., and P. Dicken. 2002. "Global Production Networks and the Analysis of Economic Development." *Review of International Political Economy* 9 (3): 436–64. Available online at http://dx.doi.org/10.1080/09692290210150842.

Henson, S., and R.J. Loader. 2001. "Barriers to Agricultural Exports from Developing Countries: The Role of Sanitary and Phytosanitary Requirements." *World Development* 29 (1): 85–102. Available online at http://dx.doi.org/10.1016/S0305-750X(00)00085-1.

Henson, S., and J. Northen. 1998. "Economic Determinants of Food Safety Controls in the Supply of Retailer Own-branded Products in the United Kingdom." *Agribusiness* 14 (2): 113–26. Available online at http://dx.doi.org/10.1002/(SICI)1520-6297(199803/04)14:2<113::AID-AGR4>3.0.CO;2-5.

Henson, S., and T. Reardon. 2005. "Private Agri-food Standards: Implications for Food Policy and the Agri-food System." *Food Policy* 30 (3): 241–53. Available online at http://dx.doi.org/10.1016/j.foodpol.2005.05.002.

Herbert, S. 2000. "For Ethnography." *Progress in Human Geography* 24 (4): 550–68.

Higgins, V., and G. Lawrence, eds. 2005. *Agricultural Governance: Globalization and the New Politics of Governance*. London; New York: Routledge.

Hindu Business Line. 2000. "The Cleaning Act." 21 August. Available online at http://www.hindu.com/businessline/2000/08/21/stories/102105mf.htm; accessed 16 July 2013.

Hong Kong. 2011. Agriculture, Fisheries and Conservation Department. "Accredited Fish Farm Scheme." Available online at http://www.hkaffs.org/en/index.html; accessed 26 September 2011.

Hopkins, T.K., and I. Wallerstein. 1986. "Commodity Chains in the World-Economy Prior to 1800." *RE:view* 10 (1): 157–70.

Humphrey, J., and H. Schmitz. 2001. "Governance in Global Value Chains." *IDS Bulletin* 32 (3): 19–29. Available online at http://dx.doi.org/10.1111/j.1759-5436.2001.mp32003003.x.

IDRC (International Development Research Centre). 2005. *Rural Poverty and Environment Program Initiative*. Ottawa. Available online at http://www.idrc.ca/en/Pages/default.aspx; accessed 4 October 2005.

IFOAM (International Federation of Organic Agriculture Movements). 2007. "Principles of Organic Agriculture Preamble." Bonn. Available online at http://www.ifoam.org/organic_facts/principles/pdfs/IFOAM_FS_Principles_forWebsite.pdf; accessed 12 November 2007.

IFOAM. 2011. "Uniting the Organic World." Bonn. Available online at http://www.ifoam.org/; accessed 26 September 2011.

ILO (International Labour Organization). 1998. *Forced Labour in Myanmar (Burma): Report of the Commission of Inquiry Appointed under Article 26 of the Constitution of the International Labour Organization to Examine the Observance by Myanmar of the Forced Labour Convention, 1930 (No. 29)*. Geneva: ILO, 2 July 1998. Available online at http://www.ilo.org/public/english/standards/relm/gb/docs/gb273/myanmar.htm; accessed 16 July 2013.

ILO. 2002. *Decent Work and the Informal Economy*. International Labour Conference, 90th Session, Report VI. Geneva. Available online at www.ilo.org/public/english/standards/relm/ilc/ilc90/pdf/rep-vi.pdf; accessed 9 March 2004.

Independent. 2005. "US firm starts shrimp certification." 18 February. Available online at http://independent-bangladesh.com/; accessed 25 February 2005.

IntelAsia. 2005. "US backed Bangladesh programme threatens Vietnam shrimpers." 20 August 2005. Available online at http://www.intellasia.net/us-backed-bangladesh-programme-threatens-vietnam-shrimpers-11423; accessed 16 July 2013.

ISEAL (International Social and Environmental Accreditation and Labelling Alliance). 2011. "ISEAL Alliance." London. Available online at http://www.isealalliance.org/; accessed 26 September 2011.

Islam, M.S. 2002. "The Rhetoric of Environmentally Sound Shrimp Aquaculture in Bangladesh." Major Review Paper, Graduate Program in Sociology, York University.

Islam, M.S. 2005. "Muslims in the Capitalist Discourse: September 11 and its Aftermath." *Journal of Muslim Minority Affairs* 25 (1): 3–12. Available online at http://dx.doi.org/10.1080/13602000500113423.

Islam, M.S. 2007. "Capitalist Development and Governance: A Post-modern Critique." *Daily Star* 5 (1116). Available online at http://thedailystar.net/2007/07/21/d707211503115.htm; accessed 21 July 2007.

Islam, M.S. 2008a. "From Pond to Plate: Towards a Twin-driven Commodity Chain in Bangladesh Shrimp Aquaculture." *Food Policy* 33 (3): 209–23. Available online at http://dx.doi.org/10.1016/j.foodpol.2007.10.002.

Islam, M.S. 2008b. "From Sea to Shrimp Processing Factories in Bangladesh: Gender and Employment at the Bottom of a Global Commodity Chain." *Journal of South Asian Development* 3 (2): 211–36. Available online at http://dx.doi.org/10.1177/097317410800300202.

Islam, M.S. 2009. "In search of 'White Gold': Environmental and agrarian changes in rural Bangladesh." *Society & Natural Resources* 22 (1): 66–78. Available online at http://dx.doi.org/10.1080/08941920801942255.

Islam, M.S. 2010. "Regimes of Environmental Regulations and Governance: Opportunities and Challenges for Shrimp Aquaculture in Bangladesh." *Journal of Bangladesh Studies* 12 (1): 44–62.

Islam, M.S. 2012. "Evolution of Shrimp Farming in Bangladesh: Myths versus Reality." *Global Aquaculture Advocate*, November-December.

Islam, M.S. 2013. *Development, Power and the Environment: Neoliberal Paradox in the Age of Vulnerability*. New York: Routledge.

Islam, M.S., R.K. Talukder, and A.A. Miah. 2004. "An Analysis of Stakeholder Profiles in Relation to Production, Marketing, and Processing of Shrimp in Bangladesh." *Bangladesh Journal of Political Economy* 20 (1): 23–40.

ISO (International Standards Organization). 2011. "International Standards for Business, Government and Society." Available online at http://www.iso.org/iso/home.html; accessed 26 September 2011.

Ito, S. 2002. "From Rice to Prawns: Economic Transformation and Agrarian Structure in Rural Bangladesh." *Journal of Peasant Studies* 29 (2): 47–70. Available online at http://dx.doi.org/10.1080/714003949.

Ito, S. 2004. "Globalization and Agrarian Change: A Case of Freshwater Prawn Farming in Bangladesh." *Journal of International Development* 16 (7): 1003–13. Available online at http://dx.doi.org/10.1002/jid.1152.

Jain, A., and D.P. Chakraborty. 2002. "Sister Alice broke off from her order to help women shrimp peelers." Subaltern Innovators Network. Information Series, January. Available online at http://www.it.bton.ac.uk/research/euindia/knowledgebase/workingpaper/pages/subalter2.htm#SISTER; accessed 16 July 2013.

Jessop, B. 1990. "Regulation Theories in Retrospect and Prospect." *Economy and Society* 19 (2): 153–216. Available online at http://dx.doi.org/10.1080/03085149000000006.

Jilani, G. 1999. "Sustainable Environment Management Programme (SEMP)." *Bangladesh Environmental News Letter* 10 (1).

Joekes, S. 1995. *Trade-Related Employment for Women in Industry and Services in Developing Countries*. Geneva: United Nations Research Institute for Social Development.

Josling, T., D. Roberts, and D. Orden. 2004. *Food Regulation and Trade: Toward a Safe and Open Global System*. Washington, DC: Institute for International Economics.

Kabeer, N. 2003. *Gender Mainstreaming in Poverty Eradication and the Millennium Development Goals: A Handbook for Policy Makers*. Ottawa: Canadian International Development Agency.

Karim, M. 2000. "Preserving Shrimp Quality." *Agribusiness Bulletin* 61 (25 February).

Kendrick, A. 1994. "The Gher Revolution: The Social Impacts of Technological Change in Freshwater Prawn Cultivation in Southern Bangladesh." Report prepared for CARE International, Bangladesh. Unpublished.

Khatun, F. 2004. "Fish Trade Liberalization in Bangladesh: Implications of SPS Measures and Co-labelling for the Export-oriented Shrimp Sector." FAO Project PR26109. Rome: Food and Agriculture Organization.

Khor, M. 1994. "The Aquaculture Disaster: Third World Communities Fight the 'Blue Revolution'." *Third World Resurgence* 59. Available online at http://www.twnside.org.sg/title/aqua-ch.htm; accessed 28 July 2011.

KRAV. 2010. "KRAV Standards." Uppsala, Sweden. Available online at http://www.krav.se/System/Spraklankar/In-English/KRAV-standards/; accessed 26 September 2011.

Kritzinger, A., S. Barrientos, and H. Rossouw. 2004. "Employment in South African Horticulture: Experiences of Contract Workers in Fruit Exports." *Sociologia Ruralis* 44 (1): 17–39. Available online at http://dx.doi.org/10.1111/j.1467-9523.2004.00259.x.

Latour, B. 1986. "The Powers of Association." In *Power, Action and Belief: A New Sociology of Knowledge?* ed. J. Law. London: Routledge and Kegan Paul.

Law, J. 1986. "On the Methods of Long-distance Control: Vessels, Navigation and the Portuguese Route to India." *Sociological Review* 32: 234–63.

Le Heron, R. 1993. *Globalized Agriculture: Political Choice*. Oxford: Pergamon Press.

Lemos, M.C., and A. Agrawal. 2006. "Environmental Governance." *Annual Review of Environment and Resources* 31 (1): 297–325. Available online at http://dx.doi.org/10.1146/annurev.energy.31.042605.135621.

Levy, D.S., and P.J. Newell, eds. 2005. *The Business of Global Environmental Governance*. Cambridge, MA: MIT Press.

Li, T. 2000. "Constituting Tribal Space: Indigenous Identity and Resource Politics in Indonesia." *Comparative Studies in Society and History* 42 (1): 149. Available online at http://dx.doi.org/10.1017/S0010417500002632.

Li, T. 2002. "Engaging Simplifications: Community-Based Resource Manage-
    ment, Market Processes and State Agendas in Upland Southeast Asia."
    World Development 30 (2): 265–83. Available online at http://dx.doi.org/
    10.1016/S0305-750X(01)00103-6.

Lockie, S., K. Lyons, and G. Lawrence. 2000. "Constructing 'Green' Foods:
    Corporate Capital, Risk, and Organic Farming in Australia and New
    Zealand." *Agriculture and Human Values* 17 (4): 315–22. Available online at
    http://dx.doi.org/10.1023/A:1026547102757.

London, C. 1997. "Class Relations and Capitalist Development: Subsumption
    in the Colombian Coffee Industry." *Journal of Peasant Studies* 24 (4): 269–95.
    Available online at http://dx.doi.org/10.1080/03066159708438651.

Lund, F., and S. Srinivas. 2000. "Learning from Experience: A Gendered Ap-
    proach to Social Protection for Workers in the Informal Economy."
    Strategies and Tools against Social Exclusion and Poverty Programme.
    Geneva: International Labour Organization.

Lynch, O., and K. Talbot. 1995. *Balancing Acts: Community-Based Forest Man-
    agement and National Law in Asia and the Pacific*. Washington, DC: World
    Resource Institute.

MAC (Marine Aquarium Council). 2009. "Marine Aquarium Council: Healthy
    Reef, Healthy Fish, Healthy Hobby." Los Angeles. Available online at
    http://www.aquariumcouncil.org/; accessed 26 September 2011.

Mangrove Action Project. 2009. "Civil society groups question industrial
    aquaculture at FAO meet." Port Angeles, WA, 5 March. Available online at
    http://mangroveactionproject.org/news/current_headlines/civil-society-
    groups-question-industrial-aquaculture-at-fao-meet; accessed: 12 February
    2012.

Mangrove Action Project. 2011. "Shrimp Farming." Port Angeles, WA. Avail-
    able online at http://mangroveactionproject.org/issues/shrimp-farming/
    shrimp-farming; accessed 16 September 2011.

Manju, T.H. 1996. "Political Economy of Shrimp Culture in Bangladesh."
    Dhaka: Grameen Bank.

Marsden, T. 1997. "Creating Space for Food: The Distinctiveness of Recent
    Agrarian Development." In *Globalising Food: Agrarian Questions and Global
    Restructuring*, ed. D. Goodman and M. Watts. London: Routledge.

Marsden, T., A. Flynn, and M. Harrison. 2000. *Consuming Interests: The Social
    Provision of Foods*. London: UCL Press.

Marsden, T., and J. Little, eds. 1990. *Political, Social and Economic Perspectives on
    the International Food System*. Aldershot,UK: Avebury.

Marsden, T., R. Munton, S. Whatmore, and J. Little. 1986. "Towards a Politi-
    cal Economy of Capitalist Agriculture: A British Perspective." *International*

Journal of Urban and Regional Research 10 (4): 488–512. Available online at http://dx.doi.org/10.1111/j.1468-2427.1986.tb00026.x.

Marsden, T., and J. Murdoch, eds. 2006. *Between the Local and the Global: Confronting Complexity in the Contemporary Agri-Food Sector*. New York: Elsevier.

Marsden, T., and D. Symes. 1984. "Landownership and Farm organization: Evolution and Change in Capitalist Agriculture." *International Journal of Urban and Regional Research* 8 (3): 388–401. Available online at http://dx.doi.org/10.1111/j.1468-2427.1984.tb00616.x.

Marx, K. 1999. *The Capital: An Abridged Edition*. New York: Oxford University Press.

Maxwell, S., and R. Slater, eds. 2004. *Food Policy: Old and New*. Oxford: Blackwell Publishing.

MBA (Monterey Bay Aquarium). "Monetary Bay Aquarium Seafood Watch." Monterey, CA. Available online at http://www.montereybayaquarium.org/cr/SeafoodWatch/web/sfw_factsheet.aspx?gid=20; accessed 26 September 2011.

McMichael, P. 1992. "Tensions between National and International Control of the World Food Order: Contours of a New Food Regime." *Sociological Perspectives* 35 (2): 343–65. Available online at http://dx.doi.org/10.2307/1389383.

McMichael, P., ed. 1994. *The Global Restructuring of Agri-Food System*. Ithaca, NY: Cornell University Press.

McMichael, P. 1995. *Food and Agrarian Orders in the World Economy*. Westport, CT: Greenwood Press.

McMichael, P. 1996. "Globalisation: Myths and Realities." *Rural Sociology* 61 (1): 25–55. Available online at http://dx.doi.org/10.1111/j.1549-0831.1996.tb00609.x.

McMichael, P. 1998. "Global Food Politics." Monthly Review 50 (3): 97–122.

McMichael, P. 1999. "Virtual Capitalism and Agri-food Restructuring." In *Restructuring Global and Regional Agricultures: Transformations in Australian Agri-food Economies and Spaces*, ed. D. Burch, J. Goss, and G. Laurence. Aldershot, UK: Ashgate.

McMichael, P. 2008. *Development and Social Change: A Global Perspective*. Thousand Oaks, CA: Pine Forge Press.

McMichael, P., and C.K. Kim. 1994. "Japanese and South Korean Agricultural Restructuring in Comparative and Global Perspective." In *Global Restructuring of Agri-food Systems*, ed. P. McMichael. Ithaca, NY: Cornell University Press.

Mehrotra, S., and M. Biggeri. 2005. "Can Industrial Outwork Enhance Homeworkers' Capabilities? Evidence from Clusters in South Asia." *World*

Development 33 (10): 1735–57. Available online at http://dx.doi.org/10.1016/j.worlddev.2005.04.013.

Metcalfe, I. 2003. "Environmental Concerns for Bangladesh." *South Asia: Journal of South Asian Studies* 26 (3): 423–38. Available online at http://dx.doi.org/10.1080/0085640032000178961.

Mol, A.P.J., and D. Sonnenfeld. 2000. *Ecological Modernization around the World: Perspectives and Critical Debates.* Ilford, UK: Frank Cass.

Montalbano, W.D. 1991. "A global pursuit of happiness." *Los Angeles Times,* 1 October, F1.

Moran, W., G. Blunden, and J. Greenwood. 1993. "The Role of Family Farming in Agrarian Change." *Progress in Human Geography* 17 (1): 22–42. Available online at http://dx.doi.org/10.1177/030913259301700102.

MSC (Marine Stewardship Council). 2007a. "About MSC." London. Available online at http://eng.msc.org/; accessed 13 August 2007.

MSC. 2007b. "MSC Principles and Criteria for Sustainable Fishing." London. Available online at http://www.msc.org/documents/email/msc-principles-criteria/; accessed 13 August 2007.

MSC. 2011. "Marine Stewardship Council: Certified Sustainable Seafood." London. Available online at http://www.msc.org/; accessed 26 September 2011.

Muradian, R., and W. Pelupessy. 2005. "Governing the Coffee Chain: The Role of Voluntary Regulatory Systems." *World Development* 33 (12): 2029–44. Available online at http://dx.doi.org/10.1016/j.worlddev.2005.06.007.

Mutersbaugh, T. 2002. "The Number Is the Beast: A Political Economy of Organic Coffee Certification and Producer Unionism." *Environment & Planning A* 34 (7): 1165–84. Available online at http://dx.doi.org/10.1068/a3435.

NACA (Network of Aquaculture Centres in Asia-Pacific). 2007. "Certification Systems." Available online at http://www.enaca.org/modules/cms/start.php?start_id=25; accessed 13 August 2007.

Naturland. 2006. *Naturland Standards for Organic Aquaculture.* Gräfelfing, Germany. Available online at http://www.naturland.de/fileadmin/MDB/documents/Richtlinien_englisch/Naturland-Standards_Aquaculture.pdf; accessed 10 January 2007.

Naturland. 2011. "Naturland: Organic Agriculture throughout the World." Gräfelfing, Germany. Available online at http://www.naturland.de/home0.html; accessed 26 September 2011.

Newby, H. 1987. *Country Life: A Social History of Rural England.* New York: Barnes & Noble Books.

Newman, B. 2006. "Indian Farmer Suicide: A Lesson for Africa's Farmers." *Food First Backgrounder* 12 (4): 2.

Nijera Kori. 1996. "The Impact of Shrimp Cultivation on Soils and Environment in Paikgacha Region, Khulna (Limited to Polders 20, 21, 22, 23 and 29)." Dhaka.

NRC (National Research Council). 1995. *Standards, Conformity Assessment and Trade*. Washington, DC.

OIE (Office international des épizooties). 2009. "A Short History of the OIE." Paris. Available online at http://web.oie.int/eng/OIE/en_histoire.htm; accessed 26 September 2011.

Ong, A. 1997. "The Gender and Labor Politics in Postmodernity." In *The Politics of Culture in the Shadow of Capital*, ed. L. Lowe and D. Lloyd. Durham, NC: Duke University Press.

Oosterveer, P. 2006. "Globalization and Sustainable Consumption of Shrimp: Consumers and Governance in the Global Space of Flows." *International Journal of Consumer Studies* 30 (5): 465–76. Available online at http://dx.doi.org/10.1111/j.1470-6431.2006.00535.x.

Ortiz, S., and S. Aparicio. 2007. "How Labourers Fare in Fresh Fruit Export Industries: Lemon Production in Northern Argentina." *Journal of Agrarian Change* 7 (3): 382–404. Available online at http://dx.doi.org/10.1111/j.1471-0366.2007.00150.x.

PAI (Product Authentication International). 2007. "Welcome to the PAI Group." Worthing, UK. Available online at http://www.thepaigroup.com/; accessed 26 September 2011.

Peluso, N., and M. Watts, eds. 2001. *Violent Environments*. Ithaca, NY: Cornell University Press.

Petit, N. 2007. "Ethiopia's Coffee Sector: A Bitter or Better Future." *Journal of Agrarian Change* 7 (2): 225–63. Available online at http://dx.doi.org/10.1111/j.1471-0366.2007.00145.x.

Philips, M.J., C.K. Lin, and M.C.M. Beveridge. 1993. "Shrimp Culture and the Environment: Lessons from the World's Most Rapidly Expanding Warmwater Aquaculture Sector." In *Environment and Aquaculture in Developing Countries*, ed. R.S.V. Pullin, H. Rosenthal, and J.L. Maclean. Bangkok: ICLARM.

Plumptre, T. n.d. "What Is Governance?" Ottawa: Institute on Governance. Available online at www.iog.ca; accessed 28 August 2007.

Pokrant, B., and P. Reeves. 2003. "Work and Labour in the Bangladesh Brackish-Water Shrimp Export Sector." *South Asia: Journal of South Asian Studies* 26 (3): 359–89. Available online at http://dx.doi.org/10.1080/0085640032000178934.

Ponte, S. 2002a. "Brewing a Bitter Cup? Deregulation, Quality and the Reorganization of Coffee Marketing in East Africa." *Journal of Agrarian Change* 2 (2): 248–72. Available online at http://dx.doi.org/10.1111/1471-0366.00033.

Ponte, S. 2002b. "The 'Latte Revolution'? Regulation, Markets and Consumption in the Global Coffee Chain." *World Development* 30 (7): 1099–122. Available online at http://dx.doi.org/10.1016/S0305-750X(02)00032-3.

Porter, M. 1990. *The Competitive Advantage of Nations.* London: Macmillan.

Princen, T. 1994. "NGOs: Creating a Niche in Environmental Diplomacy." In *Environmental NGOs in World Politics: Linking the Local and the Global*, ed. T. Princen and M. Finger. London: Routledge. Available online at http://dx.doi.org/10.4324/9780203429037.

Public Citizen. 2005. *Fishy Currency: How International Finance Institutions Fund Shrimp Farms.* Washington, DC.

QAI (Quality Assurance International). 2009. "Canadian Organic Regime (COR) and Quebec Organic Reference Standards." San Diego, CA. Available online at http://www.qai-inc.com/services/canada.asp; accessed 26 September 2011.

QAI. 2011. "Quality Assurance International: From Field to Shelf Since 1989." San Diego, CA. Available online at http://www.qai-inc.com/; accessed 26 September 2011.

Rahman, A. 1995. "Shrimp Culture and Environment in the Coastal Region." Working Paper New Series 8. Dhaka: Bangladesh Institute of Development Studies.

Rahman, S., B.K. Barmon, and N. Ahmed. 2010. "Diversification Economies and Efficiencies in a 'Blue-Green revolution' Combination: A Case Study of Prawn-Carp-Rice Farming in the '*Gher*' System in Bangladesh." *Aquaculture International* 19:665-682.

Raman, K.R., and R.D. Lipschutz, eds. 2010. *Corporate Social Responsibility: Comparative Critiques.* London: Palgrave Macmillan.

Ramsar (Ramsar Convention on Wetland). 1997. "Global group formed to counter destructive industrial shrimp farming." 24 October. Available online at http://www.ramsar.org/cda/en/ramsar-about-private-industrial-shrimp-action/main/ramsar/1-36-50%5E16909_4000_0__; accessed 12 June 2007.

Raynolds, L. 1994a. "Institutionalizing Flexibility: A Comparative Analysis of Fordist and Post-Fordist Models of Third World Agri-export Production." In *Commodity Chains and Global Capitalism*, ed. G. Gereffi and M. Korzeniewicz. Westport, CT: Praeger.

Raynolds, L. 1994b. "The Restructuring of Third World Agri-exports: Changing Production Relations in the Dominican Republic." In *The Global Restructuring of the Agri-food System*, ed. P. McMichael. Ithaca, NY: Cornell University Press.

Raynolds, L. 1997. "Restructuring National Agriculture, Agri-food Trade, and Agrarian Livelihoods in the Caribbean." In *Globalising Food: Agrarian Questions and Global Restructuring*, ed. D. Goodman and M. Watts. London: Routledge.

Raynolds, L. 2001. "New Plantations, New Workers: Gender and Production Politics in the Dominican Republic." *Gender & Society* 15 (1): 7–28. Available online at http://dx.doi.org/10.1177/089124301015001002.

Raynolds, L. 2002. "Consumer-Producer Links in Fair Trade Coffee Networks." *Sociologia Ruralis* 42 (4): 404–24. Available online at http://dx.doi.org/10.1111/1467-9523.00224.

Raynolds, L. 2004. "The Globalization of Organic Agri-food Networks." *World Development* 32 (5): 725–43. Available online at http://dx.doi.org/10.1016/j.worlddev.2003.11.008.

Raynolds, L., D. Myhre, P. McMichael, V. Carro-Figueroa, and F.H. Buttel. 1993. "The 'New' Internationalization of Agriculture: A Reformation." *World Development* 21 (7): 1101–21. Available online at http://dx.doi.org/10.1016/0305-750X(93)90002-Q.

Reardon, T., and J.A. Berdegué. 2002. "The Rapid Rise of Supermarkets in Latin America." *Development Policy Review* 20 (4): 371–88. Available online at http://dx.doi.org/10.1111/1467-7679.00178.

Resolve. 2012. "Toward Sustainability: Roles and Limitations of Certification." Washington, DC. Available online at http://www.resolv.org/site-assess ment/files/2012/06/Appendices-Only.pdf; accessed: 30 October 2012).

Rich, B. 1994. *Mortgaging the Earth: The World Bank, Environmental Impoverishment, and the Crisis of Development*. Boston: Beacon.

Rigg, J. 2001. *More than the Soil: Rural Change in Southeast Asia*. Toronto: Pearson Education Limited.

Rigg, J. 2006. "Land, Farming, Livelihoods, and Poverty: Rethinking the Links in the Rural South." *World Development* 34 (1): 180–202. Available online at http://dx.doi.org/10.1016/j.worlddev.2005.07.015.

Rigg, J., and S. Nattapoolwat. 2001. "Embracing the Global in Thailand: Activism and Pragmatism in an Era of Deagrariannization." *World Development* 29 (6): 945–60. Available online at http://dx.doi.org/10.1016/S0305-750X(01)00021-3.

Robinson, G. 1997. "Greening and Globalizing: Agriculture in 'New Times." In *Agricultural Restructuring and Sustainability: A Geographical Perspective*, ed. B. Ilbery, Q. Chiotti, and T. Rickard. Wallingford, UK: CAB International.

Rogaly, B. 1999. "Dangerous Liaisons? Seasonal Migration and Agrarian Change in West Bengal." In *Sonar Bangla? Agricultural Growth and Agrarian*

Change in West Bengal and Bangladesh, ed. B. Rogaly, B. Harriss-White, and S. Bose. New Delhi: Sage Publications.

Roheim, C.A. 2004. "Seafood, Trade Liberalization and Impacts on Sustainability." In *Global Aquacultural Trade and Developing Countries*, ed. M.A. Aksoy and J.C. Beghin. Washington, DC: World Bank Publications.

Ruigrok, W., and R. van Tulder. 1995. *The Logic of International Restructuring*. London: Routledge.

Rutherford, S. 1994. *CARE and Gher: Financing the Small Fry*. Dhaka: CARE International in Bangladesh.

Sachs, J. D. 2007. "The Promise of the Blue Revolution: Aquaculture Can Maintain Living Standards while Averting the Ruin of the Oceans." *Scientific American*, 17 June 2007. Available online at http://www.scientificamerican.com/article.cfm?id=the-promise-of-the-blue-revolution-extended; accessed 29 May 2013.

Sanderson, S. 1986. "The Emergence of 'World Steer': Internationalization and Foreign Domination in Latin American Cattle Production." In *Food, the State and International Political Economy*, ed. F.L. Tullis and W.L. Hollist. Lincoln: University of Nebraska Press.

Santiso, C. 2002. "Good Governance and Aid Effectiveness: The World Bank and Conditionality." *Georgetown Public Policy Review* 7 (1): 1–23.

Schofer, E., F. Ramirez, and J. Meyer. 2000. "The Effect of Science on National Economic Development, 1970-1990." *American Sociological Review* 65 (6): 866–87. Available online at http://dx.doi.org/10.2307/2657517.

Scott, D. 2000. "The Environmental and Social Impacts of Commercial Shrimp Farming." *Reports*, 8 November.

Scott, J.C. 1998. *Seeing Like a State: How Certain Schemes to Improve Human Condition Have Failed*. New Haven, CT: Yale University Press.

Seafood Choice Alliance. 2008. "The U.S. Marketplace for Sustainable Seafood: Are We Hooked Yet?" Silver Spring, MD. Available online at http://www.seafoodchoices.org/documents/USMarketplace2008_Full.pdf; accessed 29 October 2012.

Sernbo, K., and J. Kloth. 1996. "Prawn Farming: A Study of Intensive Aquaculture." Stockholm: Swedish Society for Nature Conservation.

Shiva, V. 1995. "The Damaging Social and Environmental Effects of Aquaculture." *Third World Resurgence* 59: 22–4.

Shiva, V. 2000. *Stolen Harvest: The Hijacking of the Global Food Supply*. London: Zed Books.

Siddique, K. 2003. "Declaration in the Export Sector of Bangladesh and Women Workers: Assessing Impacts and Identifying Coping Strategies." CPD Occasional Paper Series 26. Dhaka: Centre for Policy Dialogue.

Singh, H. 1998. *Colonial Hegemony and Popular Resistance: Princes, Peasants, and Paramount Power*. Thousand Oaks, CA: Sage Publications.

SIPPO (Swiss Import Promotion Programme). 2011. "Imports into Switzerland and the EU." Zurich. Available online at http://importers.sippo.ch/inter net/osec/en/home/import.html; accessed 26 September 2011.

Skladany, M., and C. Harris. 1995. "On Global Pond: International Development and Commodity Chains in the Shrimp Industry." In *Food and Agrarian Orders in the Global Economy*, ed. P. McMichael. Ithaca, NY: Cornell University Press.

Small, Lee-Ann. 2007. "East Meets West: Utilising Western Literature to Conceptualize Post-Soviet Agrarian Change." *Journal of Peasant Studies* 34 (1): 29–50. Available online at http://dx.doi.org/10.1080/03066150701311845.

Smyth, S., and P.W.B. Phillips. 2002. "Product Differentiation Alternatives: Identity Preservation, Segregation and Traceability." *AgBioForum* 5 (2): 30–42.

Soil Association. 2011. "Certification." Bristol, UK. Available online at http://www.soilassociation.org/certification; accessed 26 September 2011.

Soja, E., and B. Hooper. 1993. "The Space that Difference Makes." In *Place and the Politics of Identity*, ed. M. Keith and S. Pile. London, New York: Routledge.

Spaargaren, G., and A. Mol. 1992. "Sociology, Environment, and Modernity: Ecological Modernization as a Theory of Social Change." *Society & Natural Resources* 5 (4): 323–44. Available online at http://dx.doi.org/10.1080/08941929209380797.

Sperber, W.H. 2005. "HACCP and Transparency." *Food Control* 16 (6): 505–9. Available online at http://dx.doi.org/10.1016/j.foodcont.2003.10.012.

SQF (Safe Quality Food). 2011. "Safe Quality Food Institute: One World, One Standard." Arlington, VA. Available online at http://www.sqfi.com/; accessed 26 September 2011.

SSOQ (Shrimp Seal of Quality Organization). 2002. "The Seal of Quality Program: Questions and Answers on the Seal of Quality Program." Dhaka.

SSOQ. 2004. "Shrimp Seal of Quality (SSOQ) Certification Standards." Dhaka. Available online at http://library.enaca.org/certification/publications/SSOQ_Certification_Standards_March_15_2004.pdf; accessed 14 August 2007.

Stanford, L. 2002. "Constructing 'Quality': The Political Economy of Standards in Mexico's Avocado Industry." *Agriculture and Human Values* 19 (4): 293–310. Available online at http://dx.doi.org/10.1023/A:1021196219849.

Stonich, S. 2002. "Farming Shrimp, Harvesting Hunger: The Costs and Benefits of the Blue Revolution." *Backgrounder* 8 (1).

Stonich, S., and C. Bailey. 2000. "Resisting the Blue Revolution: Contending Coalitions Surrounding Industrial Shrimp Farming." *Human Organization* 59 (1): 23–36.

Sturgeon, T.J. 2001. "How Do We Define Value Chains and Production Networks?" *IDS Bulletin* 32 (3): 9–18. Available online at http://dx.doi.org/10.1111/j.1759-5436.2001.mp32003002.x.

Talbot, J.M. 2002. "Tropical Commodity Chains, Forward Integration Strategies and International Inequality: Coffee, Cocoa and Tea." *Review of International Political Economy* 9 (4): 701–34. Available online at http://dx.doi.org/10.1080/0969229022000021862.

Tanaka, K., and L. Busch. 2003. "Standardization as a Means for Globalizing a Commodity: The Case of Rapeseed in China." *Rural Sociology* 68 (1): 25–45. Available online at http://dx.doi.org/10.1111/j.1549-0831.2003.tb00127.x.

Tanner, B. 2000. "Independent Assessment by Third-party Certification Bodies." *Food Control* 11 (5): 415–7. Available online at http://dx.doi.org/10.1016/S0956-7135(99)00055-9.

Taylor, P.L. 2005. "In the Market but Not of It: Fair Trade Coffee and Forest Stewardship Council Certification as Market-Based Social Change." *World Development* 33 (1): 129–47. Available online at http://dx.doi.org/10.1016/j.worlddev.2004.07.007.

Thompson, S.J., and J.T. Cowan. 2000. "Globalizing Agri-food Systems in Asia: Introduction." *World Development* 28 (3): 401–7. Available online at http://dx.doi.org/10.1016/S0305-750X(99)00138-2.

Tutu, A. 2004. "Commercial Shrimp Farming in Bangladesh: In Respective of Environment, Land Rights and Labour Rights." Khulna, Bangladesh: Coastal Development Partnership.

UKAS (United Kingdom Accreditation Service). 2009. "About UKAS." Feltham, UK. Available online at http://www.ukas.com/about-accreditation/about-ukas/; accessed 26 September 2011.

UNESCAP (United Nations Economic and Social Commission for Asia and the Pacific). 2007. "What Is Good Governance?" Bangkok. Available online at http://www.unescap.org/pdd/prs/ProjectActivities/Ongoing/gg/governance.pdf; accessed 28 August 2007.

UNESCAP and ADB (Economic and Social Commission for Asia and the Pacific and Asian Development Bank). 2000. *State of the Environment in Asia and Pacific 2000.* New York, United Nations.

United States. 1998. Department of Labor. *Report on Labor Practices in Burma.* Washington, DC, September. Available online at http://www.dol.gov/ILAB/media/reports/ofr/burma1998/; accessed 16 July 2013.

United States. 2011. National Oceanic and Atmospheric Administration. Office of Science and Technology. National Marine Fisheries Service. "Fisheries of the United States: World Fisheries." Washington, DC. Available online at http://www.st.nmfs.noaa.gov/st1/fus/fus11/04_world2011.pdf; accessed 27 May 2013.

USAID Bangladesh. 2006. *A Pro-poor Analysis of the Shrimp Sector in Bangladesh.* Arlington, VA: U.S. Agency for International Development.

Utting, P., and J.C. Marques, eds. 2009. *Corporate Social Responsibility and Regulatory Governance: Towards Inclusive Development?* London: Palgrave Macmillan. Available online at http://dx.doi.org/10.1057/9780230246966.

Uzemeri, M. 1997. "ISO 9000 and other Metastandards: Principles for Management Practice?" *Academy of Management Executive* 11 (1): 21–36.

Vandergeest, P. 1988. "Commercialization and Commoditization: A Dialogue between Perspectives." *Sociologia Ruralis* 28 (1): 7–29. Available online at http://dx.doi.org/10.1111/j.1467-9523.1988.tb00329.x.

Vandergeest, P. 2003a. "Land to some tillers: development-induced displacement in Laos." *International Social Science Journal* 55 (175): 47–56. Available online at http://dx.doi.org/10.1111/1468-2451.5501005.

Vandergeest, P. 2003b. "Racialization and Citizenship in Thai Forest Politics." *Society & Natural Resources* 16 (1): 19–37. Available online at http://dx.doi.org/10.1080/08941920309172.

Vandergeest, P. 2004. "New Regulation and Agri-food Industrialization: Assessing Codes of Conduct for Shrimp Farming in Thailand." In *Coping with Globalization: Southeast Asian Historical and Cultural Heritage,* ed. R. de Koninck and B. Thibert. Montreal: Canadian Council for Southeast Asian Studies Trilateral Initiative.

Vandergeest, P. 2007. "Certification and Communities: Alternatives for Regulating the Environmental and Social Impacts of Shrimp Farming." *World Development* 35 (7): 1152–71. Available online at http://dx.doi.org/10.1016/j.worlddev.2006.12.002.

Vandergeest, P., M. Flaherty, and P. Miller. 1999. "A Political Ecology of Shrimp Aquaculture in Thailand." *Rural Sociology* 64 (4): 573–96. Available online at http://dx.doi.org/10.1111/j.1549-0831.1999.tb00379.x.

Wal-Mart. 2005. "New certification for Wal-Mart shrimp another example of environmental leadership." Bentonville, AK, 17 November. Available online at http://news.walmart.com/news-archive/2005/11/17/new-certification-for-wal-mart-shrimp-another-example-of-environmental-leadership; accessed 6 August 2006.

Wal-Mart. 2006. "Wal-Mart takes lead on supporting sustainable fisheries." Bentonville, AK, 3 February. Available online at http://news.walmart.com/

news-archive/2006/02/06/wal-mart-takes-lead-on-supporting-sustainable-fisheries; accessed 6 August 2006.

Walker, K.L. 2006. "Gangster Capitalism and Peasant Protest in China: The Last Twenty Years." *Journal of Peasant Studies* 33 (1): 1–33. Available online at http://dx.doi.org/10.1080/03066150600624413.

Watts, M. 1996. "Development III: The Global Agrofood System and Late Twentieth Century Development (or Kautsky Redux)." *Progress in Human Geography* 20 (2): 230–45. Available online at http://dx.doi.org/10.1177/030913259602000208.

Watts, M. 2003. "Development and Governmentality." *Singapore Journal of Tropical Geography* 24 (1): 6–34.

Wilkinson, F. 1995. "Productive Systems in Knitwear." Paper presented at the workshop on The International Organisation of Production: A "Commodity Chains" Approach, Geneva, March.

Wilkinson, F. 2002. "The Final Foods Industry and the Changing Face of Global Agri-Food System." *Sociologia Ruralis* 42 (4): 329–46. Available online at http://dx.doi.org/10.1111/1467-9523.00220.

Wilkinson, F. 2006. "Fish: A Global Value Chain Driven onto the Rocks." *Sociologia Ruralis* 46 (2): 139–53. Available online at http://dx.doi.org/10.1111/j.1467-9523.2006.00408.x.

Wood, A. 2005. "Demystifying 'Good Governance': An Overview of World Bank Governance Reforms and Conditions." Available online at http://www.trocaire.org/pdfs/policy/prsp/demystifyinggoodgovernance.pdf; accessed 28 August 2007.

World Bank. 1989. *Sub-Saharan Africa: From Crisis to Sustainable Growth*. Washington, DC.

World Bank. 1999. "World Bank to help Bangladesh boost environmentally-friendly and sustainable fish and shrimp production." News Release 2000/009/SAS. Washington, DC, 20 January. Available online at http://web.worldbank.org/WBSITE/DELETEDSITESBACKUP/0,,content MDK:20015453~menuPK:64615830~pagePK:166745~piPK:459740~the SitePK:336806,00.html; accessed 31 July 2007.

World Bank. 2007a. "Bangladesh Fourth Fisheries Project (December 1999 – June 2006)." Washington, DC. Available online at http://web.worldbank.org/WBSITE/EXTERNAL/COUNTRIES/SOUTHASIAEXT/EXTSAREGT OPAGRI/0,,contentMDK:20996590~pagePK:34004173~piPK:34003707~the SitePK:452766,00.html; accessed 1 May 2007.

World Bank. 2007b. "What Is Our Approach to Governance?" Washington, DC. Available online at http://web.worldbank.org/WBSITE/EXTERNAL/WBI/EXTWBIGOVANTCOR/0,,contentMDK:20678937~pagePK:64168445~piPK:64168309~theSitePK:1740530,00.html; accessed 28 August 2007.

World Bank. 2012. "Fisheries and Aquaculture." Washington, DC. Available online at http://web.worldbank.org/WBSITE/EXTERNAL/TOPICS/EXT ARD/0,,contentMDK:20451222~menuPK:1308455~pagePK:148956~piPK: 216618~theSitePK:336682,00.html; accessed 30 October 2012.

World Bank, NACA (Network of Aquaculture Centres in Asia-Pacific), WWF (World Wildlife Fund), and FAO (Food and Agriculture Organization). 2002. *Shrimp Farming and Environment, Synthesis Report. Work in Progress for Public Discussion.* Washington, DC.

WWF (World Wildlife Fund). 1997. *WWF Position Statement on Shrimp Aquaculture.* Washington, DC.

WWF. 2007. *Certification Programs for Aquaculture: Environmental Impacts, Social Issues and Animal Welfare.* Washington, DC.

Zadek, S., P. Prudan, and R. Evans. 1997. *Building Corporate Accountability: Emerging Practices in Social and Ethical Accounting, Auditing and Reporting.* London: New Economics Foundation.

Zuckerman, A. 1996. "European Standards Officials Push Reform of ISO 9000 and QS-9000 Registration." *Quality Progress* 29 (9): 131–4.

Index